Mastering OpenLayers 3

Create powerful applications with the most robust open source web mapping library using this advanced guide

Gábor Farkas

BIRMINGHAM - MUMBAI

Mastering OpenLayers 3

First published: January 2016

Production reference: 1220116

Published by Packt Publishing Ltd.
Livery Place
35 Livery Street
Birmingham B3 2PB, UK.

ISBN 978-1-78528-100-6

www.packtpub.com

Credits

Author
Gábor Farkas

Reviewer
Jose Troche

Commissioning Editor
Veena Pagare

Acquisition Editor
Sonali Vernekar

Content Development Editor
Anish Dhurat

Technical Editor
Jayesh Sonawane

Copy Editors
Sonia Cheema
Trishya Hajare

Project Coordinator
Bijal Patel

Proofreader
Safis Editing

Indexer
Monica Ajmera Mehta

Graphics
Disha Haria

Production Coordinator
Conidon Miranda

Cover Work
Conidon Miranda

About the Author

Gábor Farkas is a PhD student at University of Pécs's Institute of Geography. He holds a master's degree in geography, although he moved from traditional geography to pure Geoinformatics early in his academic journey. He often studies Geoinformatical solutions in his free time, keeps up with the latest trends, and is an open source enthusiast. He loves to work with GRASS GIS, PostGIS, and QGIS, but his all-time favorites are open source web mapping technologies, which mostly cover his main areas of research interest.

There have been many kind-hearted and nice people in my life who have helped me in my career or private life by giving me great advice. However, there is one significant person who has made this book possible. I would like to dedicate this book to my advisor, Titusz Bugya, who gave me the tip of starting a blog about WebGIS in English. This blog eventually led to the writing of this book. So, thanks Titusz; this book is partially the result of your trust and effort.

About the Reviewer

Jose Troche is a seasoned software development engineer with over a decade of hands-on experience in architecting and building enterprise web applications in multitiered environments. He has developed web-based applications that are capable of creating, storing, searching, retrieving, real-time sharing, and tracking geospatial data. He has also created REST APIs for advanced geospatial web services that are deployed to large-scale enterprise cloud architectures. He has integrated OpenLayers into several of his projects.

Jose has also worked as a contractor in aerospace and defense companies and agencies such as NASA, Lockheed Martin and General Dynamics; he is currently employed by Amazon Inc.

www.PacktPub.com

Support files, eBooks, discount offers, and more

For support files and downloads related to your book, please visit www.PacktPub.com.

Did you know that Packt offers eBook versions of every book published, with PDF and ePub files available? You can upgrade to the eBook version at www.PacktPub.com and as a print book customer, you are entitled to a discount on the eBook copy. Get in touch with us at service@packtpub.com for more details.

At www.PacktPub.com, you can also read a collection of free technical articles, sign up for a range of free newsletters and receive exclusive discounts and offers on Packt books and eBooks.

https://www2.packtpub.com/books/subscription/packtlib

Do you need instant solutions to your IT questions? PacktLib is Packt's online digital book library. Here, you can search, access, and read Packt's entire library of books.

Why subscribe?

- Fully searchable across every book published by Packt
- Copy and paste, print, and bookmark content
- On demand and accessible via a web browser

Free access for Packt account holders

If you have an account with Packt at www.PacktPub.com, you can use this to access PacktLib today and view 9 entirely free books. Simply use your login credentials for immediate access.

Table of Contents

Preface

As in every other computer-related field, the Web has also become a determining factor in GIS. In this new trend, with some client-based knowledge, we can easily publish our maps and layers on the Web. However, as technology rapidly develops, we can now perform some more serious GIS-related work on the Web as well. With enough browser capabilities and client-side computational power, an even newer trend has emerged from the Web-based GIS world: WebGIS. This new trend researches the possibilities of deploying powerful GIS applications on the Web, making the most general workflows of a spatial analyst possible on a browser in a platform-independent manner.

Thanks to OSGEO, OGC, and other initiatives, companies, individuals, and the open source philosophy have made a quick and great impact on this brand new field. Consequently, there is a wide palette of open source applications and libraries to work with and build upon. One of the most original and robust web mapping projects is OpenLayers. This library debuted a brand new, cutting-edge technology with a major version change. OpenLayers 3 is capable of things that we could not even imagine a few years ago.

An unplanned consequence (we could probably call it externality) of its powerful capabilities is the added difficulty of using it and a steep learning curve. The twisted version of a famous quote also states: *with great power comes great complexity*. Creating simple maps and deploying simple web mapping applications is easy with OpenLayers 3; however, if we need something more advanced, we need more stable and in-depth knowledge of the library. Gaining this knowledge is a great journey, which *Mastering OpenLayers 3* is designed to start you on and aid you through.

What this book covers

Chapter 1, Creating Simple Maps with OpenLayers 3, guides you through the process of creating a simple map with the library. It also discusses some key concepts of OpenLayers 3, an effective way of using the API documentation, and a method to debug broken code.

Chapter 2, Applying Custom Styles, shows you how you can use CSS and JavaScript to customize the appearance of your application. It discusses which parts of the library can be styled with CSS and those that can be styled with JavaScript. It provides some methods for you to use to create a custom style.

Chapter 3, Working with Layers, introduces you to layer management. In this chapter, you will learn how to modify the layer stack, what the most common and useful operations you can perform with layers, and essentially, how to build a complete layer tree.

Chapter 4, Using Vector Data, shows you various vector formats and operations. You will learn a lot about geospatial features. You will read, write, modify, and style vector layers, attributes, and geometries.

Chapter 5, Creating Responsive Applications with Interactions and Controls, guides you through the various controls in OpenLayers 3. You will learn how to use the available controls effectively and build your very own.

Chapter 6, Controlling the Map – View and Projection, discusses some essential views and projection-based concepts. You will learn how to modify the view, use extents dynamically, and use custom projections.

Chapter 7, Mastering the Renderers, is a bit of a specialized chapter. You will take a look at how rendering works in OpenLayers 3 and how you can modify these rendering mechanisms. There will be some examples using Canvas and the WebGL HTML technologies, ranging from novice to expert skill levels.

Chapter 8, OpenLayers 3 for Mobile, shows you how to create responsive applications for desktop and mobile browsers at the same time. You will be able to make some mobile-based considerations and create a mobile-friendly OpenLayers 3 application by the end of this chapter.

Chapter 9, Tools of the Trade – Integrating Third-Party Applications, introduces some other tools into your workflow, making the development of your application more efficient and enjoyable. You will get some tips about some very useful third-party applications and libraries, which can be easily integrated with OpenLayers 3.

Chapter 10, Compiling Custom Builds with Closure, shows you how to build your own version of OpenLayers 3. Along with the custom building process, you will learn how to bundle your own application with the library and generate a custom API documentation automatically.

What you need for this book

For this book, you will generally need a modern web browser on your system. For some of the chapters, you will also need some additional software. For a better experience, it is strongly advised to have a working server on your machine. It can be either an Apache, an Nginx, or a HTTP Server created from Python.

For *Chapter 8, OpenLayers 3 for Mobile,* you will either need a handheld touch device to test some touch based features, or a browser, which can emulate such a device. For emulation, any of Google Chrome, Mozilla Firefox, or Opera are good enough. Unfortunately, Microsoft browsers are not suitable for this purpose. For *Chapter 9, Tools of the Trade – Integrating Third Party Applications,* you will need a fresh version of QGIS.

Who this book is for

This book is intended for frontend developers with a basic understanding of JavaScript and GIS concepts, and preferably for those who are familiar with the fundamentals of OpenLayers 3. You might have never used OpenLayers 3 as a seasoned JavaScript developer. If this is the case, and you are ambitious and eager to learn web mapping, this book will definitely set you on the right track.

Conventions

In this book, you will find a number of text styles that distinguish between different kinds of information. Here are some examples of these styles and an explanation of their meaning.

Code words in text, database table names, folder names, filenames, file extensions, pathnames, dummy URLs, and user input are shown as follows: "To make our map's `div` element focusable, we must add a `tabindex` property to it in the HTML file." Key combinations are also distinguished from regular text: "*F12* in modern ones, or *CTRL + J*, if *F12* does not work".

A block of code is set as follows:

```
<!DOCTYPE html>
<html lang="en">
<head>
<title>Chapter 1 - Creating a simple map</title>
<link href="../../js/ol3-3.11.0/ol.css" rel="stylesheet">
<link href="ch01.css" rel="stylesheet">
```

Any command-line input or output is written as follows:

```
node tasks/build.js config/ol.json ol.js
node tasks/build.js config/ol-debug.json ol-debug.js
```

Words that you see on the screen, for example, in menus or dialog boxes, appear in the text like this: "From the available shortcuts, we will need the command prompt (**Node.js command prompt**) as we will need to start various JavaScript programs."

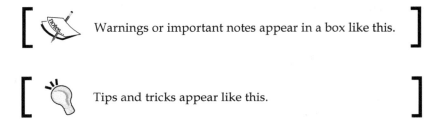

Warnings or important notes appear in a box like this.

Tips and tricks appear like this.

Reader feedback

Feedback from our readers is always welcome. Let us know what you think about this book—what you liked or disliked. Reader feedback is important for us as it helps us develop titles that you will really get the most out of.

To send us general feedback, simply e-mail feedback@packtpub.com, and mention the book's title in the subject of your message.

If there is a topic that you have expertise in and you are interested in either writing or contributing to a book, see our author guide at www.packtpub.com/authors.

Customer support

Now that you are the proud owner of a Packt book, we have a number of things to help you to get the most from your purchase.

Downloading the example code

You can download the example code files from your account at `http://www.packtpub.com` for all the Packt Publishing books you have purchased. If you purchased this book elsewhere, you can visit `http://www.packtpub.com/support` and register to have the files e-mailed directly to you.

Downloading the color images of this book

We also provide you with a PDF file that has color images of the screenshots/diagrams used in this book. The color images will help you better understand the changes in the output. You can download this file from `http://www.packtpub.com/sites/default/files/downloads/MasteringOpenlayers3_ColorImages.pdf`.

Errata

Although we have taken every care to ensure the accuracy of our content, mistakes do happen. If you find a mistake in one of our books—maybe a mistake in the text or the code—we would be grateful if you could report this to us. By doing so, you can save other readers from frustration and help us improve subsequent versions of this book. If you find any errata, please report them by visiting `http://www.packtpub.com/submit-errata`, selecting your book, clicking on the **Errata Submission Form** link, and entering the details of your errata. Once your errata are verified, your submission will be accepted and the errata will be uploaded to our website or added to any list of existing errata under the Errata section of that title.

To view the previously submitted errata, go to `https://www.packtpub.com/books/content/support` and enter the name of the book in the search field. The required information will appear under the **Errata** section.

Piracy

Piracy of copyrighted material on the Internet is an ongoing problem across all media. At Packt, we take the protection of our copyright and licenses very seriously. If you come across any illegal copies of our works in any form on the Internet, please provide us with the location address or website name immediately so that we can pursue a remedy.

Please contact us at `copyright@packtpub.com` with a link to the suspected pirated material.

We appreciate your help in protecting our authors and our ability to bring you valuable content.

Questions

If you have a problem with any aspect of this book, you can contact us at `questions@packtpub.com`, and we will do our best to address the problem.

1
Creating Simple Maps with OpenLayers 3

OpenLayers 3 is the most robust open source web mapping library out there, highly capable of handling the client side of a WebGIS environment. Whether you know how to use OpenLayers 3 or you are new to it, this chapter will help you to create a simple map and either refresh some concepts or get introduced to them. As this is a mastering book, we will mainly discuss the library's structure and capabilities in depth. In this chapter we will create a simple map with the library, and revise the basic terms related to it.

In this chapter we will cover the following topics:

- Structure of OpenLayers 3
- Architectural considerations
- Creating a simple map
- Using the API documentation effectively
- Debugging the code

Before getting started

Take a look at the code provided with the book. You should see a js folder in which the required libraries are stored. For the first few chapters, ol.js, and ol.css in the ol3-3.11.0 folder will be sufficient. The code is also available on GitHub. You can download a copy from the following URL: https://github.com/GaborFarkas/mastering_openlayers3/releases. Take a look at the following screenshot:

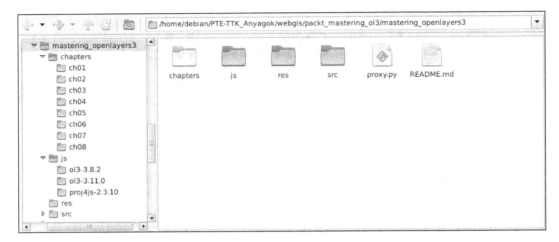

 You can download the latest release of OpenLayers 3 from its GitHub repository at https://github.com/openlayers/ol3/releases. For now, grabbing the distribution version (v3.11.0-dist.zip) should be enough.

Creating a working environment

There is a security restriction in front end development, called Cross Origin Resource Sharing (CORS). By default, this restriction prevents the application from grabbing content from a different domain. On top of that, some browsers disallow reaching content from the hard drive when a web page is opened from the file system. To prevent this behavior, please make sure you possess one of the following:

- A running web server (highly recommended)
- Firefox web browser with security.fileuri.strict_origin_policy set to false (you can reach flags in Firefox by opening about:config from the address bar)

- Google Chrome web browser started with the `--disable-web-security` parameter (make sure you have closed every other instance of Chrome before disabling security)

- Safari web browser with **Disable Local File Restrictions** (in the **Develop** menu, which can be enabled in the **Advanced** tab of **Preferences**)

 You can easily create a web server if you have Python 2 with `SimpleHTTPServer`, or if you have Python 3 with `http.server`. For basic tutorials, you can consult the appropriate Python documentation pages.

Structure of OpenLayers 3

OpenLayers 3 is a well structured, modular, and complex library, where flexibility and consistency take higher priority than performance. However, this does not mean OpenLayers 3 is slow. On the contrary, the library highly outperforms its predecessor; therefore its comfortable and logical design does not really adversely affect its performance. The relationship of some of the most essential parts of the library can be described with a radial Universal Modeling Language (UML) diagram, such as the following:

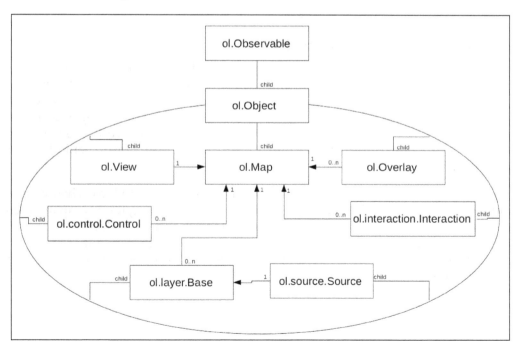

Reading a UML scheme can seem difficult, and can be difficult if it is a proper one. However, this simplified scheme is quite easy to understand. With regard to the arrows, 1 represents a one-to-one relation, while the 0..n and 1 symbols denote a one-to-many relationship.

You will probably never get into direct contact with the two superclasses at the top of the OpenLayers 3 hierarchy: ol.Observable, and ol.Object. However, most of the classes you actively use are children of these classes. You can always count on their methods when you design a web mapping or WebGIS application.

In the diagram, we can see that the parent of the most essential objects is the ol.Observable class. This superclass ensures all of its children have consistent listener methods. For example, every descendant of this superclass bears the on, once, and un functions, making registering event listeners to them as easy as possible.

The next superclass, ol.Object, extends its parent with methods capable of easy property management. Every inner property managed by its methods (get, set, and unset) are observable. There are also convenience methods for bulk setting and getting properties, called getProperties and setProperties. Most of the other frequently used classes are direct, or indirect, descendants of this superclass.

Building the layout

Now that we have covered some of the most essential structural aspects of the library, let's consider the architecture of an application deployed in a production environment. Take another look at the code. There is a chapters folder in which you can access the examples within the appropriate subfolder. If you open ch01, you can see three file types in it. As you have noticed, the different parts of the web page (HTML, CSS, and JavaScript) are separated. There is one main reason behind this: the code remains as clean as possible.

With a clean and rational design, you will always know where to look when you would like to make a modification. Moreover, if you're working for a company there is a good chance someone else will also work with your code. This kind of design will make sure your colleague can easily handle your code. On top of that, if you have to develop a wrapper API around OpenLayers 3, this is the only way your code can be integrated into future projects.

Creating the appeal

As the different parts of the application are separated, we will create a minimalistic HTML document. It will expand with time as the application becomes more complicated and needs more container elements. For now, let's write a simple HTML document:

```
<!DOCTYPE html>
<html lang="en">
    <head>
        <title>Chapter 1 - Creating a simple map</title>
        <link href="../../js/ol3-3.11.0/ol.css" rel="stylesheet">
        <link href="ch01.css" rel="stylesheet">
        <script type="text/javascript" src="../../js/ol3-
3.11.0/ol.js"></script>
        <script type="text/javascript"
src="ch01_simple_map.js"></script>
    </head>
    <body>
        <div id="map" class="map"></div>
    </body>
</html>
```

Downloading the example code

You can download the example code files from your account at http://www.packtpub.com for all the Packt Publishing books you have purchased. If you purchased this book elsewhere, you can visit http://www.packtpub.com/support and register to have the files e-mailed directly to you.

In this simple document, we defined the connection points between the external resources, and our web page. In the body, we created a simple div element with the required properties. We don't really need anything else; the magic will happen entirely in our code. Now we can go on with our CSS file and define one simple class, called map:

```
.map {
    width: 100%;
    height: 100%;
}
```

Save this simple rule to a file named ch01.css, in the same folder you just saved the HTML file.

If you are using a different file layout, don't forget to change the relative paths in the link, and script tags appropriately.

Writing the code

Now that we have a nice container for our map, let's concentrate on the code. In this book, most of the action will take place in the code; therefore this will be the most important part. First, we write the main function for our code:

```
function init() {
    document.removeEventListener('DOMContentLoaded', init);
}
document.addEventListener('DOMContentLoaded', init);
```

By using an event listener, we can make sure the code only runs when the structure of the web page has been initialized. This design enables us to use relative values for sizing, which is important for making adaptable applications. Also, we make sure the map variable is wrapped into a function (therefore we do not expose it) and seal a potential security breach. In the init function, we detach the event listener from the document, because it will not be needed once the DOM structure has been created.

> The DOMContentLoaded event waits for the DOM structure to build up. It does not wait for images, frames, and dynamically added content; therefore the application will load faster. Only IE 8 and prior versions do not support this event type, but if you have to fall back you can always use the window object's load event. To check a feature's support in major browsers, you can consult the following site: http://www.caniuse.com/.

Next, we extend the init function by creating a vector layer and assigning it to a variable. Note that in OpenLayers 3.5.0, creating vector layers has been simplified. Now, a vector layer has only a single source class, and the parser can be defined as a format in the source:

```
var vectorLayer = new ol.layer.Vector({
    source: new ol.source.Vector({
        format: new ol.format.GeoJSON({
            defaultDataProjection: 'EPSG:4326'
        }),
        url: '../../res/world_capitals.geojson',
        attributions: [
            new ol.Attribution({
                html: 'World Capitals © Natural Earth'
            })
        ]
    })
});
```

We are using a GeoJSON data source with a WGS84 projection. As the map will use a Web Mercator projection, we provide a `defaultDataProjection` value to the parser, so the data will be transformed automagically into the view's projection. We also give attribution to the creators of the vector dataset.

You can only give attribution with an array of `ol.Attribution` instances passed to the layer's source. Remember: giving attribution is not a matter of choice. Always give proper attribution to every piece of data used. This is the only way to avoid copyright infringement.

Finally, construct the map object, with some extra controls and one extra interaction:

```
var map = new ol.Map({
    target: 'map',
    layers: [
        new ol.layer.Tile({
            source: new ol.source.OSM()
        }),
        vectorLayer
    ],
    controls: [
        //Define the default controls
        new ol.control.Zoom(),
        new ol.control.Rotate(),
        new ol.control.Attribution(),
        //Define some new controls
        new ol.control.ZoomSlider(),
        new ol.control.MousePosition(),
        new ol.control.ScaleLine(),
        new ol.control.OverviewMap()
    ],
    interactions: ol.interaction.defaults().extend([
        new ol.interaction.Select({
            layers: [vectorLayer]
        })
    ]),
    view: new ol.View({
        center: [0, 0],
        zoom: 2
    })
});
```

In this example, we provide two layers: a simple OpenStreetMap tile layer and the custom vector layer saved into a separate variable. For the controls, we define the default ones, then provide a zoom slider, a scale bar, a mouse position notifier, and an overview map. There are too many default interactions, therefore we extend the default set of interactions with `ol.interaction.Select`. This is the point where saving the vector layer into a variable becomes necessary. The view object is a simple view that defaults to projection EPSG:3857 (Web Mercator).

> OpenLayers 3 also has a default set of controls that can be accessed similarly to the interactions, under `ol.control.defaults()`. Default controls and interactions are instances of `ol.Collection`, therefore both of them can be extended and modified like any other collection object. Note that the `extend` method requires an array of features.

Save the code to a file named `ch01_simple_map.js` in the same folder as your HTML file. If you open the HTML file, you should see the following map:

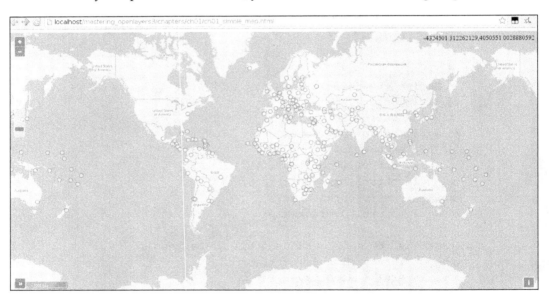

> You have different, or no results? Do not worry, not even a bit! Open up your browser's developer console (*F12* in modern ones, or *CTRL + J* if *F12* does not work), and resolve the error(s) noted there. If there is no result, double-check the HTML and CSS files; if you have a different result, check the code or the CORS requirements based on the error message. If you use Internet Explorer, make sure you have version 9 or higher.

Using the API documentation

The API documentation for OpenLayers 3.11.0, the version we are using, can be found at http://www.openlayers.org/en/v3.11.0/apidoc/. The API docs, like the library itself, are versioned, thus you can browse the appropriate documentation for your OpenLayers 3 version by changing **v3.11.0** in the URL to the version you are currently using.

 The development version of the API is also documented; you can always reach it at http://www.openlayers.org/en/master/apidoc/. Be careful when you use it, though. It contains all of the newly implemented methods, which probably won't work with the latest stable version.

Check the API documentation by typing one of the preceding links in your browser. You should see the home page with the most frequently used classes. There is also a handy search box, with all of the classes listed on the left side. We have talked about default interactions and their lengthy nature before. On the home page you can see a link to the default interactions. If you click on it, you will be directed to the following page:

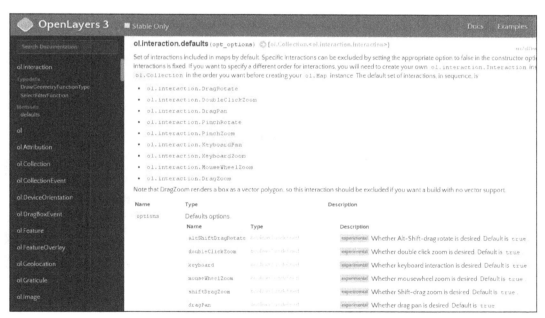

Now you can also see that nine interactions are added to the map by default. It would be quite verbose to add them one by one just to keep them when we define only one extra interaction, wouldn't it?

You can see some features marked as experimental while you browse the API documentation with the **Stable Only** checkbox unchecked. Do not consider those features to be unreliable. They are stable, but experimental, and therefore they can be modified or removed in future versions. If the developer team considers a feature is useful and does not need further optimization or refactoring, it will be marked as stable.

Understanding type definitions

For every constructor and function in the API, the input and expected output types are well documented. To see a good example, let's search for a function with inputs and outputs as well. If you search for ol.proj.fromLonLat, you will see the following function:

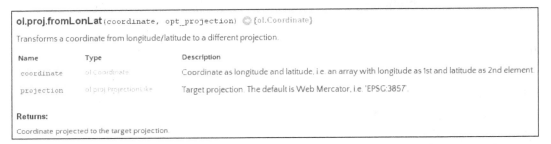

The function takes two arguments as input, one named coordinate and one named projection; projection is optional. coordinate is an ol.Coordinate type (an array with two numbers), while projection is an ol.proj.ProjectionLike type (a string representing the projection). The returned value, as we can see next to the white arrow, is also an ol.Coordinate type, with the transformed values.

A good developer always keeps track of future changes in the library. This is especially important with OpenLayers 3 when a major change occurs, as it lacks backward compatibility. You can see all of the major changes in the library in the OpenLayers 3 GitHub repository: https://github.com/openlayers/ol3/blob/master/changelog/upgrade-notes.md.

Debugging the code

As you will have noticed, there was a third file in the OpenLayers 3 folder discussed at the beginning of the chapter (js/ol3-3.11.0). This file, named ol-debug.js, is the uncompressed source file, in which the library is concatenated with all of its dependencies. We will use this file for two purpose in this book. Now, we will use it for debugging. First, open up ch01_simple_map.js. Next, extend the init function with an obvious mistake:

```
var geometry = new ol.geom.Point([0, 0]);
vectorLayer.getSource().addFeature(geometry);
```

Don't worry if you can't spot the error immediately. That's what is debugging for. Save this extended JavaScript file with the name ch01_error.js. Next, replace the old script with the new one in the HTML file, like this:

```
<script type="text/javascript" src="ch01_error.js"></script>
```

If you open the updated HTML, and open your browser's developer console, you will see the following error message:

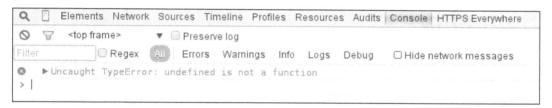

Now that we have an error, let's check it in the source file by clicking on the error link on the right side of the error message:

Quite meaningless, isn't it? The compiled library is created with Google's Closure Library, which obfuscates everything by default in order to compress the code. We have to tell it which precise part of the code should be exported. We will learn how to do that in the last chapter. For now, let's use the debug file. Change the `ol.js` in the HTML to `ol-debug.js`, load up the map, and check for the error again:

```
Q   Elements  Network  Sources  Timeline  Profiles  Resources  Audits  Console  HTTPS Everywhere
ol-dsbug.js ×  ch01_error.js
71267   * @param {string} featureKey
71268   * @param {ol.Feature} feature
71269   * @return {boolean}  true  if the feature is "valid", in the sense that it is
71270   *     also a candidate for insertion into the RTree, otherwise  false .
71271   * @private
71272   */
71273  ol.source.Vector.prototype.addToIndex_ = function(featureKey, feature) {
71274    var valid = true;
71275    var id = feature.getId();
71276    if (goog.isDef(id)) {
71277  
{}  Line 71275, Column 20
```

Finally, we can see, in a well-documented form, the part that caused the error. This is a validating method, which makes sure the added feature is compatible with the library. It requires an `ol.Feature` as an input, which is how we caught our error. We passed a simple geometry to the function, instead of wrapping it in an `ol.Feature` first.

Summary

In this chapter, you were introduced to the basics of OpenLayers 3 with a more advanced approach. We also discussed some architectural considerations, and some of the structural specialties of the library. Hopefully, along with the general revision, we acquired some insight in using the API documentation and debugging practices. Congratulations! You are now on your way to mastering OpenLayers 3.

In the next chapter, we will discuss which parts of the rendered elements can be changed with pure CSS, and what elements can be changed with CSS-like style properties. We will also learn how to change the appeal of the map, and thereby make our application blend in with our current project.

2
Applying Custom Styles

We covered the basics of the library in the previous chapter. Before moving on and learning how to code great applications with the library, we will cover the basics of applying custom styles with CSS and the methods offered by OpenLayers 3. The CSS part requires some basic knowledge in styling, but the more advanced techniques will be discussed in greater details.

In this chapter, we will cover the following topics:

- Modifying the default appearance of the map with CSS
- Applying custom styles to vector layers
- Customizing controls
- Creating a WebGIS application layout

Before getting started

Before moving on and customizing the default appearance, we should talk about its rendering process. OpenLayers 3 is a canvas-based web mapping library, which means that it draws everything it can on a single `canvas` element. This not only makes the rendering process faster, but also prevents direct styling with CSS. However, there are some parts rendered as pure DOM elements. These parts, specifically the controls, overlays, and drag boxes, can be styled directly. For the other parts, like vector data, the capabilities of the `canvas` element can be used for styling, mostly with inner methods. We will discuss rendering in a later chapter in more detail. For now, keeping this nature of the library in mind should be enough.

Using the DOM renderer opens up new possibilities in CSS styling. However, it cannot render vector data in SVG format; therefore, you can only style image layers directly. The library also loses performance; thus, using the DOM renderer should be considered as a generally bad practice. Renderers in OpenLayers 3 will be discussed in more detail in *Chapter 7, Mastering the Renderers.*

Basic considerations

From now on, step by step, we will make a simple WebGIS application with OpenLayers 3. In most of the chapters, we will extend the code created in the previous one. To make it clear, we will consider the current goal at the beginning of every chapter.

In this chapter, after a few warm-up examples, we will make the layout of our application. We will make a highly adaptable *full-screen* application; therefore, we will use relative units whenever it is possible. We will also make sure that our design does not prevent the usage of the default one. For now, the application will have three parts. The map canvas will display the map, the toolbar will contain the control buttons (the tools), and the notification bar will inform the user about the state of our application in various ways.

Customizing the default appearance

Now that we are clear about what parts can be customized with CSS, let's make an attempt to use it in practice. Firstly, we will need the code from the example in the previous chapter. If you look at the code appendix, you will see some files starting with ch02_css. The html and js files are exactly the same as we used in the last chapter. In this example, all the magic will take place in the css file.

 If you take a look at the html file, you can see our custom css file is declared after the official css file. This was done due to the phenomenon called **CSS specificity**. If two CSS file declarations are made to the same element with the same specificity, the order of the declarations will define the styling. As we have declared our custom css file after the official one, it will overwrite the default styling.

Identifying the classes

Open up the first example, called ch02_css.html, in your browser. You can see the already modified look of the previous example. The question is, how can you precisely tell which classes you have to modify to get the same results. To identify the required classes, right-click on one of the controls and then inspect the element. Your browser's inspector will open up and you will see something similar to the following screenshot:

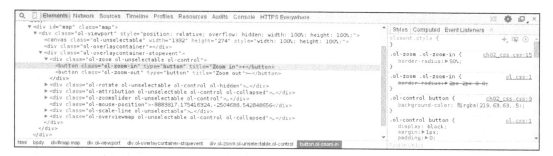

On the right, you can see the rules used by the official and our custom css file on the inspected element. On the left, you can see all the controls' DOM elements and the classes associated with them by default. These are the classes we have to modify, in order to alter the default appeal.

Styling the controls

Now that we know which elements can be changed directly with CSS and also which classes have to be changed to modify the appearance of the application, it's time to make some declarations. Firstly, let's make some small changes to the default appearance. We change the controls' original blue glow to a reddish one and make the overview map appear above the scale bar with the following rules:

```css
body {
    margin: 0px;
}
.map {
    width: 100%;
    height: 100%; /*Fallback*/
    height: 100vh;
}
.ol-control button {
    background-color: rgba(219,63,63,.5);
}
```

```
.ol-control button:focus {
    background-color: rgba(219,63,63,.5);
}
.ol-control button:hover {
    background-color: rgba(219,63,63,1);
}
.ol-scale-line {
    background-color: rgba(219,63,63,.5);
}
.ol-overviewmap {
    bottom: 2em;
}
```

Firstly, we remove the margin around the document because this will be a full-screen application.

> The unit can be omitted when the value is zero. The margin: 0; declaration would give exactly the same result as the preceding one.

Next, we define the size of the map element to match the size of the window. We declare every button control's color with RGBA values. Finally, we lift the overview map above the scale bar.

> As mentioned previously, we are using relative values for styling, to make our application is greatly adaptable. For this purpose, the em value is a great choice, as it depends on the font size of the current element. We also use the vh (viewport height) value, which is relative to the viewport; therefore, it precisely stacks with it. As the vh unit has a limited support, defining a fallback option should be considered.

Let's also change the font type the mouse position control uses to a fixed-width one:

```
.ol-mouse-position {
    font-family: monospace;
}
```

Specific font families can also be declared in the font-family property (Times New Roman) as generic families (monospace, serif, sans-serif). The browser will always try to use the defined font, but it might not be present on every system. If the defined font is not available, it tries to apply the most similar font, which can be used on the given operating system.

Keep in mind that you can provide fallback options, separating them with commas, and this is a better practice than relying on one particular font family. Alternatively, just host that particular font family and include it in a @font-face rule.

Finally, as drag boxes, the zoom box can also be styled with CSS; let's make a rule for the zoom box specifically:

```
.ol-dragzoom {
    background-color: rgba(219,63,63,.1);
    border-width: 2px;
    border-color: rgba(219,63,63,1);
}
```

If you save the current rules to a css file, link it to the example and open it up; you will see the following screenshot:

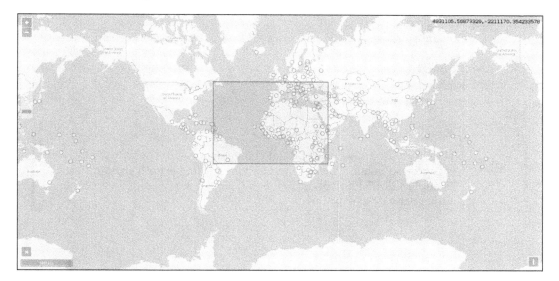

The controls have a reddish glow instead of the original blue one, the overview map is placed properly above the scale bar, and the coordinates are displayed with a fixed-width font type.

Customizing the attribution control

The attribution control has a nice inline styling by default. It is good to go when we have only a few layers to give credit to, but with more layers, it becomes more confusing to read. If you have a lot of layers to display, you might need to display those attributions in a list style. To achieve this effect, we simply overwrite the display rule of the containing element:

```
.ol-attribution li {
    display: table;
}
```

 The list-item value is also good to go with the display attribute. However, with table, you can arbitrarly resize the element, and the collapse button still remains in its place.

With this styling option, the logo will always be on top, as it is the first element of the list. This cannot be overridden, but as the element is now taller, we can provide our logo as a background and optionally disable the one provided by the library. In this case, we will use my university's seal as a logo:

```
.ol-attribution ul {
    background-image: url(../../res/university_of_pecs_transparent.
png);
    background-size: contain;
    background-position: 50%;
    background-repeat: no-repeat;
}
```

 The CSS background rules do not allow you to set the opacity for the background image. You have to modify your image with an editor (for example, GIMP, PhotoShop, and Paint.NET) if you would like to apply a transparency to your image.

If you extend your css file with these rules and open up the results, you will see the modified attribute control with our custom logo:

Creating a custom zoom control with CSS

In the next step, let's make a zoom control similar to the one in OpenLayers 2, where the slider is between the two zoom buttons. At first glance, this job might seem difficult, but it can be done with pure CSS. Firstly, alter the zoom buttons in such a way that they will be in circles without the whitish background:

```
.ol-zoom .ol-zoom-in {
    border-radius: 50%;
}
.ol-zoom .ol-zoom-out {
    border-radius: 50%;
    top: 203px;
    position: relative;
}
.ol-zoom {
    background-color: rgba(255,255,255,0);
}
.ol-zoom:hover {
    background-color: rgba(255,255,255,0);
}
```

The zoom out button is placed exactly 203 pixels below the zoom in button. This is due to a single reason: the zoom slider is declared as 200 pixels tall, the buttons have a 1 pixel margin, and the zoom slider has a 2 pixel padding. Unfortunately, we cannot do anything about the absolute height of the zoom slider, as the library uses it to calculate resolutions.

We made a note about CSS specificity before. In this case, the reason behind why we can't use the `ol-zoom-in` and `ol-zoom-out` classes without nesting is the fact that the more specific declaration wins. As the original declarations are more specific, they would overwrite our rules. For this reason, we have to make our declarations at least as specific as the original ones to overwrite them. For more information, visit the Mozilla Developer Network's related article at `https://developer.mozilla.org/en-US/docs/Web/CSS/Specificity`.

Modifying the slider is a bit trickier than customizing the buttons. There are two main elements: the rail and the thumb. The problem is that the position of the slider needs to be calculated from an absolute and a relative unit. Fortunately, we can calculate values with CSS; thus, the following lines solve our problem:

```css
.ol-zoomslider {
    top: calc(1.875em + 6px);
    left: calc(.5em + 12px);
    width: 2px;
}
.ol-zoomslider-thumb {
    background-color: rgba(219,63,63,.5);
    left: -11px !important;
}
.ol-zoomslider-thumb:hover {
    background-color: rgba(219,63,63,1);
}
```

We can use `calc` to calculate lengths with simple arithmetic operators in CSS rules. Remember that, for addition and subtraction, you always have to provide a whitespace between the operators and values.

As the rail of the slider will only be a narrow line with the thumb centered on it, the top position of the rail should be the top position of the `zoom in` button (`0.5` em) added to the height of the button (`1.375` em) added to the paddings and margins (`6` px). We have to correct this value by some pixels, which can be done by visual interpretation. The left position of the rail is calculated from the element's original left position (`0.5` em) and its original width (24 pixels).

We fix the thumb to the rail by setting it back to 11 pixels and making an important exception. We must do it this way, as its left position gets reset to 0 by the library every time the slider changes. As the code changes, the inline styling of the element and inline rules have the most specificity; we can only fix the thumb with the !important exception to the rail with CSS. If there is any other way, using !important should be avoided.

If you save the whole set of rules to a css file, or use the one provided with the example, and load it up, you will see our new zoom control in all its splendor:

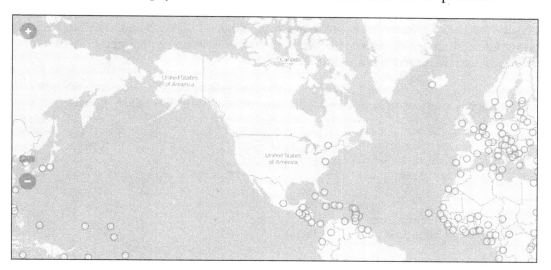

If you open the example from a touch device, it will be messy and disoriented. This is due to the library's design patterns. When the application is opened from a touch device, a class named ol-touch gets applied to the controls, and it overrides some of our rules. To make it compatible with touch devices, we have to make further declarations, which you can see in the css file named ch02_touch, too:

```css
.ol-zoomslider, .ol-touch .ol-zoomslider {
    top: calc(1.875em + 6px);
    left: calc(.5em + 12px);
    width: 2px;
}
.ol-touch .ol-zoomslider-thumb {
    width: 22px;
}
.ol-touch .ol-control button {
    font-size: 1.14em;
}
```

As the `ol-zoomslider` class under the `ol-touch` class has declarations by default, which we already made in our custom `ol-zoomslider` class, we can save lines by applying our existing rules to the more specific class, too. We can do this by using a logical OR operator, which is a simple comma in CSS. The rest of the issues can be solved by making new `ol-touch`-specific rules.

Styling vector layers

You might or you might not be familiar with vector styling at this point. If you know about the concept, however, a little revision won't hurt. In this example, we will change the default vector style of the example dataset to green stars. As vector data is drawn directly to the canvas by the library, their styles can be changed only by inner methods with a limited set of values.

You can see a `js` file named `ch02_vector` in the code appendix. You can use this file with the previous example or extend the original one with the following rules:

```
var vectorLayer = new ol.layer.Vector({
    source: new ol.source.Vector({
        format: new ol.format.GeoJSON({
            defaultDataProjection: 'EPSG:4326'
        }),
        url: '../../res/world_capitals.geojson',
        attributions: [
            new ol.Attribution({
                html: 'World Capitals © Natural Earth'
            })
        ]
    }),
    style: new ol.style.Style({
        image: new ol.style.RegularShape({
            stroke: new ol.style.Stroke({
                width: 2,
                color: [6, 125, 34, 1]
            }),
            fill: new ol.style.Fill({
                color: [25, 235, 75, 0.3]
            }),
            points: 5,
            radius1: 5,
            radius2: 8,
            rotation: Math.PI
        })
    })
});
```

In this simple style object, we define only a point symbolizer. It is a regular shape, which can be a simple, regular polygon. The polygon can be convex if it has only one radius value, and concave if it has two. Our star has five points and an outer radius of 8 pixels. The colors of its stroke, and fill, are expressed in RGBA values, which can be done by passing an array to their color parameter with four values. As the star will be upside down by default, we rotate it by 180 degrees The library only accepts radian values; thus, we have to rotate the star by π.

Using RGBA values is the only way to express opacity in vector styling. For regular styling with CSS, it is also a good practice as it takes fewer lines and all the major browsers support it.

Save the updated code, link it to the previous example, and open it up in your favorite browser. You should see the capitals represented by green stars:

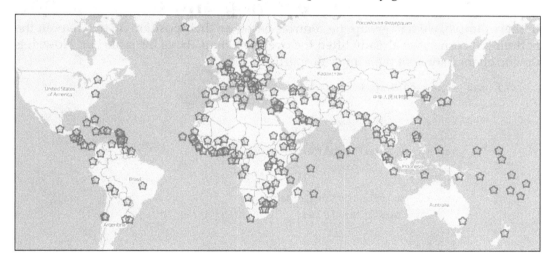

We have only defined a symbolizer for point geometries in our style object. This means that the line and polygon symbolizers are set to null. If you use this style object on line, or polygon features, they would simply not render. To make general style objects for multiple geometry types, you have to provide at least a stroke style and a fill style besides image.

Customizing the appearance with JavaScript

Apart from direct styling with CSS, OpenLayers 3 offers some methods to specify the appearance of our maps. These methods can be used to make such changes in the behavior of the controls, which would otherwise be quite hard to achieve, if not impossible. In the next example, we will look at some of the JavaScript-based customizing options.

If you open up the code attachment, you can see some files named `ch02_controls`. In these files, you can examine the changes we made to the previous example. The main changes, like the title suggests, will be in the JavaScript part of the example.

Changing the overview map and the scale bar

In this example, we will group the controls based on their position on the map. In the bottom-left corner, we already lifted the overview map above the scale bar. Now, it is time to change some of their inner properties:

```
var map = new ol.Map({
    [...]
    controls: [
        [...]
        new ol.control.ScaleLine({
            units: 'degrees'
        }),
        new ol.control.OverviewMap({
            collapsible: false
        })
        [...]
});
```

The scale bar now shows the scale in degrees, regardless of the map projection. We will later see that, in a WebGIS application, the unit of this control will be bounded to the unit of the current projection. However, the valid options for the controls are only `degrees`, `imperial`, `nautical`, `metric`, and `us`.

The overview map is now opened and cannot be closed. However, if you save these changes and open it up in a browser, you can see that the opened overview map covers up the scale bar again. To resolve this issue, we have to extend our CSS file with an additional rule:

```
.ol-overviewmap.ol-uncollapsible {
    bottom: 2em;
}
```

If we set an otherwise collapsible control to not collapsible, the library gives a specific class name to the control's DOM element called `ol-uncollapsible`. Remember the rules of CSS specificity: the more specific declaration wins. This way, we have to make our rule at least as specific as the original one, which uses a logical AND operator between the two classes. We also use this method, which can be achieved in CSS by concatenating the two class names.

 Use the overview map control with great care! It can handle the Web Mercator projection correctly, but with other projections it is unreliable. It cannot handle EPSG:4326 at all, and, in the case of custom projections, it can handle the ones with metric units.

Truncating the coordinate control

The `MousePosition` control outputs the current mouse coordinates with great precision. This can be good; however, we will fix it to exactly three digits in the next step. Luckily, the control offers a property for a preprocessing function. Let's create a function that can truncate the output to three-digit precision:

```
new ol.control.MousePosition({
    coordinateFormat: function (coordinates) {
        var coord_x = coordinates[0].toFixed(3);
        var coord_y = coordinates[1].toFixed(3);
        return coord_x + ', ' + coord_y;
    }
})
```

The function receives an array with two coordinates as an input, and requires a string as an output. We separate the array members into variables and fix them to three decimal places with JavaScript's `toFixed` function. Next, we return the fixed numbers converted to a string.

When a number is added to a string with the JavaScript's arithmetic + operator, it makes an automatic type conversion and concatenates the number(s) to the string(s). In our case, add the coordinate values to a string containing a comma, and a whitespace is enough to return an automatically converted string.

Changing the attribution

The goal of this step is to rework the attribution element's appearance and content a little bit. We will change the font type of the attribution control and the logo of the map. The logo is a rarely mentioned element of the map, but it plays an important role in every organization. This logo represents the given organization, and in most cases, it gets on the map in one way or another. OpenLayers 3, however, offers a method to define our custom logo and displays it in the attribution control.

Firstly, let's declare some rules for a new CSS class. It contains the required information to style the font of the attribution control:

```
.info-label {
    font-family: Palatino, serif;
    font-style: italic;
}
.ol-attribution img {
    max-width: 2em;
}
```

The second rule is required to create an IE-compatible application. The default `max-width` rule is interpreted differently by Internet Explorer 11 than any other major browser; therefore, we need to give it an exact value. The 2 em value is the same as declared for `max-height` by default.

Next, we create a `span` element in our JavaScript code to apply our newly created custom style on it:

```
var infoLabel = document.createElement('span');
infoLabel.className = 'info-label';
infoLabel.textContent = 'i';
```

If you would like to add some text to the element, always use `textContent` instead of `innerHTML`. As `innerHTML` tries to parse its content as HTML, `textContent` is much faster. There are also some security vulnerabilities behind `innerHTML`, but they are related to the user input and are out of the scope of this book.

Now, we just have to include our custom element in the attribution control's constructor:

```
new ol.control.Attribution({
    label: infoLabel
})
```

For the custom logo, we have to supply an object containing its attributes to the map object. Then, the logo will appear in the attribution control. The object has a mandatory url and an optional href parameter:

```
var map = new ol.Map({
    [...]
    logo: {
        src: '../../res/university_of_pecs.png',
        href: 'http://www.ttk.pte.hu/en'
    }
});
```

> If the logo does not have a link, it can be directly included as a single URL string to the logo parameter.

If you put every part of the code in place, save them and load the result in a browser; you will see the following customized map:

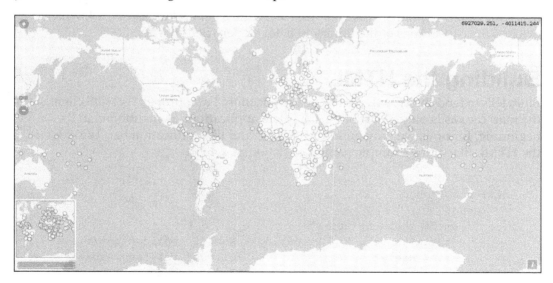

You can also customize the appearance of the attribution control with some simple CSS rules:

```
.ol-attribution span {
    font-family: Palatino, serif;
    font-style: italic;
}
```

However, these rules also apply to the » symbol shown when the control is not collapsed:

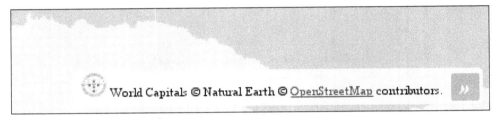

Creating a WebGIS client layout

Now that we are quite familiar with the possibilities of styling our maps with CSS and the inner methods, the next step is to create the layout of a WebGIS application. This step requires us to rethink our design patterns. The goal of this chapter is to create an application-specific design that doesn't prevent future developers from using the default options. This way, we can create a general wrapper API, which extends the capabilities of the library in a developer-friendly way.

Building the HTML

First, let's extend the HTML part of our application. For a proper WebGIS client, the map canvas is only a part of the complete application. As mentioned in the beginning, for now, we only build the tool bar and the notification bar. We extend the HTML like in the example named `ch02_webgis.html`:

```
<!DOCTYPE html>
<html lang="en">
    <head>
        <meta charset="utf-8">
        <title>Chapter 2 - Preparing a WebGIS Application</title>
        <link href="../../js/ol3-3.9.0/ol.css" rel="stylesheet">
        <link href="ch02_webgis.css" rel="stylesheet">
        <script type="text/javascript" src="../../js/ol3-
3.9.0/ol.js"></script>
```

```
        <script type="text/javascript"
src="ch02_webgis.js"></script>
    </head>
    <body>
        <div class="map-container">
            <div id="toolbar" class="toolbar"></div>
            <div id="map" class="map">
                <div class="nosupport">Your browser doesn't seem
to support this application. Please, update it.</div>
            </div>
            <div class="notification-bar">
                <div id="messageBar" class="message-bar"></div>
                <div id="coordinates"></div>
            </div>
        </div>
    </body>
</html>
```

Now we put everything in a map container. The sizes of the element are relative to the container. We also put a built-in error message in the HTML, which will be covered up by the map if the browser can load it.

 Note that, in a good API, every element is created dynamically with JavaScript. Hard coding the HTML elements is a bad practice. We only do this for the sake of simplicity. Creating an API with JavaScript is out of the scope of this book.

Styling the layout

As you have noticed, we created our HTML by defining simple elements with class names. We style these elements in a separate CSS file with class-based rules. Firstly, we style the map container element with the error message:

```
body {
    margin: 0px;
}
.map-container {
    width: 100%;
    height: 100%; /*Fallback*/
    height: 100vh;
}
.map {
    width: 100%;
```

```
        height: calc(100% - 3.5em);
    }
    .nosupport {
        position: absolute;
        width: 100%;
        top: 50%;
        transform: translateY(-50%);
        text-align: center;
    }
```

In Web design, horizontal alignment goes smoothly, but vertical alignment can be painful. In the nosupport class, you can see the most typical hack. The absolute positioning allows you to manually align the element with the parent. Setting the top attribute to 50% pushes down the element's top-side to the middle of the parent element. Giving it a -50% vertical transformation with translateY pulls back the element by 50% of its height.

Next, we style the notification bar. It has two parts, one for the mouse position control and one for the messages that the application will communicate. Now, we only style the coordinate indicator:

```
    .notification-bar {
        width: 100%;
        height: 1.5em;
        display: table;
    }
    .notification-bar > div {
        height: 100%;
        display: table-cell;
        border: 1px solid grey;
        width: 34%;
        box-sizing: border-box;
        vertical-align: middle;
    }
    .notification-bar .message-bar {
        width: 66%;
    }
    .notification-bar .ol-mouse-position {
        font-family: monospace;
        text-align: center;
        position: static;
    }
```

Regardless of using the div elements, we style the notification bar to render table-like. This way, we can vertically align the text messages that the application will output in an easy manner. It needs a parent element with the table display and child elements with the table-cell display (at least in Internet Explorer).

> In an HTML document, every visible element is rendered as a box. Every box has four edges: content, padding, border, and margin. By default, browsers use a content-box model, which applies the computed size only to the content. As we use a 100% width for the element, but we apply a 1 pixel border, the resulting box will exceed the maximum width of the screen by 4 pixels. This is why we use a border-box model, which includes the padding, and the border to the computed size of the box.

Finally, we style the tool bar for the controls. For now, it can only handle one line of buttons, but it can be expanded if more controls are needed:

```
.toolbar {
    height: 2em;
    display: table;
    padding-left: .2em;
}
.toolbar .ol-control {
    position: static;
    display: table-cell;
    vertical-align: middle;
    padding: 0;
}
.toolbar .ol-control button {
    border-radius: 2px;
    background-color: rgba(219,63,63,.5);
    width: 2em;
    display: inline-block;
}
.toolbar .ol-control button:hover {
    background-color: rgba(219,63,63,1);
}
```

As before, the styling of the control buttons are basically the same. The only difference is that we give them an inline-block display if they are in the tool bar. This way, the zoom controls, which are vertically stacked by default, become horizontally aligned. We vertically center the elements of the tool bar with the table method described above.

By specifying the style of the controls under our custom classes, they will always overwrite the default declarations. However, our styles are only applied if the controls are placed in the appropriate containers. If they are targeted at the map canvas, they won't be affected by our rules.

Writing the code

With the CSS rules and the HTML elements in place, the final task is to write the code part of the example. The code will be based on the previous example; however, we will strip it down to only contain the most necessary parts:

```
var map = new ol.Map({
    target: 'map',
    layers: [
        new ol.layer.Tile({
            source: new ol.source.OSM()
        }),
        new ol.layer.Vector({
            source: new ol.source.Vector({
                format: new ol.format.GeoJSON({
                    defaultDataProjection: 'EPSG:4326'
                }),
                url: '../../res/world_capitals.geojson',
                attributions: [
                    new ol.Attribution({
                        html: 'World Capitals © Natural Earth'
                    })
                ]
            })
        })
    ],
    controls: [
        new ol.control.Zoom({
            target: 'toolbar'
        }),
        new ol.control.MousePosition({
            coordinateFormat: function(coordinates) {
                var coord_x = coordinates[0].toFixed(3);
                var coord_y = coordinates[1].toFixed(3);
                return coord_x + ', ' + coord_y;
            },
```

```
        target: 'coordinates'
      })
  ],
  view: new ol.View({
      center: [0, 0],
      zoom: 2
  })
});
```

We cut out the entire interactions part. This way, we don't have to save the vector layer into a separate variable. We keep the base layer and the vector layer to have something for our map to display. We cut out most of the controls and only define the zoom buttons and the mouse position controls. As we do not extend the default set of controls, but instead define some, the default ones won't be present in our map, unless we add them manually.

The main extension to the previous examples is the placement of the controls. We can specify where OpenLayers 3 should place a control with the target parameter. We can provide a DOM element, or just simply the id of our element of choice. We place our controls according to our design in the tool bar and the coordinate container. If you save the complete example and open it up, you will see our application:

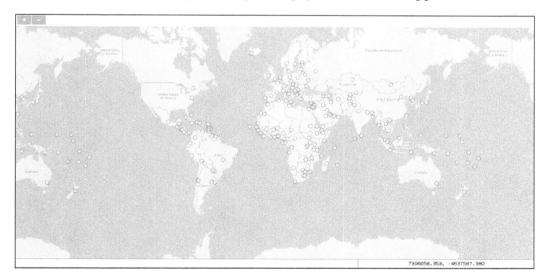

Summary

In this chapter, we learned how to style the appeal of our application with CSS and JavaScript styling methods, effectively. Take some friendly advice: in programming, there is rarely only one good solution. This rule greatly applies to CSS. It offers several methods to achieve one particular effect. If you learn to utilize most of its capabilities, you can easily create better a design than the simple ones described in this chapter (for example, with flexible boxes, filters, and other effects).

In the next chapter, we will learn how to manage layers. We will learn to dynamically add layers, remove layers, change their order, and draw them in a custom layer tree.

Working with Layers

3

Now that we have learned the basics of creating a frame for our custom WebGIS client, we will proceed to build a fully operational layer tree. Through out the chapter, we will revise how to manage the layer stack of OpenLayers 3 and utilize these capabilities in our application.

In this chapter, we will cover the following topics:

- Adding and removing layers dynamically
- Adding layers with the HTML5 File API
- Changing layer attributes based on user input
- Changing the order of a layer with the HTML5 Drag and Drop API

Before getting started

In the previous chapters, we discussed the HTML and CSS parts quite thoroughly. From now on, we will focus on the JavaScript part of the application. We will use native JavaScript (no jQuery, ExtJS, or other libraries) to build our application. This way, we will have a better understanding of the native language, rather than a library's abstraction methods. Eventually, our code will be more verbose, but this is a price we are willing to pay in order to gain better insight into JavaScript.

Using a proxy

For this chapter, I have adapted a simple Python proxy file to use from the one made by the OpenLayers Contributors for OpenLayers 2. As we will use AJAX requests to fetch features and metadata, we can easily bump into real CORS restrictions. These restrictions can only be resolved by a server-side proxy script, which requests the data from the target server and forwards it to us. From this moment on, the data will be from the same origin as the proxy script on the same server, which is similar to our application.

To use the proxy script, we will need two things: a Python interpreter and a running web server. If you don't have both of these, you won't be able to use the proxy. In this case, you will have to use a map server, which allows CORS requests.

> If you've used a Python server before, it won't be sufficient now. We need to access a CGI script; therefore, you have to start a different Python server. If you use Python 2, you can create CGIHttpServer. With Python 3, you just have to start your server with the --cgi flag.

If you have a web server and Python installed in it, you can find the proxy file in the code appendix as proxy.py. Copy the file into your server's cgi-bin folder. Note that you may have to modify the relative paths in the examples that are based on your server's layout.

> If your web server is public, don't use the proxy script! It is a dead simple script without any validation, sanitization, or security checks. If people can access your server from the Internet, they can use it for bad purposes, and as a consequence, charges can even be brought against you.

Resources to use

Through the examples used in this book, we will build a complete GUI for layer management. This involves adding layers from different sources with the help of forms. As some of the forms need valid resources to work with, called map servers, we will need some URLs to test our application on. The two most common open source map servers are MapServer and GeoServer. They have slightly different semantics that need some consideration when we automatize the data requesting process. We will use the following demo servers, layers, and projections for testing purposes:

- For WMS, refer to the following:
    - http://demo.opengeo.org/geoserver/wms (GeoServer without the CORS restriction)

- ○ `http://demo.mapserver.org/cgi-bin/wms` (MapServer with the CORS restriction)
- For WFS, refer to the following:
  - ○ `http://demo.opengeo.org/geoserver/wfs` (GeoServer with the CORS restriction)
  - ○ Layers: `topp:states` and `osm:water_areas`
  - ○ Projection: `EPSG:3857`
  - ○ `http://demo.mapserver.org/cgi-bin/wfs` (MapServer with the CORS restriction)
  - ○ Layers: `cities` and `continents`
  - ○ Projection: `EPSG:4326`

Note that these demo servers are made available for use free of cost by Boundless and the University of Minnesota Twin Cities. Respect them by using their servers responsibly and not exploiting their services.

Basic considerations

The layer tree will consist of two parts: the layer container with the layer elements and the control buttons. The buttons will be responsible to add and remove layers. The layer container will contain the layers in reverse order, which are as usual in the GIS software. Some of the layers' attributes will be ported to the elements, giving us the ability to change them through the GUI. The layer tree will have a reference to the map object and message bar, giving it the capability of making changes in the map and notifying us of every significant change.

Building a layer tree

If you look up the examples for this chapter, you will see some files with the `ch03_layertree` prefix. These files contain the first example. In this example, we will build the base of our layer tree and add the two layers from the previous example to it. First, take a look at the HTML file. We only add one single `div` element to the map, which we will dynamically fill with content:

```
[...]
<div id="layertree" class="layertree"></div>
<div id="map" class="map">
[...]
```

Styling the layer tree

In the next step, we will style the content of the layer tree with CSS. If you look at the CSS file for the example, you can see that there are quite a lot declarations in it. First, we will create some rules for the whole element:

```
.layertree {
    width: 20%;
    height: calc(100% - 3.5em);
    float: left;
    [...]
}
```

In spite of not showing the full HTML and CSS code here, in order to preserve valuable space, you must use the full versions from the example to get correct results. For the JavaScript part, you can proceed with the book. As we mainly focus on JavaScript, we won't skip any of the code contained in it.

We float the layer tree to the left-hand side of our map as expected from the GIS software. Next, we style the containers and layer elements:

```
.layertree .layertree-buttons {
    height: 2em;
    border-bottom: 1px solid grey;
}
.layertree .layercontainer {
    position: relative;
    height: calc(100% - 2em);
    overflow-y: auto;
}
.layercontainer .layer {
    position: relative;
    height: 2em;
    [...]
}
.layer span:first-of-type {
    position: absolute;
    left: 1.5em;
    max-width: calc(100% - 1.5em);
    [...]
}
```

We position the button and layer containers, respectively, give them height values for `overflow` to work, and go on to the layer elements. The first `span` in the element will be the layer's name. We give it the `absolute` position so that later on, the visibility check box can be positioned before it. Finally, we borrow OpenLayers 3's `ol-unselectable` class for our cause.

Absolutely positioned elements are positioned relative to their closest positioned ancestor. If you want to style an absolutely positioned element relative to one of its ancestors, you have to position that ancestor too. This is why we give the containers a `relative` position. The reason behind why we position the layer name absolutely is that, this way, it is taken out of the natural flow of elements; therefore, the visibility checkbox can be fitted before it.

Creating a layer tree constructor

To make the whole layer management logic clear and reusable, we choose an API-like solution. We create a layer tree object with a constructor and leave every operation to it using the object methods. This way, we only have to provide a reference to our map object, `id` of the layer tree element, and `id` of the message bar element. Everything else will be handled by our object automatically:

As a frontend developer, you are most likely to be familiar with the concept of constructor functions. However, there is one thing that we should note about them. In JavaScript, constructors can be called simple functions without using the `new` keyword. This results in an `undefined` returned by the constructor and a nicely changed global context where, in this case, `this` defaults to the global `window` object.

```
var layerTree = function(options) {
    'use strict';
    if(!(this instanceof layerTree)) {
        throw new Error('layerTree must be constructed with the
new keyword.');
    } else if (typeof options === 'object' && options.map && options.
target) {
        if (!(options.map instanceof ol.Map)) {
            throw new Error('Please provide a valid OpenLayers 3
map object.');
        }
```

```
        this.map = options.map;
        var containerDiv = document.getElementById(options.target);
        if (containerDiv === null || containerDiv.nodeType !== 1)
{
            throw new Error('Please provide a valid element id.');
        }
        this.messages = document.getElementById(options.messages)
||
                         document.createElement('span');
```

To prevent the preceding unwanted behavior, you can use the strict mode by making a use strict declaration at the beginning of your constructor function. In the strict mode, this defaults to undefined; therefore, the constructor throws an error if it is called without the new keyword (as a simple function).

In the first part of the code, we process the parameters that are provided by the user. The parameters are expected to be wrapped in an object with property names, such as map, target, and messages. As you can see, we are using two methods to validate the user input. If an essential parameter is missing or the constructor is called a simple function, we throw a user-friendly error, while in other cases, we just use a predefined value.

In further examples, we won't validate every user input to preserve space. However, you should always validate every user input and throw user-friendly errors or messages accordingly. This makes the code more stable and also improves the user experience. Remember: you can throw an error in the natural flow of the code as it acts as a return statement and stops it.

Next, we create the container elements and add them to the target element:

```
        var controlDiv = document.createElement('div');
        controlDiv.className = 'layertree-buttons';
        containerDiv.appendChild(controlDiv);
        this.layerContainer = document.createElement('div');
        this.layerContainer.className = 'layercontainer';
        containerDiv.appendChild(this.layerContainer);
```

Now that the environment is set up, we can proceed to add layers to the layer tree. For this task, we create a function that expects a layer object as input and creates a registry based on the layer properties:

```
var idCounter = 0;
this.createRegistry = function(layer) {
    layer.set('id', 'layer_' + idCounter);
    idCounter += 1;
    var layerDiv = document.createElement('div');
    layerDiv.className = 'layer ol-unselectable';
    layerDiv.title = layer.get('name') || 'Unnamed Layer';
    layerDiv.id = layer.get('id');
    var layerSpan = document.createElement('span');
    layerSpan.textContent = layerDiv.title;
    layerDiv.appendChild(layerSpan);
    this.layerContainer.insertBefore(layerDiv,
this.layerContainer.firstChild);
    return this;
};
```

There is one big consideration we have to make here: how do we link the layers to the appropriate layer tree elements? To overcome this problem, we use quite a secure method by creating a private `idCounter` member and a privileged `createRegistry` method, which can access this variable. We call it `createRegistry` as it creates a registry inside our layer tree; therefore, this name refers to our code's architectural design. This way, the code can only be broken if someone (or something) changes the `id` property of the layer object. We create the layer element, add the unique ID to it, and insert it on top of the layer stack, visually representing the order of the layers.

Private members can be created by simple `var` declarations inside a function. If a private member is created in an object constructor or method, a privileged method can access it. A privileged method is a method that's declared in the same scope as the private member that it uses (in our case, the constructor function).

Finally, we close our constructor by throwing an error if the input is not an object or any of the parameters are missing:

```
    } else {
        throw new Error('Invalid parameter(s) provided.');
    }
};
```

When a method makes local changes to your object, you can always return the modified object at the end of the method. This way, the object's methods will be chainable and it will be more convenient to use. However, as the new keyword always tries to return an object, if it is used with a valid constructor, the constructor functions should be void (there should not be a return statement in the end).

There's only one thing left to do: instantiate the layer tree in the init function, and add the layers to the layer tree via its createRegistry method. We also have to add a name parameter to our layers as the method will try to use it to display the layer's name. As we created the constructor function and the chainable method earlier, we can execute the whole process in one call:

```
var tree = new layerTree({map: map, target: 'layertree', messages:
'messageBar'})
    .createRegistry(map.getLayers().item(0))
    .createRegistry(map.getLayers().item(1));
```

As layers are wrapped in an ol.Collection object in OpenLayers 3, we can call them with the item method one by one. If you save the whole code and open it in a browser, you will see our layer tree up and running in the way that we have designed it:

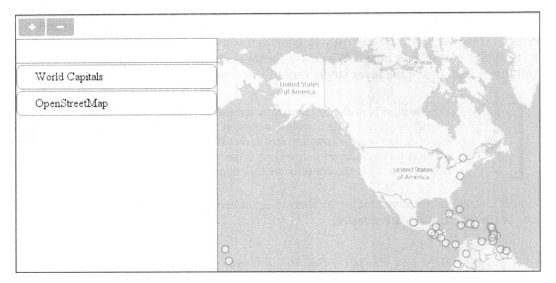

Adding layers dynamically

Now that we have a basic layer tree, it's time to add some logic when adding layers. In this example, called `ch03_addlayer`, we will extend our code so far with some layer requesting and WMS metadata fetching capabilities. We will add every additional method to the object's prototype for the sake of clarity and performance.

Creating the interface

To keep things simple, we first hard code some forms in the HTML part. We will be able to add layers by filling out and submitting these forms. This will only need some event listeners in the JavaScript code. As these forms are quite verbose, we will only discuss the most important parts here. You can see the full code in the example's HTML file:

```
<div id="addwms" class="toggleable" style="display: none;">
    <form id="addwms_form" class="addlayer">
        [...]
                <td><input id="wmsurl" name="server" type="text"
                    required="required" value="http://demo.opengeo.
org/geoserver/wms"></td>
                <td><input id="checkwmslayer" name="check"
type="button"
                    value="Check for layers"></td>
            [...]
                <td><select name="layer"
required="required"></select></td>
            [...]
                <td><input name="displayname" type="text"></td>
            [...]
                <td><select name="format" required="required"></
select></td>
            [...]
                <td><input type="checkbox" name="tiled"></td>
            [...]
                <td><input type="submit" value="Add layer"></td>
                <td><input type="button" value="Cancel"
                    onclick="this.form.parentNode.style.display =
'none'"></td>
            [...]
```

The forms basically consist of a `div` and `form` element with ids, some required fields, optional fields, a submit button, and a cancel button. The cancel button hides the form with a simple inline expression. We default the URL to the demo GeoServer instance, which is provided by Boundless.

Giving form members a name makes them accessible from the form's DOM object as properties. Just make sure that the names are unique in a single form.

Showing the appropriate form will be handled by our object, but the actions that are triggered by clicking on a form button, other than cancel, won't be. We assign events to these buttons manually using the `init` function:

```
document.getElementById('checkwmslayer').addEventListener('click',
function () {
    tree.checkWmsLayer(this.form);
});
document.getElementById('addwms_form').addEventListener('submit',
function (evt) {
    evt.preventDefault();
    tree.addWmsLayer(this);
    this.parentNode.style.display = 'none';
});
document.getElementById('wmsurl').addEventListener('change', function
() {
    tree.removeContent(this.form.layer)
        .removeContent(this.form.format);
});
document.getElementById('addwfs_form').addEventListener('submit',
function (evt) {
    evt.preventDefault();
    tree.addWfsLayer(this);
    this.parentNode.style.display = 'none';
});
```

The first event triggers our object's WMS metadata fetching capability. The second event disables the browser's default behavior of redirecting on form submission, and then it adds a WMS layer to the map with our object. The third event is a security consideration, which includes clearing out the layer and format options when we change the URL. Don't worry about these unknown methods as yet; we will cover them later on in this chapter.

 Note that forms and form-related events should be generated dynamically by the object in the production code.

Extending the constructor

As we would like to add two buttons to the button container automatically, we first add a helper method to our object's prototype:

```
layerTree.prototype.createButton = function (elemName, elemTitle,
elemType) {
    var buttonElem = document.createElement('button');
    buttonElem.className = elemName;
    buttonElem.title = elemTitle;
    switch (elemType) {
        case 'addlayer':
            buttonElem.addEventListener('click', function () {
                document.getElementById(elemName).style.display =
'block';
            });
            return buttonElem;
        default:
            return false;
    }
};
```

This method creates a button and adds properties provided as arguments. It uses a switch statement as we will need to extend it later when we add a delete button to the layer switcher. For now, it registers an event to the button, which makes the appropriate form visible when it's clicked. Next, we extend the constructor function:

```
[...]
controlDiv.appendChild(this.createButton('addwms', 'Add WMS
Layer', 'addlayer'));
controlDiv.appendChild(this.createButton('addwfs', 'Add WFS
Layer', 'addlayer'));
[...]
this.map.getLayers().on('add', function (evt) {
    if (evt.element instanceof ol.layer.Vector) {
        this.createRegistry(evt.element, true);
    } else {
        this.createRegistry(evt.element);
    }
}, this);
[...]
```

You can call any method that is added to an object's prototype directly in its constructor function. The naked object gets all of its prototype methods on instantiation before it gets shaped by the constructor function. Adding methods to an object's prototype also speeds up instantiation; therefore, the whole code.

As the `createButton` method returns the button element that it creates, we can directly append it to its container in a single call. Next, we add an event listener to the layers' collection object.

In OpenLayers 3, every change event that is triggered is handled by the nearest `ol.Observable` child to the source of the event. For example, layer events are triggered by the layers collection object, feature change events are triggered by their source object, while rotation change events are triggered by the view object.

As you have probably noticed, we use two versions of the `createRegistry` method. If the layer is a vector, we add an additional `true` to the arguments. Let's see the modified method to clear things up:

```
this.createRegistry = function (layer, buffer) {
    [...]
    layerDiv.className = buffer ? 'layer ol-unselectable
buffering' :
        'layer ol-unselectable';
    [...]
};
```

We use a ternary operator to decide whether we have to add an additional buffering class to the layer element's class list. But why? To put the last part of the puzzle in place, let's take a look at our `addBufferIcon` method:

```
layerTree.prototype.addBufferIcon = function (layer) {
    layer.getSource().on('change', function (evt) {
        var layerElem = document.getElementById(layer.get('id'));
        switch (evt.target.getState()) {
            case 'ready':
                layerElem.className = layerElem.className.replace(/
(?:^|\s)(error|buffering)(?!\S)/g, '');
                break;
            case 'error':
                layerElem.classList.add('error');
                break;
```

```
      default:
          layerElem.classList.add('buffering');
          break;
  }
});
};
```

 You can use JavaScript's ternary (conditional) operator to substitute a simple if-else statement with a single operator. The syntax is `condition ? expression, if condition is true : expression, if condition is false`.

With this method, we register an event listener to a layer's source object. The listener listens to every change event, which only occurs if the source's state changes. However, the event won't carry the state of the source (which can be classified as undefined, error, ready, or loading); we have to ask the source for it using the source's `getState` method.

 You can listen to a single image source's ready status by registering a listener on its `imageloadend` event. However, tiled sources only have a `tileloadend` event, which fires every time a single tile has been loaded.

If the source's status is ready, then we remove the `error` or `buffering` classes from the element with a regular expression, while in other cases, we add them to it accordingly. The reasons behind this are that we use this check only for vector layers; they need some time to get processed, and they fire their `change` event consistently. For raster layers, defining their state can be cumbersome (especially for tile sources).

 Knowing how to use regular expressions can be a powerful tool for string manipulation. The preceding expression consists of a noncapturing group (`(?:^|\s)`), capturing group (`(error|buffering)`), negative look ahead (`(?!\S)`), and a global flag (`g`). It says this: look for the start of the line or a whitespace. Found one? Don't capture it, just stay sharp! Look for the `error`, or `buffering`strings. Got one? Capture it! Now, look at the character after the captured string. Is it a whitespace? No? Great, then we have a match. Don't stop, we have a global flag, so search the entire input string for possible matches!

Before going further, let's refer to the CSS file of the example. There are some rules for the forms, which we won't discuss here, but there are also some more important declarations that determine the look of our buttons and vector layer states:

```css
.layertree .layertree-buttons button {
    height: 2em;
    width: 2em;
    [...]
    position: relative;
    top: 50%;
    transform: translateY(-50%);
    vertical-align: middle;
}
.layertree-buttons .addwms {
    background-image: url(../../res/button_wms.png);
}
[...]
.buffering span::after {
  content: '*';
}
.error {
  border-color: red;
}
```

The buttons are positioned with both of the methods that are mentioned in the previous chapter. This ensures compatibility with Firefox, which uses the `vertical-align` rule. The other browsers use the vertical transformation. We provide visual identifiers to the buttons via background images. Finally, the loading sign will be a simple star that's appended to the layer's name. An erroneous layer will have a red border, but this is a very rare phenomenon in OpenLayers 3. If you load the example, you will see the two buttons in their place:

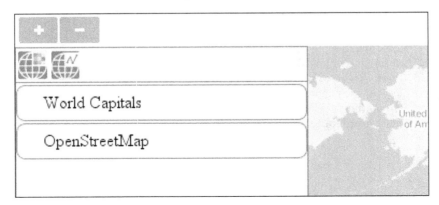

Fetching the WMS metadata

OpenLayers 3, like its predecessor, provides a great perk such as knowing how to serialize the GetCapabilities response from a map server. Up until now, it only allowed us to use it for WMS and WMTS. The lack of a WFS capabilities object is not necessarily a problem, and we will see why later on in the chapter. For now, let's create a method that helps us create options for the available layers and formats on a WMS server from its capabilities response. First, let's create some utility methods:

```
layerTree.prototype.removeContent = function (element) {
    while (element.firstChild) {
        element.removeChild(element.firstChild);
    }
    return this;
};

layerTree.prototype.createOption = function (optionValue) {
    var option = document.createElement('option');
    option.value = optionValue;
    option.textContent = optionValue;
    return option;
};
```

The first method clears out the entire element that's been given as an argument, while the second one creates an option element, gives it properties based on our input value, and returns it. As we will use both of them multiple times, it is a good practice to export them as individual methods. Next, let's create the metadata processing method:

```
layerTree.prototype.checkWmsLayer = function (form) {
    form.check.disabled = true;
    var _this = this;
    this.removeContent(form.layer).removeContent(form.format);
    var url = form.server.value;
    url = /^((http)|(https))(:\/\/)/.test(url) ? url : 'http://' +
url;
    form.server.value = url;
```

The method expects a form DOM object and requests capabilities based on the form's input values. The first part disables the check button from the time of processing. It goes on and prepends `http://` to the URL if the protocol is missing. It also updates the form's URL field as the `addWmsLayer` method will use the same form object. Now, we can go on and create the AJAX request:

```
var request = new XMLHttpRequest();
request.onreadystatechange = function () {
    if (request.readyState === 4 && request.status === 200) {
        var parser = new ol.format.WMSCapabilities();
        try {
            var capabilities =
parser.read(request.responseText);
            var currentProj = _this.map.getView().getProjection().
getCode();
            var crs;
            var messageText = 'Layers read successfully.';
            if (capabilities.version === '1.3.0') {
                crs = capabilities.Capability.Layer.CRS;
            } else {
                crs = [currentProj];
                messageText += ' Warning! Projection compatibility
could not be checked due to version mismatch (' +
capabilities.version + ').';
            }
```

The parser can only read the list of projections from the WMS 1.3.0 responses. If you have to deal with a previous version, you can default the projection to the currently used one. Eventually, if the WMS does not support the default projection, the layer simply won't load.

As the request can fail due to a mistype of the URL and other bad URLs, we will wrap the whole process in a try-catch-finally clause. AJAX requests (as the acronym suggests) are asynchronous; therefore, we have to assign a listener to its `readystatechange` event and check if everything went well. If this is the case, we can go on and process the serialized results. We check the projections the WMS supports, and grab a reference to our current projection.

By default, the `this` keyword refers to the context it has been called from. In our methods, the context is our object. However, as we define an event listener, we scope our object and scope into the one we assigned the listener to. Because we need our object's methods inside the listener function, we have to solve this issue. One way to do it is by assigning `this` to a variable while it still refers to our object.

Next, we check conditions against the layers from the response. If our current map projection is supported and there is at least one layer served, the function creates options based on the layer names and the propagated format values:

```
var layers = capabilities.Capability.Layer.Layer;
if (layers.length > 0 && crs.indexOf(currentProj)
 > -1) {
        for (var i = 0; i < layers.length; i += 1) {
            form.layer.appendChild(_this.
createOption(layers[i].Name));
        }
        var formats = capabilities.Capability.Request.
GetMap.Format;
        for (i = 0; i < formats.length; i += 1) {
            form.format.appendChild(_this.
createOption(formats[i]));
        }
        _this.messages.textContent = messageText;
    }
```

Next, we display the error message in the notification bar if something bad has happened during the parsing process. We also enable the check button, regardless of the error type:

```
    } catch (error) {
        _this.messages.textContent = 'Some unexpected
error occurred: (' + error.message + ').';
    } finally {
        form.check.disabled = false;
    }
} else if (request.status > 200) {
    form.check.disabled = false;
}
};
```

Finally, we send the request to the destination server after doing a final check on the URL:

```
url = /\?/.test(url) ? url + '&' : url + '?';
url = url + 'REQUEST=GetCapabilities&SERVICE=WMS';
request.open('GET', '../../../cgi-bin/proxy.py?' +
encodeURIComponent(url), true);
//request.open('GET', url, true);
request.send();
};
```

As a final check, we decide how to parameterize the URL. If we use GeoServer, it probably does not have any parameters in the URL so far; therefore, we need to start them with a ? token. In the case of using MapServer, the URL is possibly pointing to a `mapfile` as a parameter; therefore, we need to continue and add some more parameters with the help of an & token. Next, if we use the proxy file, we encode the final URL because sending special characters to the server (especially with Python 2's `SimpleHttpCGIServer`) can cause an error. Finally, we can send the request through our proxy script.

> This is the part where you have to use the second open method if you can't use the proxy file. If you can use it but the relative path does not match, just modify it to the correct path.

If you save and load up the example so far, you can see the layers and formats popping up on a valid URL input:

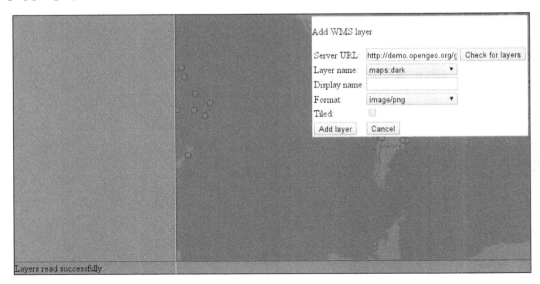

Adding WMS layers

Now that we have a working metadata parser, we create a method to add WMS layers from the list as shown in preceding screenshot. This method requires the same form, creates a layer object based on the parameters, and adds it to the map:

```
layerTree.prototype.addWmsLayer = function (form) {
    var params = {
        url: form.server.value,
        params: {
            layers: form.layer.value,
            format: form.format.value
        }
    };
    var layer;
    if (form.tiled.checked) {
        layer = new ol.layer.Tile({
            source: new ol.source.TileWMS(params),
            name: form.displayname.value
        });
    } else {
        layer = new ol.layer.Image({
            source: new ol.source.ImageWMS(params),
            name: form.displayname.value
        });
    }
    this.map.addLayer(layer);
    this.messages.textContent = 'WMS layer added successfully.';
    return this;
};
```

First, we create an object based on the general WMS parameters in a structure; the library accepts the URL, layer name, and the format. Next, as the user can choose between a single image layer and a tiled layer, we create the layer and the source object accordingly. Finally, we add the layer to the map.

Both tiled and single-image WMS layers have their ups and downs. Tiled layers significantly outperform single image layers. On the other hand, if the map server renders some content on top of the layer dynamically (such as labels or charts), tiled layers can have duplicated content or artifacts near tile edges.

Adding WFS layers

As the last step of this example, we create a simple method to add WFS layers to the map. WFS capabilities in OpenLayers 3 are strongly limited. The library can't read capabilities or build queries; it just requests features based on a URL and some parameters. Furthermore, it only supports WFS 1.0.0 and 1.1.0. In this simple method, we request vector layers based on basic parameters. First, we process the input form and create some related objects:

```
layerTree.prototype.addWfsLayer = function (form) {
    var url = form.server.value;
    url = /^((http)|(https))(:\/\/)/.test(url) ? url : 'http://' +
url;
    url = /\?/.test(url) ? url + '&' : url + '?';
    var typeName = form.layer.value;
    var mapProj = this.map.getView().getProjection().getCode();
    var proj = form.projection.value || mapProj;
    var parser = new ol.format.WFS();
    var source = new ol.source.Vector({
        strategy: ol.loadingstrategy.bbox
    });
```

Strategies in vector sources affect the rendering process, not the feature requests. As OpenLayers 3 uses an internal R-tree to index spatial data, it can easily select features based on an extent. With bbox, or tile strategy, you can speed up your application, as features with a minimum bounding rectangle out of the viewport are not even considered for rendering.

Next, we construct an AJAX request, default the version to 1.1.0, register an event listener to it, and send the request to the destination server:

```
var request = new XMLHttpRequest();
request.onreadystatechange = function () {
    if (request.readyState === 4 && request.status === 200) {
        source.addFeatures(parser.readFeatures(request.
responseText, {
            dataProjection: proj,
            featureProjection: mapProj
        }));
    }
};
```

```
    url = url + 'SERVICE=WFS&REQUEST=GetFeature&TYPENAME=' +
typeName + '&VERSION=1.1.0&SRSNAME=' + proj;
    request.open('GET', '../../../cgi-bin/proxy.py?' +
encodeURIComponent(url));
    //request.open('GET', url);
    request.send();
```

The same rule applies here when you use the proxy script. If you can't use it, just use the second open method, which is commented out. If we get a response from the server, we process it with our WFS parser and add the features to the source object.

Note that in OpenLayers 3, every feature needs to be present in the map's projection. You can ask the library to perform this transformation automatically by setting the appropriate projection parameters in the readFeatures method or in the format object itself. However, only readFeatures is consistent among the different formats.

Meanwhile, when the features are being downloaded, we construct the layer object, call the addBufferIcon method on it (which registers listeners related to the layer's status), and add it to the map:

```
var layer = new ol.layer.Vector({
    source: source,
    name: form.displayname.value
});
this.addBufferIcon(layer);
this.map.addLayer(layer);
this.messages.textContent = 'WFS layer added successfully.';
return this;
};
```

Now, it's time to save and test our code. Take your time to do this and check some of the resources that we mentioned at the beginning of this chapter. Check the water areas layer last. While it loads, you can go and grab a coffee. What do you experience when you play with the layer?

WFS considerations

Web Feature Service is designed to be able to support datasets in variable sizes. It has a logical server side and spatial filtering capabilities, which depend on the implementation of WFS and can be accessed via a GetCapabilities request. Sadly, only the GML support is mandatory in the service specifications, which is very verbose and produces large responses when bigger datasets are requested.

It is also a common practice to store large datasets in a single WFS layer and leave the filtering to the user. This was the reason behind the long loading time in our case, too. To effectively use a WFS server, we would need native support for the parsing of capabilities and query building from OpenLayers 3.

On the other hand, requesting already filtered data is quite unusual in the GIS field. Users are used to seeing the layer as a whole and apply their own filtering logic in it. Using canvas-based rendering, OpenLayers 3 has achieved an immense rendering performance. However, it still relies on the CPU, and rendering 28,539 polygons is just too much for it. Without proper hardware acceleration (WebGL), rendering large datasets should be avoided.

OpenLayers 3 can request WFS features based on a loading function. With this approach, we can request features in the current spatial extent. This can speed up our larger-scale applications. Dynamic loading is good enough for simple web mapping; however, in WebGIS, based on the preceding considerations, it should be avoided. You can see an example of dynamic WFS in the ch03_dynamicwfs.js file between lines 177 and 196.

Adding vector layers with the File API

The HTML5 File API makes it possible for us to load nearly any kind of file from our hard drive to a browser and process these files with JavaScript. It has capabilities way beyond our use case (it can even handle binary files); thus, it is advisable for every frontend developer to look into it in further detail. The files for this example are named ch03_fileapi.

First, we create a new form as usual. You can grab it from the HTML file.

Creating the interface

The basic interface to access our new functionality is the same, as shown in the previous examples. First, we extend our layer constructor, adding a new button to the layer tree:

```
var layerTree = function (options) {
[...]
        controlDiv.appendChild(this.createButton('addvector', 'Add
Vector Layer', 'addlayer'));
[...]
};
```

Next, we create a new rule for its button class in our CSS file:

```
.layertree-buttons .addvector {
    background-image: url(../../res/button_vector.png);
}
```

We also add a new event listener to our `init` function to link the form to our object:

```
document.getElementById('addvector_form').addEventListener('submit',
function (evt) {
    evt.preventDefault();
    tree.addVectorLayer(this);
    this.parentNode.style.display = 'none';
});
```

Adding a new button to the layer tree, which is based on our knowledge from the previous example, is simple. If you save the code and load it, you will see the new option in the button container:

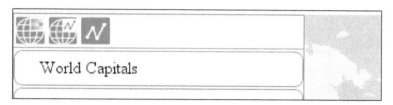

Building the method

As usual, the method accepts a form as an argument. As you have seen in the HTML file, the parameters are the usual ones, with one exception: the format. We use some predefined formats for our users to choose from and construct our new layer accordingly. First, we start our method by initializing some essential parameters and constructing a new file reader:

```
layerTree.prototype.addVectorLayer = function (form) {
    var file = form.file.files[0];
    var currentProj = this.map.getView().getProjection();
    var fr = new FileReader();
    var sourceFormat;
    var source = new ol.source.Vector();
```

File readers, similar to AJAX requests, are asynchronous. We have to register a listener to the file reader's `load` event to reliably get all of the fetched data:

 The easiest way to get access to files is using an `input` element with a `file` type. The element has multiple file supports; hence, we have to grab the first element from its file array.

```
fr.onload = function (evt) {
    var vectorData = evt.target.result;
    switch (form.format.value) {
        case 'geojson':
            sourceFormat = new ol.format.GeoJSON();
            break;
        case 'topojson':
            sourceFormat = new ol.format.TopoJSON();
            break;
        case 'kml':
            sourceFormat = new ol.format.KML();
            break;
        case 'osm':
            sourceFormat = new ol.format.OSMXML();
            break;
        default:
            return false;
    }
    var dataProjection = form.projection.value || sourceFormat.
readProjection(vectorData) || currentProj;
    source.addFeatures(sourceFormat.readFeatures(vectorData, {
        dataProjection: dataProjection,
        featureProjection: currentProj
    }));
};
```

When the data is available to be processed, we assign it to a variable. Based on the user's choice, we construct a format object and then try to guess the data's projection. Note that the order is important. First, we check whether the user has provided a projection by enabling manual overriding. We start guessing whether the form's projection field is empty. As all of the spatial formats have some way to store their projection, we try to access it. If we have no luck, we default the projection to our map's projection. Finally, we finish our method by telling the file reader to start reading, and while it's working, we create the layer and add it to the map:

TopoJSON is the new cutting-edge ASCII format to store vector data. It reduces redundancy in the coordinates by mapping topological connections, and it further decreases the file size by quantizing the coordinates. If you are not obligated to use a specific format, always consider using TopoJSON.

```
fr.readAsText(file);
var layer = new ol.layer.Vector({
    source: source,
    name: form.displayname.value,
    strategy: ol.loadingstrategy.bbox
});
this.addBufferIcon(layer);
this.map.addLayer(layer);
this.messages.textContent = 'Vector layer added
successfully.';
return this;
};
```

You can try out our new functionality with the vector layers that are located in the code appendix's res folder. All of the layers are in the EPSG:4326 projection.

Adding vector layers with a library

OpenLayers 3 offers similar capabilities out of the box. It is an interaction that combines the File API and the Drag and Drop API. As it is a completely automatic solution to add vector data from the hard drive, it needs different considerations. It is more restrictive when it comes to projection handling. We can define the projection in the constructor. If we don't, it tries to read the projection from the data itself. If it cannot find one, the interaction defaults it to the map projection.

You cannot access the interaction's default projection. If you want to change it, you have to remove the interaction from the map and construct a new one with a different projection.

Look at the file named `ch03_draganddrop.js`. We will extend our previous example based on its content. First, replace `ch03_fileapi.js` with `ch03_draganddrop.js` in the previous example's HTML file's `head` section. The only thing we have to do for this interaction to work is add it to the map and define its behavior when a vector file is added:

```
var dragAndDrop = new ol.interaction.DragAndDrop({
    formatConstructors: [
        ol.format.GeoJSON,
        ol.format.TopoJSON,
        ol.format.KML,
        ol.format.OSMXML
    ]
});
dragAndDrop.on('addfeatures', function (evt) {
    var source = new ol.source.Vector()
    var layer = new ol.layer.Vector({
        source: source,
        name: 'Drag&Drop Layer'
    });
    tree.addBufferIcon(layer);
    map.addLayer(layer);
    source.addFeatures(evt.features);
});
var map = new ol.Map({
    [...]
    interactions: ol.interaction.defaults().extend([
        dragAndDrop
    ]),
    [...]
});
```

There are two customizable features in the interaction. Passing an array of formats is mandatory as the interaction will check whether the data can be parsed with an instance of one of the formats. If it finds a match, it fires an `addfeatures` event with the parsed features. Adding a projection parameter is optional, as noted previously.

As it does not process the features automatically, we have to register an event listener to it. We split the process into parts so that the buffer icon will be displayed, while the features are loaded into the source object.

Now, go ahead and test our newly implemented feature. Grab a vector file from the **res** folder, and drop it on the map canvas.

Removing layers dynamically

Now that we can add layers dynamically with our layer tree, it's time to add the capability of removing layers. For this task, we create a button that's designated to removing a selected layer, and add some logic to select a single layer in the layer tree. You can see this example if you look for ch03_deletelayer.

Extending a constructor

First of all, we need to make the layers selectable, and we can do this by registering further events to the layer elements in the constructor function. To make it simple and clear, we create a utility method to add this event type to the layer element:

```
layerTree.prototype.addSelectEvent = function (node, isChild) {
    var _this = this;
    node.addEventListener('click', function (evt) {
        var targetNode = evt.target;
        if (isChild) {
            evt.stopPropagation();
            targetNode = targetNode.parentNode;
        }
        if (_this.selectedLayer) {
            _this.selectedLayer.classList.remove('active');
        }
        _this.selectedLayer = targetNode;
        targetNode.classList.add('active');
    });
    return node;
};
```

The function adds an event listener to the input element, which grabs a reference of it and saves it to the object's selectedLayer property. It also grants some visual feedback by appending an active class to the clicked layer element and removes it from the previously selected layer.

There is one problem with this. If we click on the layer name, which is a child of the layer element, we get a reference that doesn't make sense. To resolve this issue, our method accepts an isChild Boolean. If the boolean is set to true, the method simply grabs the reference of the clicked element's parent node and stops propagating to the layer element itself. Next, we create rules for the active class and the remove button in our CSS file:

```
.layertree-buttons .deletelayer {
    background-image: url(../../res/button_delete.png);
}
```

```
.layercontainer .layer.active {
    border-color: orange;
}
```

Next, we extend our constructor by adding the remove button and selection logic:

```
var layerTree = function (options) {
        [...]
        controlDiv.appendChild(this.createButton('deletelayer',
'Remove Layer', 'deletelayer'));
        [...]
        this.selectedLayer = null;
        this.createRegistry = function (layer, buffer) {
            [...]
            this.addSelectEvent(layerDiv);
            [...]
            layerDiv.appendChild(this.addSelectEvent(layerSpan,
true));
            [...]
        };
        [...]
        this.map.getLayers().on('remove', function (evt) {
            this.removeRegistry(evt.element);
        }, this);
        [...]
};
```

 Don't forget about chaining methods! As we made `addSelectEvent` chainable by returning the input node, we can directly append it to the layer element in a single call.

We also register an event to the map's layer stack. If a layer gets deleted, we also remove its element from the layer tree with the `removeRegistry` method:

 When we register an event to one of the library's objects, we scope it out of our object, as done in traditional event listeners. However, in OpenLayers 3, the on method accepts an optional `this` as a third argument; therefore, we don't have to grab a reference of it.

```
layerTree.prototype.removeRegistry = function (layer) {
    var layerDiv = document.getElementById(layer.get('id'));
    this.layerContainer.removeChild(layerDiv);
    return this;
};
```

As you must have noticed, in the button creation, we used a different button type. Remember when we used a switch statement in the button creation method? It's time to extend it with the `deletelayer` case:

```
layerTree.prototype.createButton = function
(elemName, elemTitle, elemType) {
    [...]
        case 'deletelayer':
            var _this = this;
            buttonElem.addEventListener('click', function () {
                if (_this.selectedLayer) {
                    var layer = _this.getLayerById(_this.
selectedLayer.id);
                    console.log(layer);
                    _this.map.removeLayer(layer);
                    _this.messages.textContent = 'Layer removed
successfully.';
                } else {
                    _this.messages.textContent = 'No selected
layer to remove.';
                }
            });
            return buttonElem;
        [...]
};
```

When we click on the remove button, it tries to decide which layer we would like to remove. As it has the layer's `id`, it can easily search for it in the map's layer stack. To make things even more transparent, we create a `getLayerById` method for this task:

```
layerTree.prototype.getLayerById = function (id) {
    var layers = this.map.getLayers().getArray();
    for (var i = 0; i < layers.length; i += 1) {
        if (layers[i].get('id') === id) {
            return layers[i];
        }
    }
    return false;
};
```

This method grabs a reference to the internal array of the layer stack and searches for the one with the input ID. When it finds the layer, the method returns.

One valid case for using the internal array of an OpenLayers 3 collection object is this method used previously. As we can have many layers, we don't want to iterate through all of them, just as many as necessary. With the collection's `forEach` method, we can't use a return statement to save some time.

If you save and load the example, you can try out our new functionality:

 You can easily implement simple logic to deselect layers by registering a listener to the layer container, which clears the selected layer property. If you do this, don't forget to stop the layer elements from propagating; otherwise, the selected layers will be deselected instantly.

Changing layer attributes

We've almost reached the state of a fully operational layer tree. The next step in the process is to add the capabilities of changing layer attributes. In this example, we will make sure that we can change any layer's visibility, opacity, and its name from the GUI. The example files are named `ch03_attributes`. As we are only adding further parts to the layer element, we mostly have to extend our `createRegistry` method.

Styling active layers

In our concept, only active layers can be modified. With this consideration, only the active layer element's options are exposed. The other layers will have the same nice, uniform height that shows only the layer's name and the visibility checkbox. We can easily implement this behavior with CSS:

```
.layercontainer .layer.active {
    border-color: orange;
```

```css
    min-height: 2em;
    height: auto;
}
.layer div {
    display: none;
}
.layer.active div {
    display: block;
}
```

 In most browsers, the `initial` value works just fine when resetting values to their defaults. However, Internet Explorer won't interpret `initial`, and as all the browsers know `auto`, it is advisable to use it for increased compatibility.

Extending the method

Now that the styling of the elements is complete, we can create logic to manage the layer attributes. First, we add some listeners to the layer's name element so that we can change it by double-clicking on it:

```javascript
this.createRegistry = function (layer, buffer) {
    […]
    layerSpan.addEventListener('dblclick', function () {
        this.contentEditable = true;
        layerDiv.classList.remove('ol-unselectable');
        this.focus();
    });
    layerSpan.addEventListener('blur', function () {
        if (this.contentEditable) {
            this.contentEditable = false;
            layer.set('name', this.textContent);
            layerDiv.classList.add('ol-unselectable');
            layerDiv.title = this.textContent;
            this.scrollTo(0, 0);
        }
    });
```

If we double-click on the layer name, our code changes its content to be editable, makes it selectable (otherwise, the editable attribute just wouldn't work on some browsers), and gives focus to it. If the element loses focus (the `blur` event), we restore the element's original status and update everything with the layer's new name. In the last step, we scroll to the start of the text as Firefox won't do it automatically.

 Making an element's content editable is an easy solution, but it is not stable (add some line breaks to the layer name and see for yourself). As a more stable solution, you can add a hidden text input to the element, make it visible when it's double-clicked, bind it to the layer name and layer object correctly, and make it disappear on losing focus.

Next, we create a checkbox that controls the visibility of the layer. We control the top of it with CSS, and then bind it to the layer. We also gather its initial value from the layer object (luckily, both of them operate with Booleans):

```
var visibleBox = document.createElement('input');
visibleBox.type = 'checkbox';
visibleBox.className = 'visible';
visibleBox.checked = layer.getVisible();
visibleBox.addEventListener('change', function () {
    if (this.checked) {
        layer.setVisible(true);
    } else {
        layer.setVisible(false);
    }
});
layerDiv.appendChild(this.stopPropagationOnEvent
(visibleBox, 'click'));
    [...]
```

With the layer object given to the method, we only have to toggle its visibility based on the status of the checkbox. However, we are faced with a new issue. If we click on the checkbox, we trigger the selection event, making our code select the checkbox and messing up our entire logic. To prevent this behavior, we create a `stopPropagationOnEvent` utility method, which has a quite meaningful name:

```
layerTree.prototype.stopPropagationOnEvent = function
(node, event) {
    node.addEventListener(event, function (evt) {
        evt.stopPropagation();
    });
    return node;
};
```

In the last step, we return to the `createRegistry` method and define a slider, which we use to control the layer's opacity. We create a div element to store future controls and make sure that we can't deselect a layer by clicking on it. Next, we append the slider to it. Its initial value depends on the layer's current opacity, and it has a direct binding to the layer. Similar to the checkbox, we have to stop the slider from propagating, too:

> We defined our bindings to work in only one way (GUI map). If you would like to have your layer tree updated in terms of the changes made to the map object, you have to register some listeners there, too.

```
var layerControls = document.createElement('div');
this.addSelectEvent(layerControls, true);
var opacityHandler = document.createElement('input');
opacityHandler.type = 'range';
opacityHandler.min = 0;
opacityHandler.max = 1;
opacityHandler.step = 0.1;
opacityHandler.value = layer.getOpacity();
opacityHandler.addEventListener('input', function () {
    layer.setOpacity(this.value);
});
opacityHandler.addEventListener('change', function () {
    layer.setOpacity(this.value);
});
layerControls.appendChild(this.stopPropagationOnEvent
(opacityHandler, 'click'));
layerDiv.appendChild(layerControls);
    [...]
};
```

> You must be wondering why we have registered a listener to the change event when we have one on the input event that fires immediately when we move the slider. Well, because of Internet Explorer, of course. Most major browsers fire an input event in this case, while IE 11 fires a change event.

If you save the code and load the example, you will see the attribute controls working. If you want to map other attributes to the GUI, you can easily do so by creating elements for them and appending them to `layerControls`:

Changing the layer order with the Drag and Drop API

In the final step, we implement some logic to change the layer order. The code for this example is named `ch03_layerorder`. As we want to have a convenient and full GUI implementation, we use the HTML5 Drag and Drop API to achieve our task.

This API needs a simple `draggable` declaration on an element and a set of dragging-related events. The browser needs to know what to do when an element is dragged; when it is over, another element is declared `draggable` in a case where it is dropped due to such an element. First, we prepare our layer elements by creating a CSS class to give visual feedback when a layer is dragged over another one:

```
.layer.over {
    border-top: 3px solid black;
}
```

Next, we extend our `createRegistry` function to make this process possible:

```
this.createRegistry = function (layer, buffer) {
    [...]
    var _this = this;
    layerDiv.draggable = true;
    layerDiv.addEventListener('dragstart', function (evt) {
        evt.dataTransfer.effectAllowed = 'move';
        evt.dataTransfer.setData('Text', this.id);
    });
    layerDiv.addEventListener('dragenter', function (evt) {
        this.classList.add('over');
    });
    layerDiv.addEventListener('dragleave', function (evt) {
        this.classList.remove('over');
    });
    layerDiv.addEventListener('dragover', function (evt) {
        evt.preventDefault();
        evt.dataTransfer.dropEffect = 'move';
    });
```

The events that are associated with the Drag and Drop API may need some explanation. The first event is fired when we drag the element. All other events fire when the element acts as a target. Note that only those elements that also bear the `draggable` attribute are recognized as target elements.

As the main concept behind the API is pure data transfer with the help of DOM elements, we need to define the data we would like to transfer in the `dragstart` event. As we don't have to deal with data from other sources, the simplest approach for this is to send the element's `id` as a string. We also notify the browser that we will move the element; therefore, it can assign a move cursor to the dragging process.

 We defined our type of transferred data as `Text`, unlike the general `text/plain` type definition. Can you guess why? Yes, I can hear you mumbling Internet Explorer, and you are totally right!

The dragenter and dragleave events are quite unequivocal ones. If we drag over a possible target, it will have a wider top border, while if we drag out of it, it returns to its normal state. There is some magic behind the dragover event, though. It has the default behavior of canceling the drop; thus, we have to prevent it. We also have to state that we would like to do this in a completely valid operation, which is in the list of allowed effects. Most of the magic is due to the drop event, though, where we change the order of the layers:

```
layerDiv.addEventListener('drop', function (evt) {
    evt.preventDefault();
    this.classList.remove('over');
    var sourceLayerDiv = document.getElementById(evt.dataTransfer.
getData('Text'));
    if (sourceLayerDiv !== this) {
        _this.layerContainer.removeChild(sourceLayerDiv);
        _this.layerContainer.insertBefore(sourceLayerDiv,
this);
        var htmlArray =
[].slice.call(_this.layerContainer.children);
        var index = htmlArray.length -
htmlArray.indexOf(sourceLayerDiv) - 1;
        var sourceLayer =
_this.getLayerById(sourceLayerDiv.id);
        var layers = _this.map.getLayers().getArray();
        layers.splice(layers.indexOf(sourceLayer), 1);
        layers.splice(index, 0, sourceLayer);
        _this.map.render();
    }
});
```

It also has a nasty default behavior in some browsers, which is to redirect based on the given information in the dataTransfer object; therefore, our first task is *defusing the bomb*. Now we can go on and grab a reference to the dragged element based on id. If the source and its target elements are not the same, we can talk about a valid order change and go on with our logic.

First, we insert the dragged element before the target (that is why we have highlighted the target's top border to indicate the destination). Then, we calculate the layer's position in the layer stack from the array of layer elements. As the layer stack has an inverse order and starts with 0, we use the preceding formula.

Querying the child elements of a node returns an HTML collection, not an array. To check the index of a given element in the collection, though, we need the indexOf method, which is exclusive to arrays. The JavaScript array object's slice method is perfect to convert array-like objects to arrays when called without any arguments. The full call would have been Array.prototype.slice.call, but instead, we used a shortcut.

Finally, we grab a reference to the map's layer collection's internal array, cut it out from its original position, and insert it into its a new position. We also have to call a rendering frame as performing operations on the internal array of an ol.Collection object does not fire any events.

This is the other valid case for using a collection's array instead of the collection's methods. As using the methods would fire a remove and an add event, the layer tree would recreate the layer registry on the top of the stack, crashing our logic.

Now, we only have to solve one final problem. As the elements can be dragged, we can't change the opacity of the layers with the slider because we would drag the entire element. We can solve this by registering two events to the slider. One of them disables dragging when we keep our mouse button on the slider, while the other one reactivates it when we release our mouse button:

```
opacityHandler.addEventListener('mousedown', function () {
    layerDiv.draggable = false;
});
opacityHandler.addEventListener('mouseup', function () {
    layerDiv.draggable = true;
});
```

The code we've just created is operational but far from perfect. For example, it has a weakness of not letting you place a layer at the bottom of the stack. You can fix this by adding an empty dummy layer element to the bottom of the stack and defining every drag event on it except for dragstart.

If you save the code and look it up in your favorite browser, you can try out our dragging mechanism:

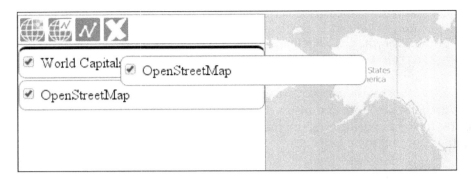

Clearing the message bar

In this very last example, called ch03_clearmessages, we make a mechanism to clear the actual message in the message bar after 10 seconds. For some applications, this is an absolutely useless feature, but for others, especially those with a less frequent notification output, this can come in handy. One way to achieve this is by manually removing the actual message after 10 seconds every time we create an output. However, there must be a more optimal and convenient way to do this. As we know that we cannot listen to change events on DOM elements without values and text contents are special DOM nodes, we will use the Mutation Observer API.

To achieve our new goal, we extend our layerTree constructor function:

```
var layerTree = function (options) {
    [...]
        var observer = new MutationObserver(function (mutations) {
            if (mutations[0].target.textContent) {
                var oldText = mutations[0].target.textContent;
                var timeoutFunction = function () {
                    if (oldText !== mutations[0].target.textContent) {
                        oldText = mutations[0].target.textContent;
                        setTimeout(timeoutFunction, 10000);
                    } else {
                        oldText = '';
                        mutations[0].target.textContent = '';
                    }
                };
                setTimeout(timeoutFunction, 10000);
            }
```

```
    });
    observer.observe(this.messages, {childList: true});
    [...]
};
```

Mutation Observer can notify us about a variety of changes in the observed DOM element and its children; however, it cannot track the changes in a text node. If we observe the changes in our `messages` element's `childList`, it will notify us about adding a text node or removing one (changing `textContent` to an empty string).

We use a recursive method to track the changes that are not observed by our observer. As we nonrecursively observe the message bar, every possible mutation event (even if someone mocks our application) will have the same target: the message bar. If we have a valid message, we store it in a variable, called `oldText`, and create a recursive function. This function compares the current message in the message bar with our stored message after 10 seconds. If it is the same, the function clears the message bar. If it is not, the function updates the variable and calls itself again after 10 seconds.

 This method is not very precise as it does not count the 10 seconds from the change of the text message but from the last check. However, for this purpose, it is completely sufficient.

Summary

Congratulations! You just created a GUI that is able to modify the layer stack in several ways. In this chapter we learned how to create a simple but fully operational layer tree. We also gained some valuable insight into JavaScript. You might have been familiar with most of the concepts discussed in this chapter. Or, this chapter might have taught you lots of new things. If this is the case, take some rest. You are on your way to not only mastering OpenLayers 3 but also becoming a great frontend developer.

We went through a small subset of the valid compatibility issues with Internet Explorer. It has been developed in its own way for quite a long time, causing quite a lot nuisance for frontend developers. However, most of these problems do not persist in Microsoft Edge.

In the next chapter, we will discuss various vector-data-based concepts. We will take a look at how we can manage vector data effectively by validating attributes, creating input forms, constraining feature types, or creating thematic layers. Let's vectorize our maps and learn how to get the most out of them!

4
Using Vector Data

When we work with vector sources, we basically have to deal with two types of data: geometry and attributes. The geometry part is responsible for storing the position of our shapes in one of the projections. We make spatial (topological) analysis with the geometries of our data.

Attribute data is responsible for storing the related information for every feature. It is also used for various analysis. Furthermore, it is utterly important when it comes to querying or styling. These are considered as basic or core capabilities in GIS software, although modern web mapping libraries tend to lack in effective attribute management. This is the reason why we will mainly focus on attribute data.

In this chapter, we will cover the following topics:

- Object-oriented attribute management
- Relational considerations
- Creating thematic layers dynamically
- Saving spatial data to our server
- Modifying geometries in place

Before getting started

As we will mainly focus on attribute management in this chapter, we will need a vector layer with lots of attributes. I have prepared such a layer to work with. It can be located in the `res` folder of the code annex, and its name is `world_countries.geojson`. Before we make some progress, let's change our default vector layer from the capitals of the world to this one:

```
var map = new ol.Map({
    [...]
        new ol.layer.Vector({
            source: new ol.source.Vector({
                format: new ol.format.GeoJSON({
                    defaultDataProjection: 'EPSG:4326'
                }),
                url: '../../res/world_countries.geojson',
            }),
            name: 'World Countries'
        })
    ],
    [...]
});
```

Accessing attributes

In the first example (`ch04_getattribute`), we will learn how to access attribute data stored in the features and communicate them to the user. We will use a very particular feature of OpenLayers 3: **the overlay**. As a first step, we will create some simple rules to be applied on our overlays:

```
.popup {
    border: 1px solid grey;
    background-color: rgba(255,255,255,1);
    border-radius: .5em;
}
```

 Overlays are geographically bounded HTML elements, which scale with the current resolution. They are stored separately from layers and other elements of the library, allowing us to have full control over them. As they are not parts of the canvas, we can easily style them with CSS.

Writing the code

For this task, we simply register a `click` event to our map, querying the underlying vector layers:

```
map.on('click', function (evt) {
    var pixel = evt.pixel;
    var coord = evt.coordinate;
    var attributeDiv = document.createElement('div');
    attributeDiv.className = 'popup';
    this.getOverlays().clear();
```

Firstly, we store the pointer's pixel and map coordinate value; then, we create a `div` element to store our attributes. Next, we clear out the existing overlays, implementing a lazy cancel effect. If the user opens a new overlay, the previous one disappears:

```
    this.forEachFeatureAtPixel(pixel, function (feature, layer) {
        var attributes = feature.getProperties();
        for (var i in attributes) {
            if (typeof attributes[i] !== 'object') {
                var attributeSpan = document.createElement('span');
                attributeSpan.textContent = i + ': ' + attributes[i];
                attributeDiv.appendChild(attributeSpan);
                attributeDiv.appendChild(document.
createElement('br'));
            }
        }
        if (attributeDiv.children.length > 0) {
            this.addOverlay(new ol.Overlay({
                element: attributeDiv,
                position: coord
            }));
        }
    }, map, function (layerCandidate) {
        if (this.selectedLayer !== null && layerCandidate.get('id')
=== this.selectedLayer.id) {
            return true;
        }
        return false;
    }, tree);
});
```

The geometry of a feature is stored as a property; therefore, the getProperties method returns it. It can also return style objects related to a given feature. To avoid falsely mapping out these objects, you can type check every attribute if it is a primitive value with the JavaScript's typeof operator.

Next, we use the map's forEachFeatureAtPixel method to query the vector layers under a given pixel. The method is not an easy one; it requires five parameters from which two are functions. In order to have a better understanding in the method, you can set some break points in the method using the developer tools of your browser.

The method's syntax is forEachFeatureAtPixel(pixel, callback, this for callback, layer filter, this for layer filter). It calls the layer filter function on all visible layers. If the filter function returns true, it queries the layer for features at the given pixel. Finally, it returns all the matched features and applies the callback function on them one by one.

In our callback function, we query the feature's attributes. Next, we iterate through its attributes object and append the attributes to our container element. If we have at least one attribute in our container in the end, we display it as an overlay. For the callback function, we specify this as the map object.

To iterate through plain objects, which have only properties inside, you can always use the in keyword with the for iterator, making your code simpler.

Next, we create our layer filter. As we only want to get features from the selected layer in the layer tree, we simply query every layer candidate against the layer tree's selectedLayer property. To make things more simple, we specify our layer tree object as the function's context. If you save the code and load the example, you can query features for their attributes. Don't forget to select the vector layer first:

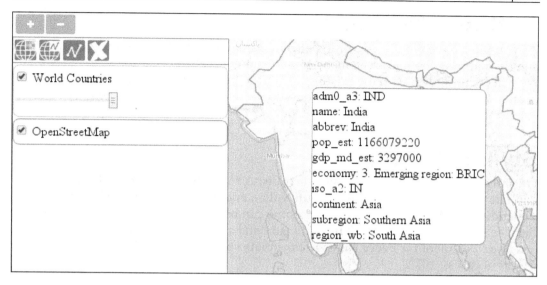

The only drawback of this method is that you can select multiple features if they are under the same pixel. How many features can you select at once?

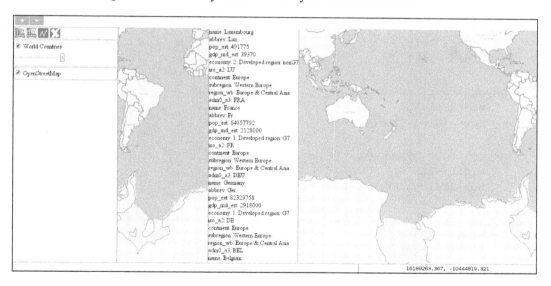

Setting attributes

As you must have wondered, setting attributes requires much more consideration than simply mapping them to an element. In this example, called ch04_setattributes, we will create a form with the existing attributes. In the form, the user will be able to change the attribute values, add new ones to the feature, and remove them. We will extend the previous example to achieve our goal.

Styling the form

Our form can have multiple possible layouts. A row with attributes will surely contain the attribute name, the attribute value, and a remove button. However, depending on the attribute's state, the name can be a span or a text input element. Besides the rows, the form will have the add and save buttons. As we will create a new div element for every row, we can create some simple CSS logic for these different cases:

```css
.popup span {
    display: inline-block;
    width: 5%;
}
.popup span:first-child {
    float: left;
    width: 40%;
}
.popup input[type=text] {
    width: 50%;
    box-sizing: border-box;
}
.popup input[type=text]:first-child {
    width: 35%;
    box-sizing: border-box;
}
.popup input[type=button], .popup input[type=submit] {
    width: 10%;
    float: right;
    [...]
}
.popup .delete {
    background-image: url(../../res/button_delete.png);
}
.popup .save {
    background-image: url(../../res/button_save.png);
}
```

You can select elements in CSS based on their attributes. You have to provide the attribute name and the value in KVP format in brackets after the element definition.

Writing the code

Firstly, unlike the previous example, we create a `form` element. Basically, as we create the possibility to rewrite and append attributes, we take advantage of the `form` element's submitting capability. We also dedicate a function to build rows based on some arguments:

```
map.on('click', function (evt) {
    [...]
    var attributeForm = document.createElement('form');
    [...]
    var deletedAttributes = [];
    var firstFeature = true;
    function createRow (attributeName, attributeValue, isNew) {
        var rowElem = document.createElement('div');
        if (isNew) {
            var nameInput = document.createElement('input');
            nameInput.type = 'text';
            rowElem.appendChild(nameInput);
        }
        var attributeSpan = document.createElement('span');
        attributeSpan.textContent = isNew ? ': ' : attributeName +
': ';
        rowElem.appendChild(attributeSpan);
        var attributeInput = document.createElement('input');
        attributeInput.name = attributeName;
        attributeInput.type = 'text';
        attributeInput.value = attributeValue;
        rowElem.appendChild(attributeInput);
        var removeButton = document.createElement('input');
        removeButton.type = 'button';
        removeButton.className = 'delete';
        removeButton.addEventListener('click', function () {
            rowElem.parentNode.removeChild(rowElem);
            deletedAttributes.push(attributeName);
        });
        rowElem.appendChild(removeButton);
        return rowElem;
    }
```

We store the deleted attribute names, so we can remove them from the feature on form submission. We use a `firstFeature` Boolean variable for a trick to limit the queried features to the first one in the given pixel. The `createRow` function creates a row based on the attribute's name and value. If it has to create an empty row, it creates a text input for the attribute's name, too.

Next, we modify our `forEachFeatureAtPixel` method's callback function. Firstly, we create the rows based on the feature's attributes and append the `add` and `save` buttons to the end of the element:

```
this.forEachFeatureAtPixel(pixel, function (feature, layer) {
    if (firstFeature) {
        var attributes = feature.getProperties();
        for (var i in attributes) {
            if (typeof attributes[i] !== 'object') {
                attributeForm.appendChild(createRow
(i, attributes[i]));
            }
        }
        if (attributeForm.children.length > 0) {
            var addAttribute = document.createElement('input');
            addAttribute.type = 'button';
            addAttribute.value = '+';
            addAttribute.addEventListener('click', function ()
{
                attributeForm.insertBefore(createRow
('', '', true), this);
            });
            attributeForm.appendChild(addAttribute);
            var saveAttributes = document.createElement('input');
            saveAttributes.type = 'submit';
            saveAttributes.value = '';
            saveAttributes.className = 'save';
```

If the user clicks on the `add` button, we can simply create a new row with two empty strings and insert the new row before the buttons. This way, the new attributes' elements will be nameless, which is required for the next part of our logic. As the final step, we add a `submit` event listener to the form and close our function:

```
            attributeForm.addEventListener('submit', function
(evt) {
                evt.preventDefault();
                var attributeList = {};
                var inputList = [].slice.call(this.querySelectorAl
l('input[type=text]'));
```

```
                               while (inputList.length > 0 && inputList[0].name
!== '') {
                           attributeList[inputList[0].name] =
inputList[0].value;
                           inputList.splice(0,1);
                       }
                       for (i = 0; i < inputList.length; i += 2) {
                           if (inputList[i].value !== '') {
                               attributeList[inputList[i].value] =
inputList[i + 1].value;
                           }
                       }
                       feature.setProperties(attributeList);
                       for (i = 0; i < deletedAttributes.length; i += 1) {
                           feature.unset(deletedAttributes[i]);
                       }
                        map.getOverlays().clear();
                   });
                   attributeForm.appendChild(saveAttributes);
                   this.addOverlay(new ol.Overlay({
                       element: attributeForm,
                       position: coord
                   }));
                   firstFeature = false;
               }
           }
       }
```

 You can query any element's children with a crafted CSS selector and JavaScript's querySelector or querySelectorAll methods. The returned element(s) will be the first matching the selector or an array in order, respectively.

On form submission, we grab all the text inputs from the form. We convert them to a regular array and create an attribute object based on some regularities. As we get an ordered array, we first check all the named inputs. If there are no named inputs left, we clearly have only new attributes in the array that come in pairs: one for the name and one for the value. If we are at the end of the list, we can move on and remove the unwanted attributes with OpenLayers 3's unset method. Finally, we set the firstFeature variable to false, ensuring that the function won't check any further features.

If you save the example and load it up, you will see the new attribute management interface at work:

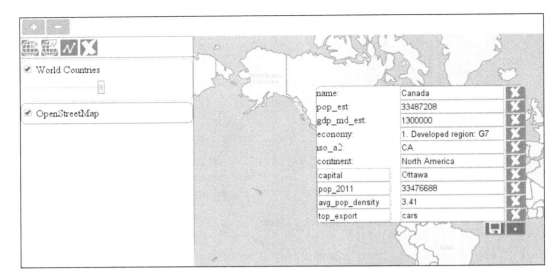

Feeling the power of modifying attributes as you like? This is one of the perks of object-oriented data management. As most of the ASCII formats used by web mapping libraries store their data as independent objects, and JavaScript is a purely object-oriented language, supporting this schema is a necessity in a WebGIS application.

Validating attributes

Object-oriented databases lack one very important thing that relational databases have: consistency. As consistent data handling and relational database support is a very important consideration in GIS software (at least to support a server-side spatial database), we need to implement some restrictions in our data management system. In this example, called `ch04_validation`, we will extend our application with typed attributes and validation.

One possible solution for easy RDBMS support is using the Web SQL Database API. However, this API is deprecated and not supported by any of the Firefox and Microsoft browsers. In supported browsers, it uses an SQLite backend.

Adjusting the styles

As we are using a form for attribute management, we can harness its validating capability as we use typed attributes. For numeric fields, we will use a number input, which does not process strings. In non-Microsoft browsers, numeric fields also prevent us from submitting the form if it detects a string in such an input. As a first step, we modify our CSS to extend our rules to numeric inputs, too:

```
.popup input[type=text], .popup input[type=number] {
    width: 60%;
    box-sizing: border-box;
}
```

Building headers

An easy way to store the types associated with the attributes is using headers like relational databases do. In our implementation, headers are objects stored in the layer object that contain the attribute names as keys and the types as values. For added convenience, we extend the OpenLayers 3 vector layer with a header builder method outside the init function:

```
ol.layer.Vector.prototype.buildHeaders = function () {
    var headers = this.get('headers') || {};
    var features = this.getSource().getFeatures();
    for (var i = 0; i < features.length; i += 1) {
        var attributes = features[i].getProperties();
        for (var j in attributes) {
            if (typeof attributes[j] !== 'object' && !(j in headers))
{
                headers[j] = 'string';
            }
        }
    }
    this.set('headers', headers);
    return this;
};
```

It simply grabs the headers property of the layer object, if it has one, and checks every feature's attributes; if it finds a missing attribute from the header object, it defaults the attribute's type to the string. This way, we have to provide every numeric attribute at layer construction.

It would be more logical to store the headers in the source object. However, unlike layer objects, source objects do not accept extra properties at construction.

Writing the code

This is one of the rare cases when we head from a complicated to a more simple example. As we manage our attributes at a higher level now, we cannot do local changes to them.

 To keep up the consistency of our data, we do not add or remove attributes at a feature level. Instead, you can build an attribute table and export those functions there.

In this step, we modify our `click` event on the map. We have to alter our `createRow` function and the `forEachFeatureAtPixel` method's `callback` function:

```
map.on('click', function (evt) {
    [...]
    function createRow (attributeName, attributeValue, type) {
        var rowElem = document.createElement('div');
        var attributeSpan = document.createElement('span');
        attributeSpan.textContent = attributeName + ': ';
        rowElem.appendChild(attributeSpan);
        var attributeInput = document.createElement('input');
        attributeInput.name = attributeName;
        attributeInput.type = 'text';
        if (type !== 'string') {
            attributeInput.type = 'number';
            attributeInput.step = (type === 'float') ? 1e-6 : 1;
        }
        attributeInput.value = attributeValue;
        rowElem.appendChild(attributeInput);
        return rowElem;
    }
```

In this rewritten function, we don't have to deal with new attributes. We only check the type of the attribute that we have to create the row for. If it is not a string, we create a numeric `input` element for it and check further. If it is a float, we set the precision to six decimal places. If it is an integer, we set the `step` attribute to 1.

You can create more complex attribute types with additional parameters. For example, if you want to implement a byte type, you can set the input's min parameter to 0, its max parameter to 255, and step to 1.

Next, we modify our main function to add validating capabilities:

```
this.forEachFeatureAtPixel(pixel, function (feature, layer) {
    [...]
        for (var i in attributes) {
            if (typeof attributes[i] !== 'object' && i in headers)
{
                attributeForm.appendChild(createRow(i,
attributes[i], headers[i]));
            }
        }
        [...]
            attributeForm.addEventListener('submit', function
(evt) {
                evt.preventDefault();
                var attributeList = {};
                var inputList = [].slice.call(this.querySelectorAl
l('input[type=text], input[type=number]'));
                for (var i = 0; i < inputList.length; i += 1) {
                    switch (headers[inputList[i].name]) {
                        case 'string':
                            attributeList[inputList[i].name] =
inputList[i].value.toString();
                            break;
                        case 'integer':
                            attributeList[inputList[i].name] =
parseInt(inputList[i].value);
                            break;
                        case 'float':
                            attributeList[inputList[i].name] =
parseFloat(inputList[i].value);
                            break;
                    }
                }
                [...]
});
```

The first part of the modification only maps out attributes that are present in the `headers` object of the layer. The second part is a lot more interesting. It collects all the form elements that can represent an attribute in an array. Based on the type of the attribute stored in the `headers` object, it parses the attribute accordingly. As inputs propagate their values as strings, converting them to numbers is a necessity. Converting them to text when we have to deal with a string type is just an extra layer of defense. Finally, we add some extra parameters and an event listener to invoke our new mechanism correctly:

```
var map = new ol.Map({
    [...]
        new ol.layer.Vector({
            [...]
            headers: {
                pop_est: 'integer',
                gdp_md_est: 'integer'
            }
        })
    [...]
});
[...]
map.getLayers().item(1).getSource().on('change', function (evt) {
    if (this.getState() === 'ready') {
        map.getLayers().item(1).buildHeaders();
    }
});
```

 As you can see, the event is just a hack for our logic to work. In a product, it should be implemented into the layer tree's most appropriate section. Furthermore, the manual initialization of the `headers` object is also hacky; however, doing it right would expand the code far beyond the scope of this book.

If you save the code and load it up, you will see our validating mechanism in action. Note that the numeric input's UI widgets do not work in Microsoft browsers:

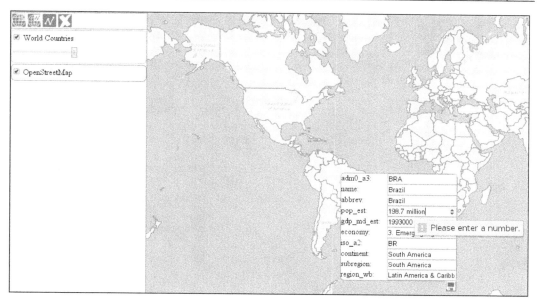

Creating thematic layers

In this example, called `ch04_thematic`, we will create an automatic solution for thematic mapping. It will include graduated and categorized symbology. To keep the example as simple as possible, we will make some generally incorrect assumptions. Firstly, we assume that we only have to style polygon layers. For graduated symbology, we hard code the intervals to five and also the color ramp starting from a beige tone and ending in a burgundy color. We will implement the whole code into our layer tree.

Extending the layer tree

We create the required GUI options in the layer tree. Firstly, we check against the origin of the layer. If it is a vector layer, we create an empty list and three buttons for the different styling options. Then, we save the default style in the layer, as it will enable us to restore the original styling. Finally, we register an event listener to the layer object. If the headers are changed, we rebuild the attribute list in the layer tree:

```
this.createRegistry = function (layer, buffer) {
    [...]
    if (layer instanceof ol.layer.Vector) {
        layerControls.appendChild(document.createElement('br'));
```

```
        var attributeOptions = document.createElement('select');
        layerControls.appendChild(this.stopPropagationOnEvent(attribut
eOptions, 'click'));
        layerControls.appendChild(document.createElement('br'));
        var defaultStyle = this.createButton('stylelayer', 'Default',
'stylelayer', layer);
        layerControls.appendChild(this.stopPropagationOnEvent(defaultS
tyle, 'click'));
        var graduatedStyle = this.createButton('stylelayer',
'Graduated', 'stylelayer', layer);
        layerControls.appendChild(this.stopPropagationOnEvent(graduate
dStyle, 'click'));
        var categorizedStyle = this.createButton('stylelayer',
'Categorized', 'stylelayer', layer);
        layerControls.appendChild(this.stopPropagationOnEvent(categori
zedStyle, 'click'));
        layer.set('style', layer.getStyle());
        layer.on('propertychange', function (evt) {
            if (evt.key === 'headers') {
                this.removeContent(attributeOptions);
                var headers = layer.get('headers');
                for (var i in headers) {
                    attributeOptions.appendChild(this.
createOption(i));
                }
            }
        }, this);
    }
    [...]
```

 In prior versions of OpenLayers 3, there was an undocumented method for firing custom events called dispatchEvent. From Version 3.8.0, this feature is gone; therefore, you must listen to existing events instead of creating new ones.

As we are building on the existing functionality, we extend our createButton method to support styling buttons. For this, we need to pass the layer object to it, obligating us to add a new argument to it:

```
layerTree.prototype.createButton = function (elemName, elemTitle,
elemType, layer) {
    [...]
        case 'stylelayer':
```

```
        var _this = this;
        buttonElem.textContent = elemTitle;
        if (elemTitle === 'Default') {
            buttonElem.addEventListener('click', function () {
                layer.setStyle(layer.get('style'));
            });
        } else {
            var styleFunction = elemTitle === 'Graduated' ? this.
styleGraduated : this.styleCategorized;
            buttonElem.addEventListener('click', function () {
                var attribute = buttonElem.parentNode.
querySelector('select').value;
                styleFunction.call(_this, layer, attribute);
            });
        }
        return buttonElem;
    [...]
};
```

We shape our default styling button to its final form, restoring the default style
stored in the layer object. The other buttons invoke the appropriate styling method.
As we grab those methods out of their default context, we have to manually provide
them with the JavaScript's call method and the reference to our layer tree.

 Extending the createButton method slowly leads to creating a
good object. Creating a method that has too much and too diverse a
functionality often leads to complicated, unmanageable code. Always
try to keep your methods clean and write quality code.

Creating choropleth maps

In this step, we need to calculate the color ramps for the classes first. We calculate a
linear transition between two arbitrary colors. To calculate the colors for the different
classes, we use an RGB color generator:

```
layerTree.prototype.graduatedColorFactory = function (classNum, rgb1,
rgb2) {
    var colors = [];
    var steps = classNum - 1;
    var redStep = (rgb2[0] - rgb1[0]) / steps;
    var greenStep = (rgb2[1] - rgb1[1]) / steps;
    var blueStep = (rgb2[2] - rgb1[2]) / steps;
```

```
        for (var i = 0; i < steps; i += 1) {
            var red = Math.ceil(rgb1[0] + redStep * i);
            var green = Math.ceil(rgb1[1] + greenStep * i);
            var blue = Math.ceil(rgb1[2] + blueStep * i);
            colors.push([red, green, blue, 1]);
        }
        colors.push([rgb2[0], rgb2[1], rgb2[2], 1]);
        return colors;
    };
```

As we have colors for the first and the last class already, we only have to partition the intervals of the color components to one part less than the number of classes we need:

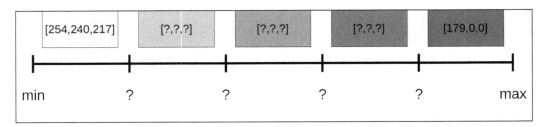

Next, we can start to write our styling function. Firstly, we calculate some statistics based on the input attribute and generate a linear gradient accordingly:

```
layerTree.prototype.styleGraduated = function (layer, attribute) {
    if (layer.get('headers')[attribute] === 'string') {
        this.messages.textContent = 'A numeric column is required for
graduated symbology.';
    } else {
        var attributeArray = [];
        layer.getSource().forEachFeature(function (feat) {
            attributeArray.push(feat.get(attribute));
        });
        var max = Math.max.apply(null, attributeArray);
        var min = Math.min.apply(null, attributeArray);
        var step = (max - min) / 5;
        var colors = this.graduatedColorFactory(5, [254, 240,
217], [179, 0, 0]);
```

You can use JavaScript's `apply` method with its `Math.min` and `Math.max` methods to calculate the minimum and the maximum value of an array. The `apply` method calls a function with a context and also an array of arguments.

Finally, we build a style function based on the generated colors and calculated intervals:

```
layer.setStyle(function (feature, res) {
    var property = feature.get(attribute);
    var color = property < min + step * 1 ? colors[0] :
        property < min + step * 2 ? colors[1] :
        property < min + step * 3 ? colors[2] :
        property < min + step * 4 ? colors[3] : colors[4];
    var style = new ol.style.Style({
        stroke: new ol.style.Stroke({
            color: [0, 0, 0, 1],
            width: 1
        }),
        fill: new ol.style.Fill({
            color: color
        })
    });
    return [style];
});
    }
};
```

Remember our assumptions: we can only style polygons with this method with five intervals and a predefined start and end color. In order to make a general styling method, you have to make a lot of checks and validations. If you test this part of the application, you can create choropleth maps with the numeric attributes:

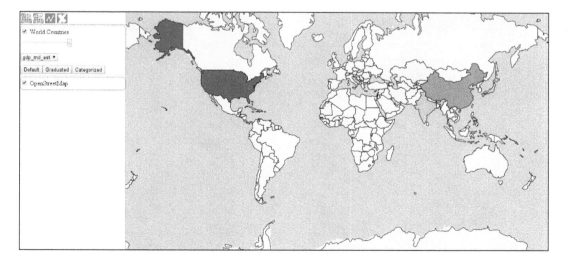

The simple equal interval symbology described above shows representative results only with data that has a nearly normal distribution. For a decent GIS software, more advanced functions are needed for graduated symbology.

Creating categorized maps

For a categorized symbology, we only need to collect the different attribute values from the features and assign random colors to them. For this purpose, we use a random color generator function:

```
layerTree.prototype.randomHexColor = function() {
    return '#' + Math.floor(Math.random() * 16777215).toString(16);
};
```

This simple method can work because the `Math.random` method returns a floating point number between 0 and 1. The biggest hexadecimal value for a color is `0xFFFFFF`. Its decimal value is `16777215`. Finally, the `Number.prototype.toString` method accepts a radix argument to support conversions between different numeral systems.

Next, we can collect the different attribute values and generate a random color for each of them:

```
layerTree.prototype.styleCategorized = function (layer, attribute) {
    var attributeArray = [];
    var colorArray = [];
    var randomColor;
    layer.getSource().forEachFeature(function (feat) {
        var property = feat.get(attribute).toString();
        if (attributeArray.indexOf(property) === -1) {
            attributeArray.push(property);
            do {
                randomColor = this.randomHexColor();
            } while (colorArray.indexOf(randomColor) !== -1);
            colorArray.push(randomColor);
        }
    }, this);
```

Our method builds two consequent arrays, where the indices of the attribute values and the colors match. This way, we can easily check whether a newly generated color already exists. If it does, the method just simply generates a new color and checks again. Now that we have the attribute and color arrays, we can build the `style` function:

```
layer.setStyle(function (feature, res) {
    var index = attributeArray.indexOf(feature.get(attribute).
toString());
    var style = new ol.style.Style({
        stroke: new ol.style.Stroke({
            color: [0, 0, 0, 1],
            width: 1
        }),
        fill: new ol.style.Fill({
            color: colorArray[index]
        })
    });
    return [style];
});
};
```

In the `style` function, we check every feature's corresponding attribute value against the attribute array, and assign a color based on the returned index number. If you save the code and load it up, you can test our new styling functionality. If you choose the `continent` column for the categorized styling, you will get the following result:

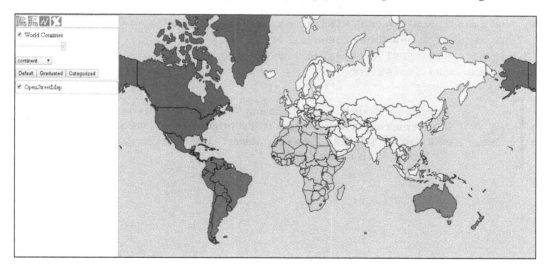

Note that features from a KML source use internal styling (as KML data can store styles); therefore, these styling functions won't work on them.

Saving vector data

In this book, we are concentrating on loading, mapping, and modifying spatial data on the client-side. However, we should be able to send our modified data to our server. Server-side applications are out of the scope of this book, though we cover how to initialize a saving process. Note that this example, called `ch04_save`, will produce errors as we don't have server-side support for receiving spatial data. Don't worry about that; the client side part works perfectly fine.

 If you would like to see the output of the last two examples, you can send them to the console before or after the AJAX request with `console.log`.

Saving in arbitrary formats

OpenLayers 3 offers powerful parser objects that are not only capable of reading strings representing vector data, but can also write features back to well-recognized formats. We can easily send a GeoJSON file with the following code:

```
var geoJSONSerializer = new ol.format.GeoJSON();
var featString = geoJSONSerializer.writeFeatures(this.getFeatures());
var request = new XMLHttpRequest();
request.open('POST', 'myserver/myscript');
request.send(featString);
```

 The GET methods have a limit in length, which depends on the browser used and also on the server configuration. As vector data can easily exceed this limit (generally at least 4,000 characters), using the POST methods is recommended.

Saving with WFS-T

Using a WFS-Transaction service usually requires less server-side configuration, but more considerations on the client side. OpenLayers 3 can write WFS-T requests; however, it is hard coded to support only Version 1.1.0. We can create a minimalistic WFS-T request with the following code:

```
var WFSTSerializer = new ol.format.WFS();
var featObject = WFSTSerializer.writeTransaction(this.getFeatures(),
null, null, {
    featureType: 'ne:countries',
    featureNS: 'http://naturalearthdata.com',
    srsName: 'EPSG:3857'
});
var serializer = new XMLSerializer();
var featString = serializer.serializeToString(featObject);
var request = new XMLHttpRequest();
request.open('POST', 'myowsserver?SERVICE=WFS');
request.setRequestHeader('Content-Type', 'text/xml');
request.send(featString);
```

As WFS-T services can insert, update, and delete features with POST, the writeTransaction method requires three arrays of features (insert, update, and delete). It also needs some options regarding the GML schema the method has to use. The method returns an XML node that needs to be serialized and then we can send it to the server. We also have to notify the server; we send XML data in the request body, by setting a Content-Type header.

> As you will possibly use a third-party WFS implementation, always test it before deployment. Possibly, nothing will go wrong with this projection; however, GeoServer tends to swap the coordinates with the projection EPSG:4326.

Modifying the geometry

Based on the reasons from the beginning of this chapter, our main focus is on attribute management. However, we cannot get past the geometry part without a word. In this example, called `ch04_geometry`, we pull out the swiss army knife of modifying geometries in OpenLayers 3. As we made a note of issues with the coordinate order in GeoServer, we swap the coordinates of a whole layer. Note that, for now, we only modify the geometries internally. We will do some visual and GUI modifications in the next chapter:

```
var modifiedFeatures = [];
var features = this.getFeatures();
for (var i = 0; i < features.length; i += 1) {
    var modifiedFeature = features[i].clone();
    modifiedFeature.getGeometry().applyTransform(function
(flatCoordinates, flatCoordinates2, stride) {
            for (var j = 0; j < flatCoordinates.length; j += stride) {
            var y = flatCoordinates[j];
            var x = flatCoordinates[j + 1];
            flatCoordinates[j] = x;
            flatCoordinates[j + 1] = y;
        }
    });
    modifiedFeatures.push(modifiedFeature);
}
```

 With the geometry objects' `applyTransform` method, we can get a reference to a feature's underlying flat coordinates and its layout in a numeric format called `stride`. The flat coordinates are a simple array with all the coordinates in bulk.

Firstly, we use `stride` to know how much further we have to step our iteration to get to the next pair of coordinates. We clone the features, modify them in place, and then save them in an array. The only thing left is writing a WFS-T request based on the new features:

```
var WFSTSerializer = new ol.format.WFS();
var featObject = WFSTSerializer.writeTransaction(null,
modifiedFeatures, null, {
    featureType: 'ne:countries',
    featureNS: 'http://naturalearthdata.com',
    srsName: 'EPSG:4326'
});
```

As GeoServer's coordinate swapping issue is well known, when updating existing features with WFS-T in the projection `EPSG:4326`, we include the features in the update array.

Summary

Congratulations! You have gained a very good control over your vector data. In this chapter, we learned effective feature management. We modified attributes, organized them in a different way, and even created thematic maps based on them. We also learned a basic yet very powerful method to modify the features' geometries.

In the next chapter, we will learn how to create custom controls and interactions. Among the different interactions, we will implement our attribute management system in a proper way. In the end, we will create a complete editing toolbar.

5

Creating Responsive Applications with Interactions and Controls

Now that we are familiar with extending OpenLayers 3 classes and vector management, we can go on and create some interactions and controls. These two terms became distinct in the library, unlike its predecessor. In a nutshell, interactions are special controls that involve a pointer and pointer events, while controls are the traditional controls that are static in nature and can be mapped to a GUI button or DOM element. This is not a bad thing, but it requires more architectural considerations when we create an application. We need to create a structure that can handle both of them in a nice, responsive GUI way.

In this chapter, we will cover the following topics:

- Creating a toolbar for control management
- Building custom controls and interactions
- Selecting, drawing, modifying, and removing features
- Measuring distances and areas on the map

Before getting started

In this chapter, we won't use any special APIs or libraries, we just play with OpenLayers 3 and native JavaScript. However, this is the chapter where we will use a feature that is not exported in the compiled library; therefore, we will need the debug version of OpenLayers 3, called ol-debug.js. The debug version of the library is in the same folder as the compiled version.

Basic considerations

As we would like to build a complete toolbar that can manage our controls and interactions, we need to make some considerations first. In the next examples, we will build a constructor function, which is similar to our layer tree. The constructed object will take care of the management of its internal controls. If you have used OpenLayers 2, you must be familiar with the panel control. Ours will be similar to it.

Right after this, we will create a general purpose control that has only one job: mapping an interaction to a button correctly. As the interaction and control have become distinct features, there is a gap between them, which we will fill. We will reuse this general control for our various purposes, and build a rich application with it, and various interactions assigned to it.

Building the toolbar

In the first example, called ch05_toolbar, we create the constructor function for our management system and add some methods to it to add and remove controls. We don't need any styling at this point. Firstly, we create the constructor:

```
var toolBar = function (options) {
    'use strict';
    if (!(this instanceof toolBar)) {
        throw new Error('toolBar must be constructed with the new
keyword.');
    } else if (typeof options === 'object' && options.map && options.
target && options.layertree) {
        if (!(options.map instanceof ol.Map)) {
            throw new Error('Please provide a valid OpenLayers 3
map object.');
        }
        this.map = options.map;
        this.toolbar = document.getElementById(options.target);
        this.layertree = options.layertree;
        this.controls = new ol.Collection();
    } else {
        throw new Error('Invalid parameter(s) provided.');
    }
};
```

Similar to the layer tree, we use the use strict paradigm to avoid bad invokes. The constructor takes an object with properties as an argument. The object must contain a reference to our map, a target element, and a reference to our layer tree. If everything is in place, we create an empty collection object in which we will store the controls associated with the given instance of our toolbar. Next, we add an addControl method to its prototype:

```
toolBar.prototype.addControl = function (control) {
    if (!(control instanceof ol.control.Control)) {
        throw new Error('Only controls can be added to the
toolbar.');
    }
    if (control.get('type') === 'toggle') {
        control.on('change:active', function () {
            if (control.get('active')) {
                this.controls.forEach(function (controlToDisable)
{
                    if (controlToDisable.get('type') === 'toggle'
&& controlToDisable !== control) {
                        controlToDisable.set('active', false);
                    }
                });
            }
        }, this);
    }
    control.setTarget(this.toolbar);
    this.controls.push(control);
    this.map.addControl(control);
    return this;
};
```

The method checks whether a valid OpenLayers 3 control has been given to it. If not, it simply returns a user-friendly error message. Next, it checks the type of the control, which we have to set manually later. In our structure, only one control can be active with a toggle type at a time. Every toggle control will get a listener associated with it. If it gets activated, every other toggle control in the toolbar gets deactivated (except the activated control). As a last step, we set the control's target and add it to the toolbar's collection and the map as well.

 You can only set a control's target before you add it to the map. After that, the setTarget method won't change the control's current target.

Next, we extend our toolbar further with a `removeControl` method:

```
toolBar.prototype.removeControl = function (control) {
    this.controls.remove(control);
    this.map.removeControl(control);
    return this;
};
```

This very simple method removes the control from the toolbar and also from the map. As every event is associated with the removed control, the library takes care of cleaning up automatically.

As a last step, we remove the zoom control from the map's constructor in our `init` function and add it to our toolbar instead:

```
var tools = new toolBar({
    map: map,
    target: 'toolbar',
    layertree: tree,
}).addControl(new ol.control.Zoom());
```

Now save the example and load it up in your browser. Do you see any changes? No? This means, everything works fine. From now on, our own control management system handles the zoom controls.

> Note that, if you create a general purpose API with a similar mechanism, you will synchronize the map's controls with the toolbar. This way, you can prevent an inattentive developer breaking the application by removing a toolbar control directly from the map.

Mapping interactions to controls

In this example, called `ch05_select`, we fill the gap between interactions and controls, and create a simple feature selecting the control. As we need to inform the user about the control's status, we create some CSS rules for active controls. Activated controls will have a nice orange color, which won't change, if we hover over them. We also extend the `ol-unselectable` class to our controls:

```
.layertree, .toolbar .ol-unselectable {
[...]
.toolbar .ol-control button.active {
    background-color: rgba(234,129,8,1);
}
.toolbar .ol-control button.active:hover {
    background-color: rgba(234,129,8,1);
}
```

Creating the control

Next, we can go on and build a custom control that has only one job: managing the underlying interaction. Firstly, we set up the control's properties and GUI elements based on the supplied options:

```
ol.control.Interaction = function (opt_options) {
    var options = opt_options || {};
    var controlDiv = document.createElement('div');
    controlDiv.className = options.className || 'ol-unselectable
ol-control';
    var controlButton = document.createElement('button');
    controlButton.textContent = options.label || 'I';
    controlButton.title = options.tipLabel || 'Custom interaction';
    controlDiv.appendChild(controlButton);
    var _this = this;
    controlButton.addEventListener('click', function () {
        if (_this.get('interaction').getActive()) {
            _this.set('active', false);
        } else {
            _this.set('active', true);
        }
    });
    var interaction = options.interaction;
```

We create a standard OpenLayers 3 control button: a `button` element inside a `div` element. We set up its style, title, and content; then, we add a listener to it. If we click on it in an active status, we deactivate it and vice versa.

 Interactions in OpenLayers 3 can be activated and deactivated by default. This is not true for controls; therefore, we have to implement it via giving the control an `active` property and registering listeners to it.

Next, we call the original control constructor with our custom control setting it up. This is one of the two key steps in extending a class in OpenLayers 3. Only after this step, we can use the control's factory methods.

After we set up the control, we can set its properties. This is where we give it a `toggle` type. We also store the associated interaction in the control and a function that will remove the interaction from the map, if the control is removed:

```
ol.control.Control.call(this, {
    element: controlDiv,
    target: options.target
});
this.setProperties({
    interaction: interaction,
    active: false,
    type: 'toggle',
    destroyFunction: function (evt) {
        if (evt.element === _this) {
            this.removeInteraction(_this.get('interaction'));
        }
    }
});
```

Next, we close our control with a listener on its `active` property. If the control is activated, we activate the interaction and add the `active` class to it's class list. Finally, we copy the prototype chain of `ol.control.Control` to our control with `ol.inherits` method. This is the second key step in extending an OpenLayers 3 class:

```
this.on('change:active', function () {
    this.get('interaction').setActive(this.get('active'));
    if (this.get('active')) {
        controlButton.classList.add('active');
    } else {
        controlButton.classList.remove('active');
    }
}, this);
};
ol.inherits(ol.control.Interaction, ol.control.Control);
```

The `ol.inherits` method is a simple reference to the Closure Library's `goog.inherits`. It takes two constructor functions; let's call them A and B. It simply copies the constructor B's prototype to the constructor A's `prototype.constructor` property. This not only exposes the constructor B's and all its parents' methods to the constructor A, but also makes an A instance of B and all its parents. One constructor can only have one inheritance with this method, it cannot be used as a mixin.

Adding and removing the control

As our control has an underlying interaction, we have to make sure that it is correctly added to the map on addition and removed on removal. For this purpose, we already created a function that will act as an event listener on the map's control collection. However, as we add an event listener to an object, which doesn't get destroyed, we have to manually take care of unlistening on the removal of the control, thus, cleaning up after ourselves:

```
ol.control.Interaction.prototype.setMap = function (map) {
    ol.control.Control.prototype.setMap.call(this, map);
    var interaction = this.get('interaction');
    if (map === null) {
        ol.Observable.unByKey(this.get('eventId'));
    } else if (map.getInteractions().getArray().indexOf(interaction)
=== -1) {
        map.addInteraction(interaction);
        interaction.setActive(false);
        this.set('eventId', map.getControls().on('remove',
this.get('destroyFunction'), map));
    }
};
```

Control objects have a `setMap` public method that can be overridden. This method gets the map object, the control is added to, and takes care of every map-related initialization. By calling the original method first, we can extend this functionality to our own needs.

If the control is added to a map or removed from it, this method gets invoked with the map object or a `null` value, respectively. This way, we can easily add the underlying interaction to the map, if it hasn't been added yet. However, we will have a hard time on the removal, as we don't have a reference to the map object then.

To overcome this problem, we register a listener to our map's control collection. If the listener detects that our control has been removed, it removes the associated interaction. If we save the key returned by the listener in a variable or a property (`eventId`), we can call the `ol.Observable.unByKey` static function with the key to remove the listener. This way, we do not need to have a reference to our map object.

Adding a selection control

Now that we have a fully operational custom control for mapping interactions to control buttons, we can add a simple selection control to our map. We leave everything on their default values and pass only an `ol.interaction.Select` method to the constructor, which can select any feature from any vector layer when it is clicked on:

```
tools.addControl(new ol.control.Interaction({
    interaction: new ol.interaction.Select()
}));
```

If you save the code and open it in your favorite browser, you will see our new control in action:

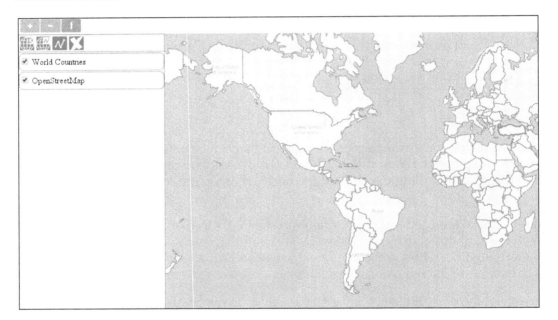

Building a set of feature selection controls

Interactions in OpenLayers 3 are related to the view or vector layers. These interactions related to vector data mostly have only this in common. Their working mechanism is highly inconsistent, it depends on the type of the given interaction. This peculiarity requires us to customize every interaction individually for our needs. In this example, called `ch05_select_complex`, we will create three selection tools.

Styling the controls

Firstly, we create some styles for the control buttons. We will use some nice background images to describe the controls. As we leave the text content of the buttons empty, we have to vertically center the buttons, not just the container `div` element. We also need to set some rules for the background images to render them properly:

```
.toolbar .ol-control button {
[...]
    vertical-align: middle;
    background-size: 1em;
    background-repeat: no-repeat;
    background-position: 50%;
}
[...]
.toolbar .ol-singleselect button {
    background-image: url(../../res/button_select.png);
}
.toolbar .ol-multiselect button {
    background-image: url(../../res/button_multiselect.png);
}
.toolbar .ol-deselect button {
    background-image: url(../../res/button_deselect.png);
}
```

Creating the selection tools

To set up and manage the selection controls, we extend the toolbar with a method that creates the required controls and adds them to the map. We will use one central select interaction. This way, if we ever need to make operations on the current selection, we only have to query a single interaction:

```
toolBar.prototype.addSelectControls = function () {
    var layertree = this.layertree;
    var selectInteraction = new ol.interaction.Select({
        layers: function (layer) {
            if (layertree.selectedLayer) {
                if (layer === layertree.getLayerById(layertree.
selectedLayer.id)) {
                    return true;
                }
            }
            return false;
        }
    });
    var selectSingle = new ol.control.Interaction({
        label: ' ',
        tipLabel: 'Select feature',
        className: 'ol-singleselect ol-unselectable ol-control',
        interaction: selectInteraction
    });
```

Luckily, the select interaction accepts a filter function, with which we can narrow down the candidate layers to the currently selected one. Next, we create another custom control with a drag box interaction attached to it:

```
    var boxInteraction = new ol.interaction.DragBox();
    var selectMulti = new ol.control.Interaction({
        label: ' ',
        tipLabel: 'Select features with a box',
        className: 'ol-multiselect ol-unselectable ol-control',
        interaction: boxInteraction
    });
```

Next, we assign an event to the drag box. When a box is drawn, we clear the selected interaction's underlying feature collection, detect every feature intersecting the box in the selected layer, and add them to the collection. Note that the selected interaction doesn't have to be active to highlight selected features:

```
boxInteraction.on('boxend', function (evt) {
    selectInteraction.getFeatures().clear();
    var extent = boxInteraction.getGeometry().getExtent();
    if (this.layertree.selectedLayer) {
        var source = this.layertree.getLayerById(this.layertree.
selectedLayer.id).getSource();
        if (source instanceof ol.source.Vector) {
            source.forEachFeatureIntersectingExtent(extent,
function (feature) {
                selectInteraction.getFeatures().push(feature);
            });
        }
    }
}, this);
```

The ol.source.Vector class has two methods for hit detection. The first one, forEachFeatureInExtent, compares the supplied extent with every feature's extent. This is a very fast method, as OpenLayers 3 uses an R-Tree for spatial indexing, but often yields incorrect results. The second one, forEachFeatureIntersectingExtent, compares the supplied extent with every feature's geometry. It is slower, but also more accurate.

Finally, we close our method by creating a third control to remove selections. This control is plain simple, and cannot be toggled; thus, we build it as a custom ol.control.Control. We also add the newly created controls to the toolbar:

```
var controlDiv = document.createElement('div');
controlDiv.className = 'ol-deselect ol-unselectable ol-control';
var controlButton = document.createElement('button');
controlButton.title = 'Remove selection(s)';
controlDiv.appendChild(controlButton);
controlButton.addEventListener('click', function () {
    selectInteraction.getFeatures().clear();
});
var deselectControl = new ol.control.Control({
    element: controlDiv
});
this.addControl(selectSingle)
    .addControl(selectMulti)
    .addControl(deselectControl);
return this;
};
```

The only thing left to do is to call our new method in the init function:

```
var tools = new toolBar({
    map: map,
    target: 'toolbar',
    layertree: tree,
}).addControl(new ol.control.Zoom()).addSelectControls();
```

If you save the example and load it up, you can play around with our selecting mechanism. Just don't forget to select the vector layer first:

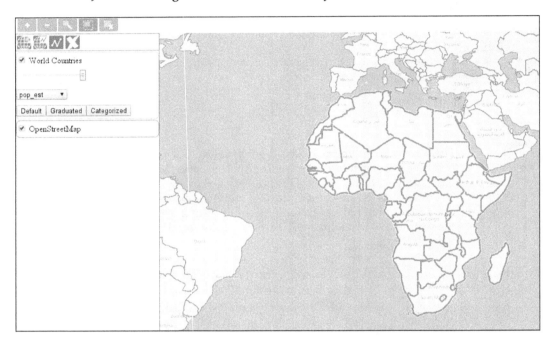

Adding new vector layers

In this example, ch05_newvector, we take a little detour back to our layer tree model. We have to make some inevitable enhancements to it before we can proceed to our next goal. We are going to create an option to add new, typed vector layers. We also need to create an event firing mechanism that can be used to detect changes in the currently active layer.

Creating the HTML and the CSS

As we extend our layer tree with a new layer addition option, we have to create the required HTML form and CSS rule for it. Both of them are very simple. The rule only contains the URL of the background image as usual:

```css
.layertree-buttons .newvector {
    background-image: url(../../res/button_newvector.png);
}
```

The HTML form enables us to name the layer and choose a type for it. The type can be one of the main vector types: point, line, or polygon. We also allow you to choose a collection type: geometry collection. Later, we will restrict the drawing options based on the layer's type:

```html
<div id="newvector" class="toggleable" style="display: none;">
    <form id="newvector_form" class="addlayer">
        <p>New Vector layer</p>
        <table>
            <tr>
                <td>Display name:</td>
                <td><input name="displayname" type="text"></td>
            </tr>
            <tr>
                <td>Type:</td>
                <td><select name="type" required="required">
                    <option value="point">Point</option>
                    <option value="line">Line</option>
                    <option value="polygon">Polygon</option>
                    <option value="geomcollection">Geometry
Collection</option>
                </select></td>
            </tr>
            <tr>
                <td><input type="submit" value="Add layer"></td>
                <td><input type="button" value="Cancel"
onclick="this.form.parentNode.style.display = 'none'"></td>
            </tr>
        </table>
    </form>
</div>
```

Extending the layer tree

Now that we have a form for the new vector layer, we can extend the layer tree with the necessary parts. Firstly, we extend the constructor function with a new button and the empty `ol.Observable` object:

```
var layerTree = function (options) {
    [...]
        controlDiv.appendChild(this.createButton('newvector', 'New
Vector Layer', 'addlayer'));
    [...]
        this.selectEventEmitter = new ol.Observable();
    [...]
        this.map.getLayers().on('remove', function (evt) {
            this.removeRegistry(evt.element);
            this.selectEventEmitter.changed();
    [...]
};
```

The reason behind our choice of event object is that `ol.Observable` is the most lightweight class that can create events, and be listened to. Practically, this is the only task of this class. We can immediately find a place to fire a change event in our constructor — when we remove the selected layer. Next, we find the other occurrence where firing the change event is appropriate:

```
layerTree.prototype.addSelectEvent = function (node, isChild) {
    var _this = this;
    node.addEventListener('click', function (evt) {
    [...]
        _this.selectEventEmitter.changed();
    [...]
};
```

Next, we create the method responsible for reading the form and add the vector layer to the map accordingly:

```
layerTree.prototype.newVectorLayer = function (form) {
    var type = form.type.value;
    if (type !== 'point' && type !== 'line' && type !== 'polygon'
&& type !== 'geomcollection') {
        this.messages.textContent = 'Unrecognized layer type.';
        return false;
    }
    var layer = new ol.layer.Vector({
        source: new ol.source.Vector(),
```

```
        name: form.displayname.value || 'Unnamed Layer',
        type: type
    });
    this.addBufferIcon(layer);
    this.map.addLayer(layer);
    layer.getSource().changed();
    this.messages.textContent = 'New vector layer created
successfully.';
    return this;
};
```

Note that, if we try to manually alter the type of the layer and provide a custom value, it will get stuck on the first check. Also, as vector layers generally get a buffering icon from the layer tree and our layer's source is empty, we must manually trigger a change event on it for the buffering icon to disappear. The order matters as we have to trigger the change event after the layer's `div` element has been created.

Finally, we add the required event listener for the form, as usual, and see the results:

```
document.getElementById('newvector_form').addEventListener('submit',
function (evt) {
    evt.preventDefault();
    tree.newVectorLayer(this);
    this.parentNode.style.display = 'none';
});
```

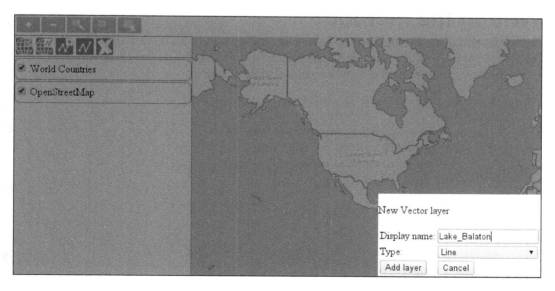

Building a set of drawing tools

In this example, called `ch05_draw`, we extend our toolbar with a method that creates a set of drawing tools. We store these tools in a new collection, as we would like to enable them, only if a vector layer is selected. As they are placed in a collection, we can easily iterate through them. Firstly, we create some new rules in our CSS file for the buttons and the disabled controls:

```css
.toolbar .ol-control button:disabled {
    background-color: rgba(0,0,0,.2);
}
.toolbar .ol-control button:disabled:hover {
    background-color: rgba(0,0,0,.2);
}
.toolbar .ol-addpoint button {
    background-image: url(../../res/button_addpoint.png);
}
.toolbar .ol-addline button {
    background-image: url(../../res/button_addline.png);
}
.toolbar .ol-addpolygon button {
    background-image: url(../../res/button_addpolygon.png);
}
```

Writing the method

Before starting our method, we extend our custom interaction control with the disabling capability. It is a very simple method that sets the `disabled` property of the button element, if the argument is a Boolean literal:

```js
ol.control.Interaction = function (opt_options) {
    [...]
    this.setDisabled = function (bool) {
        if (typeof bool === 'boolean') {
            controlButton.disabled = bool;
            return this;
        }
    };
    [...]
};
```

Next, we can create our new method that constructs the three necessary drawing controls and adds them to the collection of editing controls:

 By default, `ol.interaction.Draw` finishes the current sketch if you click within the 12 pixels radius of one of the sketch's vertices. For precise digitizing, this behavior is unacceptable; therefore, we set the `snapTolerance` parameter to 1. This way, we can only finish our sketch with a double-click on the last vertex, but we also help the library to identify a double-click, especially when our snapping control will be active.

```
toolBar.prototype.addEditingToolBar = function () {
    var layertree = this.layertree;
    this.editingControls = new ol.Collection();
    var drawPoint = new ol.control.Interaction({
        label: ' ',
        tipLabel: 'Add points',
        className: 'ol-addpoint ol-unselectable ol-control',
        interaction: this.handleEvents(new ol.interaction.Draw({
            type: 'Point',
            snapTolerance: 1
        }), 'point')
    }).setDisabled(true);
    this.editingControls.push(drawPoint);
    var drawLine = new ol.control.Interaction({
        label: ' ',
        tipLabel: 'Add lines',
        className: 'ol-addline ol-unselectable ol-control',
        interaction: this.handleEvents(new ol.interaction.Draw({
            type: 'LineString',
            snapTolerance: 1
        }), 'line')
    }).setDisabled(true);
    this.editingControls.push(drawLine);
    var drawPolygon = new ol.control.Interaction({
        label: ' ',
        tipLabel: 'Add polygons',
        className: 'ol-addpolygon ol-unselectable ol-control',
        interaction: this.handleEvents(new ol.interaction.Draw({
            type: 'Polygon',
            snapTolerance: 1
        }), 'polygon')
    }).setDisabled(true);
    this.editingControls.push(drawPolygon);
```

We can assign a layer filter in the select interaction, which is considered an easy case. However, the draw interactions require a source object to work with, which cannot be changed after instantiation. To tackle this problem, we do not specify a source in the interactions, but we will add the features to the appropriate source manually via event listeners.

Note that, later, we will dedicate a method to register listeners on the drawing interactions called `handleEvents`. Don't worry about that now, we will discuss it right after we finish this method.

We disable every editing control by default as, in the application's default state, none of the layers are selected. Next, we close our method by registering an event on the layer tree's `selectEventEmitter` object and add the controls to the toolbar:

```
layertree.selectEventEmitter.on('change', function () {
    var layer = layertree.getLayerById(layertree.selectedLayer.
id);
        if (layer instanceof ol.layer.Vector) {
            this.editingControls.forEach(function (control) {
                control.setDisabled(false);
            });
            var layerType = layer.get('type');
            if (layerType !== 'point' && layerType !==
'geomcollection') drawPoint.setDisabled(true).set('active',
false);
            if (layerType !== 'line' && layerType !==
'geomcollection') drawLine.setDisabled(true).set('active', false);
            if (layerType !== 'polygon' && layerType !==
'geomcollection') drawPolygon.setDisabled(true).set
('active', false);
        } else {
            this.editingControls.forEach(function (control) {
                control.set('active', false);
                control.setDisabled(true);
            });
        }
    }, this);
    this.addControl(drawPoint).addControl(drawLine).addControl
(drawPolygon);
    return this;
};
```

If the selected layer changes, we check the new selection. We follow two different logics based on the layer's type. If the layer has a vector type, we use a permissive logic. We enable every editing control, check for the type of the layer, and disable the inappropriate drawing controls. We also deactivate them; therefore, they do not get stuck if we change the selected layer during an editing session. If the layer is not a vector, we use a restrictive logic and disable every editing control.

We have called the layer tree's `getLayerById` method several times in our code. If you write production code, it sounds like a reasonable optimization to store a reference to the currently selected layer in the layer tree besides its DOM element.

Now, it's time to define a method to register events to the draw interactions. There is a mandatory event on finishing a sketch where we add the feature to the selected vector layer's source, if there is a vector layer selected. However, it is advisable to do a check when we start drawing. Disabling controls can be considered as a good visual feedback for users, as to whether they can use a given drawing tool or not. On the other hand, the `disabled` property of a DOM element can be overridden from the browser; thus, we should make the drawing process completely foolproof. We start with a listener that implements this extra security consideration:

```
toolBar.prototype.handleEvents = function (interaction, type) {
    if (type !== 'point') {
        interaction.on('drawstart', function (evt) {
            var error = false;
            if (this.layertree.selectedLayer) {
                var selectedLayer = this.layertree.getLayerById(this.
layertree.selectedLayer.id);
                var layerType = selectedLayer.get('type');
                error = (layerType !== type && layerType !==
'geomcollection') ? true : false;
            } else {
                error = true;
            }
            if (error) {
                interaction.finishDrawing();
            }
        }, this);
    }
}
```

If we are working with a `draw line` or `draw polygon` tool, we check for the active layer. If it is not a vector, we simply call the interaction's `finishDrawing` method. Note that calling this method in a `draw point` tool results in an error as the sketch feature becomes `null`. Next, we add an event when a sketch is finished, which is responsible for adding a feature to the source and displaying errors:

> We can check for an empty string in a conditional statement, as it is a false value in JavaScript. This means, not only the Boolean literal `false` can be used for conditional checking, but any other value can get evaluated to `true` or `false` in such cases. You can see the full list by searching for `JavaScript truthy falsey`.

```
interaction.on('drawend', function (evt) {
    var error = '';
    errorcheck: if (this.layertree.selectedLayer) {
        var selectedLayer = this.layertree.getLayerById(this.
layertree.selectedLayer.id);
        error = selectedLayer instanceof ol.layer.Vector ? ''
: 'Please select a valid vector layer.';
        if (error) break errorcheck;
        var layerType = selectedLayer.get('type');
        error = (layerType === type || layerType ===
'geomcollection') ? '' : 'Selected layer has a different vector
type.';
    } else {
        error = 'Please select a layer first.';
    }
    if (! error) {
        selectedLayer.getSource().addFeature(evt.feature);
    } else {
        this.layertree.messages.textContent = error;
    }
}, this);
return interaction;
};
```

> You can use the `break` statement to break out of any labeled code block, not just from the `switch` statements or the `for` loops. This is considered as not a good practice because using this technique can decrease the readability of your code, especially in case of poor label name choice. However, in some cases, like ours (as we do not want our error to be overwritten), this can come handy.

If you save the code so far and open it up, you will see the drawing controls in action. Add some new typed layers and draw some shapes with the corresponding tool(s) that can be activated when the layer is selected. For an extra experience, manually enable a disabled drawing control with your preferred browser's Developer Tools, try to draw something, and see what happens:

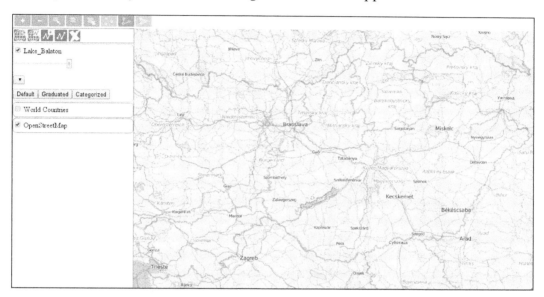

Modifying and snapping to features

In this example, called ch05_modify, we will customize the remaining feature editing interactions before we go on and create our own. Firstly, we create some further CSS rules for our new controls:

```
.toolbar .ol-modifyfeat button {
    background-image: url(../../res/button_modifyfeat.png);
}
.toolbar .ol-snap button {
    background-image: url(../../res/button_snap.png);
}
```

Extending the method

Now that we have the required rules, we can extend our addEditingToolBar method with two additional interactions. As both the modify and the snap interactions accept a collection of features to work with, we go that way and store the selected layer's features in a new collection object:

```
toolBar.prototype.addEditingToolBar = function () {
    [...]
    this.activeFeatures = new ol.Collection();
    var modifyFeature = new ol.control.Interaction({
        label: ' ',
        tipLabel: 'Modify features',
        className: 'ol-modifyfeat ol-unselectable ol-control',
        interaction: new ol.interaction.Modify({
            features: this.activeFeatures
        })
    }).setDisabled(true);
    this.editingControls.push(modifyFeature);
    var snapFeature = new ol.control.Interaction({
        label: ' ',
        tipLabel: 'Snap to paths, and vertices',
        className: 'ol-snap ol-unselectable ol-control',
        interaction: new ol.interaction.Snap({
            features: this.activeFeatures
        })
    }).setDisabled(true);
    snapFeature.unset('type');
    this.editingControls.push(snapFeature);
```

We created two new custom controls with two interactions. As the snapping control can be and must be active along another editing control, we manually remove its type attribute before adding it to the toolbar. We also linked our new collection to the interactions, making it possible to dynamically modify the features they will work with. Next, we make sure to correctly update our activeFeatures object on the layer change and add our new controls to the toolbar:

```
layertree.selectEventEmitter.on('change', function () {
    [...]
        var _this = this;
        setTimeout(function () {
            _this.activeFeatures.clear();
```

```
                _this.activeFeatures.extend(layer.getSource().
getFeatures());
            }, 0);
        [...]
    }, this);        this.addControl(drawPoint).addControl(drawLine).
addControl(drawPolygon)
        .addControl(modifyFeature).addControl(snapFeature);
    return this;
};
```

As creating a copy from our selected layer's features takes some time, rendering our layer tree unresponsive for a few seconds even with a smaller dataset, we make it asynchronous by calling it in a `setTimeout` function set to zero milliseconds. Note that this method will not speed up our code, but makes our application more responsive.

A responsive application is technically a matter of chunking time-consuming code blocks into smaller and faster ones, and timing their executions when the user doesn't notice. The physical reaction of the human body is significantly slower than visual reaction; thus, by placing the few seconds loading time after the visual feedback with an asynchronous call, the users won't even notice that there was any loading time. Of course, this theorem only applies to small datasets.

 If you have to work with large datasets, this will definitely be a bottleneck of your application. In this case, you can construct vector layers with a new collection object and call the source's `getFeaturesCollection` method on the layer change, avoiding the need for duplicating features. However, as the inner collection of the interactions cannot be changed, you have to construct a new interaction and remove the old one from the map every time.

Finally, we only have to add every newly created feature to our collection, so the interactions can be applied on them without changing the active layer:

```
toolBar.prototype.handleEvents = function (interaction, type) {
    [...]
    interaction.on('drawend', function (evt) {
        [...]
            this.activeFeatures.push(evt.feature);
        [...]
};
```

If you save and load up the example, you can see our new controls in action:

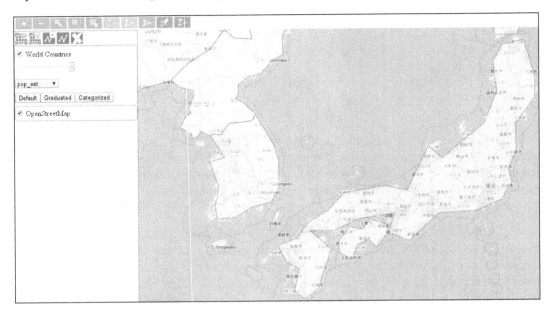

Creating new interactions

Creating new interactions is a little different than creating new controls. Instead of using a single root class, we can use `ol.interaction.Pointer` and `ol.interaction.Interaction`. We will cover, in this chapter, why we should use the pointer class. In this example, called `ch05_pointer`, we will implement two custom interactions. One for removing features and one for dragging features. Firstly, we define some CSS rules for our new controls, as usual:

```
.toolbar .ol-removefeat button {
    background-image: url(../../res/button_removefeat.png);
}
.toolbar .ol-dragfeat button {
    background-image: url(../../res/button_dragfeat.png);
}
```

Understanding ol.interaction.Pointer

Before creating some custom interaction, let's discuss how the pointer interaction works and how we can utilize it for our needs. This simple class can be constructed with five different event handler functions. The `handleEvent` function overrides every other handler and allows us to freely decide what to do with every different mouse events. If we would like to use it, we can use `ol.interaction.Interaction` instead; thus, we won't discuss it further here.

The first important handler is `handleDownEvent`. It fires every time when the left-mouse button is pushed down. If it returns `true`, the map freezes and our custom interaction gets into work. In the other case, the event is propagated to other handlers; thus, in a default scenario, a map panning occurs.

The second one is `handleDragEvent`. If `handleDownEvent` returns `true`, for every pointer that move afterwards, this function gets called. Finally, the `handleUpEvent` fires when we release the mouse button. Theoretically, if it returns `false`, the drag session is finished. In practice, however, its return value doesn't really matter. There are other checks to end the drag session, if it returns `true` or doesn't return anything at all.

There is one other handler called `handleMoveEvent`. It does not have much significance in our current use cases; however, it fires every time. We move our cursor while our interaction is active. It also fires during drag events along with the drag handler.

 As you can see, this class has a very limited vocabulary. For example, it cannot distinguish between clicks and pointer down events. However, it is easier to use and takes fewer considerations to yield less error-prone results.

Removing features

Now that we have completely understood the mechanics of the pointer interaction, it's time to create our first custom interaction: removing features. All our new interactions will operate on a user-provided collection of features; thus, we make them compatible with our editing toolbar's architectural design. Our new interactions consist of two parts: calling the `ol.interaction.Pointer` constructor with our handler functions, and setting some properties. Of course, we also have to make some inheritance, as usual:

```
ol.interaction.RemoveFeature = function (opt_options) {
    ol.interaction.Pointer.call(this, {
        handleDownEvent: function (evt) {
            this.set('deleteCandidate', evt.map.
forEachFeatureAtPixel(evt.pixel,
                function (feature, layer) {
                    if (this.get('features').getArray().
indexOf(feature) !== -1) {
                        return feature;
                    }
                }, this
            ));
            return !!this.get('deleteCandidate');
        },
        handleUpEvent: function (evt) {
            evt.map.forEachFeatureAtPixel(evt.pixel,
                function (feature, layer) {
                    if (feature === this.get('deleteCandidate')) {
                        layer.getSource().removeFeature(feature);
                        this.get('features').remove(feature);
                    }
                }, this
            );
            this.set('deleteCandidate', null);
        }
    });
    this.setProperties({
        features: opt_options.features,
        deleteCandidate: null
    });
};
ol.inherits(ol.interaction.RemoveFeature, ol.interaction.Pointer);
```

In this simple interaction, we define two handlers, one for pushing down the mouse button and one for releasing it. If we push down our mouse button, we check for features under the pixel of the event. If there is a feature under the pixel, which is also in our provided collection object, we save it and return `true`. Otherwise, we return `false`.

You can convert any value to its Boolean representative by using negation or double negation. As we double negate our saved feature, our function only returns `true` if we have a stored value (which is not `null`).

If our mouse down handler returns `true`, we check for features again when we release the mouse button. If the saved feature is still under the pointer, we remove the feature from the layer and also from the collection. With this logic, we not only implement a primitive, but also an effective cancel method. Finally, we null down our stored feature, set the default values for the interaction, and build the inheritance.

Dragging features

Our next custom interaction, which is capable of dragging features through the viewport, is slightly more difficult. We start it with the usual feature checking handler function:

```
ol.interaction.DragFeature = function (opt_options) {
    ol.interaction.Pointer.call(this, {
        handleDownEvent: function (evt) {
            this.set('draggedFeature', evt.map.
forEachFeatureAtPixel(evt.pixel,
                function (feature, layer) {
                    if
(this.get('features').getArray().indexOf(feature) !== -1) {
                        return feature;
                    }
                }, this
            ));
            if (this.get('draggedFeature')) {
                this.set('coords', evt.coordinate);
            }
            return !!this.get('draggedFeature');
        },
```

As you can see, there is only one difference between our previous interaction and this. If we have a catch, we save the event coordinates. Next, we implement the magic by moving the dragged feature by the difference between the consecutive event coordinates:

```
        handleDragEvent: function (evt) {
            var deltaX = evt.coordinate[0] -
this.get('coords')[0];
            var deltaY = evt.coordinate[1] -
this.get('coords')[1];
            this.get('draggedFeature').getGeometry().translate(deltaX,
deltaY);
            this.set('coords', evt.coordinate);
        },
```

```
        handleUpEvent: function (evt) {
            this.setProperties({
                coords: null,
                draggedFeature: null
            });
        }
    });
```

After we translate the feature with the calculated delta values, we update our stored coordinates; thus, we can move the feature further on the next drag event. After we finish with moving the feature, we simply null our properties. Finally, we set up the default values and build the inheritance.

All the geometry manipulating methods (transform, translate, applyTransform, and type-specific ones) modify the geometry in place. If you need to keep your original geometry, you must clone it first with it's clone method:

```
    this.setProperties({
        features: opt_options.features,
        coords: null,
        draggedFeature: null
    });
};
ol.inherits(ol.interaction.DragFeature, ol.interaction.Pointer);
```

> Note that there is a built-in interaction for dragging features, called
> ol.interaction.Translate. This interaction, however, moves
> all the features passed to it at once.

Extending the method

As the last step, we only have to extend our addEditingToolBar method in order to see our new interactions in action:

```
    toolBar.prototype.addEditingToolBar = function () {
        [...]
        var removeFeature = new ol.control.Interaction({
            label: ' ',
            tipLabel: 'Remove features',
            className: 'ol-removefeat ol-unselectable ol-control',
            interaction: new ol.interaction.RemoveFeature({
                features: this.activeFeatures
            })
```

```
    }).setDisabled(true);
    this.editingControls.push(removeFeature);
    var dragFeature = new ol.control.Interaction({
        label: ' ',
        tipLabel: 'Drag features',
        className: 'ol-dragfeat ol-unselectable ol-control',
        interaction: new ol.interaction.DragFeature({
            features: this.activeFeatures
        })
    }).setDisabled(true);
    this.editingControls.push(dragFeature);
    [...]
    this.addControl(drawPoint).addControl(drawLine).addControl
(drawPolygon)
        .addControl(modifyFeature).addControl(snapFeature).addControl
(removeFeature)
        .addControl(dragFeature);
    return this;
};
```

As we calibrate our interactions to accept a collection object with features in it, we can simply pass our `activeFeatures` object to them. If you save the code and load it up, you can play with removing and dragging features:

Building a measuring control

We have come to our last example in this chapter. In this example, called `ch05_ measure`, we will harness the full power of interactions and build a completely custom one in which we manually handle every event type. This example has three parts, so stay sharp. Firstly, as usual, we create a CSS rule for our new control button:

```
.toolbar .ol-measure button {
    background-image: url(../../res/button_measure.png);
}
```

One button is enough for this control, as we will implement two functionalities (length and area measurement) into a single interaction.

Creating the interaction

In the interaction's constructor, we accept two properties in an object literal: a reference to our map object and an optional style object or style function. As interactions do not have the exposed `setMap` and `getMap` methods, we need a reference to our map; thus, if it is not there, we return an error. If the style is not defined, we simply assign a default style, which is a simplified version of the OpenLayers 3 default editing style:

```
ol.interaction.Measure = function (opt_options) {
    var options = opt_options || {};
    if (!(options.map instanceof ol.Map)) {
        throw new Error('Please provide a valid OpenLayers 3
map');
    }
    var style = opt_options.style || new ol.style.Style({
        image: new ol.style.Circle({
            radius: 6,
            fill: new ol.style.Fill({
                color: [0, 153, 255, 1]
            }),
            stroke: new ol.style.Stroke({
                color: [255, 255, 255, 1],
                width: 1.5
            })
        }),
        stroke: new ol.style.Stroke({
            color: [0, 153, 255, 1],
            width: 3
        }),
```

```
        fill: new ol.style.Fill({
            color: [255, 255, 255, 0.5]
        })
    });
    var cursorFeature = new ol.Feature();
    var lineFeature = new ol.Feature();
    var polygonFeature = new ol.Feature();
```

We also create some empty sketch features. Next, we call the interaction's factory constructor with our custom `handleEvent` handler function:

```
    ol.interaction.Interaction.call(this, {
        handleEvent: function (evt) {
            switch (evt.type) {
                case 'pointermove':
                    cursorFeature.setGeometry(new ol.geom.Point(evt.
coordinate));
                    var coordinates = this.get('coordinates');
                    coordinates[coordinates.length - 1] = evt.
coordinate;
                    if (this.get('session') === 'area') {
                        if (coordinates.length < 3) {
                            lineFeature.getGeometry().
setCoordinates(coordinates);
                        } else {
                            polygonFeature.getGeometry().
setCoordinates([coordinates]);
                        }
                    }
                    else if (this.get('session') === 'length') {
                        lineFeature.getGeometry().
setCoordinates(coordinates);
                    }
                    break;
```

 The `handleEvent`'s return value defines whether the event needs to be propagated further. If it returns `true`, other interactions will also get the event; thus, we can pan or zoom the map while our interaction is active.

Firstly, we handle the move events. If we move our cursor while the interaction is active, a point feature is displayed on our cursor, which is similar to the draw interaction. Furthermore, it grabs a reference to our stored coordinate array representing the sketch feature. It switches the array's last pair of coordinates to the pointer's current location, pulling the last vertex of the sketch with the cursor.

If we are in a drawing session, it checks whether we are drawing a line or a polygon. If it is a polygon, it draws a line until our polygon is displayable (has a minimum of three vertices). After this, it draws a polygon. If it is a line, it simply draws a line.

 Note that we do not have to erase the line when we switch to a polygon, as they share the same coordinates. If we leave the existing line segment there, it will not make any kind of visual noise.

Next, we handle click events. Basically, this is a simple function that starts a drawing session or appends new coordinates to the coordinate array when we are in a session:

```
case 'click':
    if (!this.get('session')) {
        if (evt.originalEvent.shiftKey) {
            this.set('session', 'area');
            polygonFeature.setGeometry
(new ol.geom.Polygon([[[0, 0]]]));
        } else {
            this.set('session', 'length');
        }
        lineFeature.setGeometry
(new ol.geom.LineString([[0, 0]]));
        this.set('coordinates', [evt.coordinate]);
    }
    this.get('coordinates').push(evt.coordinate);
    return false;
```

If we are not in a session, we check the original browser event. If the *Shift* key is pressed, we start an area measurement, otherwise we measure a length. This is the part where we set up the geometries of the features. Note that, at this point, we only define some dummy geometries so they can pass the library's error checks. We will dynamically overwrite them with our stored coordinate array later.

 It seems to be a habit of using *Alt* and the *Platform* key as modifiers in applications. Be cautious with those keys. The *Platform* key opens up the **Start** menu in Windows, while the *Alt* key drags the active window in Linux.

If we start a new drawing session, as you can see, we add two pairs of coordinates to our array. This way, we can store the last clicked coordinate safe and sound, while we also prepare a new pair of coordinates to be modified by the move handler. Finally, we return `false`, as we don't want our interaction to be hooked up with some other interaction when we click on the map.

As the last pair of coordinates only indicate the place that the move handler should modify, its original form won't influence the shape of our geometry; therefore, the results in the accuracy of our measurement. You can replace the penultimate line with `this.get('coordinates').push(['chicken', 'nuggets']);` and the interaction will still work as intended.

Next, we handle the double-click events. We stop the drawing, calculate the results, and restore every significant property to their default values:

```
case 'dblclick':
    var unit;
    if (this.get('session') === 'area') {
        var area =
polygonFeature.getGeometry().getArea();
        if (area > 1000000) {
            area = area / 1000000;
            unit = 'km²';
        } else {
            unit = 'm²';
        }
        this.set('result', {
            type: 'area',
            measurement: area,
            unit: unit
        });
```

If we measure an area, we calculate the polygon's area, convert the result if necessary, and then update the `result` property:

```
    } else {
        var length =
lineFeature.getGeometry().getLength();
        if (length > 1000) {
            length = length / 1000;
            unit = 'km';
        } else {
            unit = 'm';
        }
        this.set('result', {
            type: 'length',
            measurement: length,
            unit: unit
        });
    }
```

If there is any other case, we must be dealing with a length measurement. We calculate the line feature's length and follow our previous logic. In this handler, we also return `false` as we do not want to propagate the event. Otherwise, in a default setting, the event would be propagated to `ol.interaction.DoubleClickZoom`, and we would unintentionally zoom into the map. If we have any other events, we just return `true` propagating the event to other interactions:

 With regard to unit notations, we currently only deal with metric coordinate systems. As the `getLength` and `getArea` methods return measurements in the projected plane, the interaction in its current form returns correct results in any coordinate system (until it converts them), but wrong units in non-metric systems.

```
                    cursorFeature.setGeometry(null);
                    lineFeature.setGeometry(null);
                    polygonFeature.setGeometry(null);
                    this.setProperties({
                        session: null,
                        coordinates: []

                    });
                    return false;
                }
                return true;
            }
        });
```

Finally, we remove the overlay when the interaction is inactive, and add it to the map when it is active. We also set up the default properties and the inheritance. It is important to set the line's and the polygon's geometry to `null` when we deactivate the interaction. This way, if we disable the interaction during a drawing session, it won't get stuck:

```
        this.on('change:active', function (evt) {
            if (this.getActive()) {
                this.get('overlay').setMap(this.get('map'));
            } else {
                this.get('overlay').setMap(null);
                this.set('session', null);
                lineFeature.setGeometry(null);
                polygonFeature.setGeometry(null);
            }
        });
```

```
        this.setProperties({
            overlay: new ol.layer.Vector({
                source: new ol.source.Vector({
                    features: [cursorFeature, lineFeature, polygonFeature]
                }),
                style: style
            }),
            map: options.map,
            session: null,
            coordinates: [],
            result: null
        });
    };
    ol.inherits(ol.interaction.Measure, ol.interaction.Interaction);
```

 You can add a layer with the map object's addLayer method while you can also add it with the layer object's setMap method. The latter adds the layer to the map silently, skipping it from the map's layer collection, but still drawing its content to the canvas.

Only one thing is left to do: we add a measurement control to our map. We do it in our init function as this control is not part of the editing toolbar. We also assign an event listener to it. If the result property changes, we annotate the results. As we saved the overlay layer as a property too, you can add the newly created features to a permanent layer in the same event before they become null:

```
var measureControl = new ol.control.Interaction({
    label: ' ',
    tipLabel: 'Measure distances and areas',
    className: 'ol-measure ol-unselectable ol-control',
    interaction: new ol.interaction.Measure({
        map: map
    })
});
measureControl.get('interaction').on('change:result', function
(evt) {
    var result = evt.target.get('result');
    tree.messages.textContent = result.measurement + ' ' +
result.unit;
});

tools.addControl(measureControl);
```

If you save the code and load it up, you can see our measurement control in action:

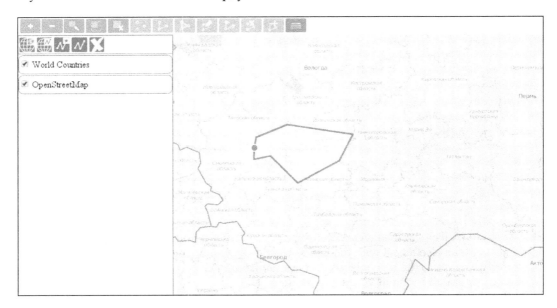

 You can keep the geometry of the last measurement with some modifications in the code. For additional help, you can see the official example at http://www.openlayers.org/en/master/ examples/measure.html. It also provides some great styling tips.

Doing geodesic measurements

One thing I know for sure, Hungary's exact size is 93030 km^2 and it does not correspond with 207186 km^2 measured with our tool. Of course, the measurement wasn't precise, but the difference is by orders of magnitude. As you must have known, projections distort spatial data in more ways. There are better and worse projections from this aspect, and Web Mercator is one of the worst. In some applications, measuring in the projected plane is sufficient, or it is the expected behavior, but in others, more precise measurements are required. The good news is: you can calculate lengths and areas accurately in basically any projection.

The next example is in a separate JavaScript file, called `ch05_measure_geodesic.js`. You can link it to the example's HTML file (`ch05_measure.html`) or modify our interaction in place. In this example, we will modify the interaction in such a way that it will always calculate lengths and areas of a sphere. Our sphere will have a radius of the semi-major axis of the WGS 84 ellipsoid used by the `EPSG:4326` projection. Firstly, we create the sphere inside our interaction:

```
ol.interaction.Measure = function (opt_options) {
    [...]
    var sphere = new ol.Sphere(6378137);
    [...]
```

Next, we modify our double-click handler where the calculations are done:

```
case 'dblclick':
    var unit;
    var mapProjection = this.get('map').getView().
getProjection();
    if (this.get('session') === 'area') {
        var lonLatPolygon = polygonFeature.
getGeometry().transform(mapProjection, 'EPSG:4326');
        var area = Math.abs(sphere.
geodesicArea(lonLatPolygon.getCoordinates()[0]));
        [...]
    } else {
        var lonLatLine = lineFeature.getGeometry().
transform(mapProjection, 'EPSG:4326');
        var lineCoordinates = lonLatLine.
getCoordinates();
        var length = 0;
        for (var i = 0; i < lineCoordinates.length
- 1; i += 1) {
            length += sphere.haversineDistance(lineCoo
rdinates[i], lineCoordinates[i +
1]);
        }
        [...]
```

When we measure a sphere, we have to provide the coordinates in a longitude/latitude format. Therefore, we have to transform the coordinates first from whatever projection we use to `EPSG:4326`. For calculating areas, we have an easy job. We simply have to pass a polygon's coordinates to our sphere's `geodesicArea` method.

The sign of the result depends on the orientation of the passed polygon's coordinates. If the coordinates have a clockwise orientation, the result will be positive, while in the other case, it will be negative. Calculating the result's absolute value is recommended.

For calculating lengths, we can use the sphere's `haversineDistance` method. As it calculates length between two given pairs of coordinates, we have to iterate through the transformed line feature's coordinates.

If you update your interaction with these modifications, you will see that now you can measure quite accurately. The new result for Hungary's area is 93051 km^2, which is quite good.

Calculating lengths even more precisely

The Haversine formula can be considered as quite accurate; however, in a few use cases, millimeters to a 10th of a meter precision is required. In such cases, using spherical geometry is not accurate enough.

An ellipsoidal approach, however, can provide the required accuracy at the expense of performance. There is a third JavaScript file for this example, called `ch05_measure_vincenty.js`. In this example, we will use a WGS 84 ellipsoid to define the shape of the Earth and measure distances on it with the Vincenty formula. As the `ol.Ellipsoid` class is not exposed in the compiled library, we have to use the `ol-debug.js` file. As the ellipsoid class was removed from OpenLayers 3.9.0, we use the debug file from version 3.8.2.

If you have an error, double check the link in the HTML file. It must connect the debug version of OpenLayers 3.8.2 to our application.

Firstly, we define an ellipsoid in our interaction. The constructor needs the length of the ellipsoid's semi-major axis in meters and also its flattening as arguments:

```
ol.interaction.Measure = function (opt_options) {
    [...]
    var ellipsoid = new ol.Ellipsoid(6378137, 1 / 298.257223563);
    [...]
```

Next, we only have to modify the calculations of the length measurement:

```
case 'dblclick':
    [...]
    } else {
        [...]
        for (var i = 0; i < lineCoordinates.length
- 1; i += 1) {
            length += ellipsoid.vincentyDistance(lineC
oordinates[i], lineCoordinates[i +
1]);
            [...]
        }
        [...]
```

Now, our application can calculate distances and areas as accurately as OpenLayers 3 allows it to.

Summary

In this chapter, we mastered the heart of any web mapping, or WebGIS application, interactions, and controls. We learned how to make brand new interactions and controls, and how to modify or customize existing ones to our needs effectively. We also learned how to implement some very useful controls for a web mapping application. We didn't see directly how we can implement the attribute controls from the previous chapter; however, you are most certainly able to do it based on the other examples.

In the next chapter, we will learn how to customize the view and how to use multiple, or even custom projections, with OpenLayers 3. We will see how deeply Proj4JS is integrated into the library and how easily we can use its capabilities almost directly from OpenLayers 3, if we include it in our project. We will also play with extents, rotation values, and animations, just to mention a few.

Controlling the Map – View and Projection

In the last few chapters, we gained a firm grip on using and customizing the most essential parts of OpenLayers 3. In this chapter, we will take a further step in creating a great application by focusing on user experience. A good web mapping or WebGIS application has a lot of convenient GUI options to modify the view. In some cases, your users will be more than happy if they are able to go through the view history with some button clicks, or if they can change the map's rotation, projection, or just zoom in to the selected feature. We will also learn how animations work and ways in which they can utilized in order to create our own special camera effects. We'll take a look at these topics in this chapter:

- Customizing and constraining the view
- Building a navigation history
- Zooming into arbitrary extents
- Changing the rotation and projection of the map
- Creating custom animations

Before getting started

For this chapter, we will need exactly one-third of a party library: PROJ4JS. It is included in the code appendix, located at js/proj4js-2.3.10/proj4.js. We will see how this library is not really a third-party application with regard to OpenLayers 3, but rather an optional extension.

Furthermore, we have to modify our base layer as OpenStreetMap only supports Web Mercator, but we need a layer that comes in multiple projections. For this purpose, we utilize Natural Earth's 50m Land layer provided by Boundless's demo GeoServer.

 We use this layer for printing purposes. You can try out NASA's Blue Marble layer (`bluemarble`) instead; it's truly beautiful.

First, let's make the necessary changes in our `init` function:

```
var map = new ol.Map({
    target: 'map',
    layers: [
        new ol.layer.Tile({
            source: new ol.source.TileWMS({
                url: 'http://demo.opengeo.org/geoserver/wms',
                params: {
                    layers: 'ne_50m_land',
                    format: 'image/png'
                }
            }),
            name: 'Natural Earth Land'
        }),
        [...]
};
```

Basic considerations

As we've focused enough on interactions and controls in the previous chapters, we would rather focus on controlling the view in this one. We will create some tools and add them to the toolbar, but we will not build further structures to support our example project. In this chapter, we will take the final step in creating a WebGIS application by filling out the remaining gaps and consider it to then be complete.

Customizing a view

Customizing the view is not a hard task; it manly consists of considerations regarding the nature of the project and expected outcome. For our application, wrapping the map around the x axis is completely needless. Also, we can restrict the extent to the projection's extent. In the first example, called ch06_customize, we make such modifications in our application. First, we disable the layer wrapping in our base layers:

```
var map = new ol.Map({
    [...]
        new ol.layer.Tile({
            source: new ol.source.TileWMS({
                [...]
                wrapX: false
            [...]
        new ol.layer.Vector({
            source: new ol.source.Vector({
                [...]
                wrapX: false
            }),
```

 Unlike in OpenLayers 2, you cannot make a high level decision to disable layer wrapping for the entire map. You have to disable it layer-wise in the layer's source object, as it is enabled in most of the sources by default.

With this consideration, we gained an instant boost in performance. However, we have to say goodbye to it instantly as this will make our map more responsive. By default, when we are interacting with the map or an animation takes place, tile and vector layers wait for us to finish before they get updated. We can disable this phenomenon with two options. In case of vector layers, we have to disable it in the layer level, but for tile layers, we can disable it in the map object. We can do it in this way:

```
        new ol.layer.Vector({
            [...]
            updateWhileAnimating: true,
            updateWhileInteracting: true
        })
    [...]
    loadTilesWhileAnimating: true,
    loadTilesWhileInteracting: true
});
```

In the next step, we'll modify the `view` object to restrict the maximum extent. Note that we can pan outside the map's extent since this option only constrains the center of the map:

```
view: new ol.View({
    [...]
    extent: ol.proj.get('EPSG:3857').getExtent()
}),
```

 As the Web Mercator projection is provided by the library, we can use a shortcut to access it. Later, we will see how to add new projections to the library's projection list.

Finally, we enable some keyboard interactions. There are two interactions related to the keyboard events in OpenLayers 3, and both of them get added to the map by default. However, we cannot use them as only focused elements can receive keyboard events, and only input-related elements can be focused by default. To make our map's `div` element focusable, we must add a `tabindex` property to it in the HTML file:

```
[...]
<div id="map" class="map" tabindex="-1"></div>
[...]
```

Now, if we click on the `map`, we can pan with the arrow keys and zoom in with the + (plus) and - (minus) keys.

 You can provide `-1`, `0`, or any positive integer to the `tabindex` property. The `-1` value opts out the element from focusing with the *Tab* key, but it makes it focusable with a mouse click or with the `focus` method. The `0` value does not alter the natural focusing order with the *Tab* key, while a positive integer determines its order.

If a focusable element gains focus, some browsers render an outline on the border of the element. As we do not want to have an outline on our map, we will disable it in our css file by extending our `map` class with a single rule:

```
.map {
    [...]
    outline: 0;
}
```

Constraining a view

There are some cases when restricting the center is not enough; the users should not pan outside an arbitrary extent. There is an easy method to do this; however, it is hard to calculate with rotations and impossible to show every part of a rotated map with a hard constrained view. In the next example, called ch06_constrain, we will implement this method.

 We will learn how to rotate the map later in this chapter.

An easy implementation calculates a new extent based on a more permissive, full extent for a given resolution. Then, we simply check the value of the center in every change in the map's view and snap it to our new extent's border if it tries to escape it:

```
map.getView().on('propertychange', function (evt) {
    var projExtent = this.getProjection().getExtent();
    if (projExtent) {
        var currentCenter = this.getCenter();
        var currentResolution = this.getResolution();
        var mapSize = map.getSize();
        var newExtent = [projExtent[0] + currentResolution *
mapSize[0] / 2,
            projExtent[1] + currentResolution * mapSize[1] / 2,
            projExtent[2] - currentResolution * mapSize[0] / 2,
            projExtent[3] - currentResolution * mapSize[1] / 2];
        if (!(new ol.geom.Point(currentCenter).
intersectsExtent(newExtent))) {
            currentCenter[0] = Math.min(Math.max(currentCenter[0],
newExtent[0]), newExtent[2]);
            currentCenter[1] = Math.min(Math.max(currentCenter[1],
newExtent[1]), newExtent[3]);
            this.setCenter(currentCenter);
        }
    }
});
```

We can calculate our new extent, which the center should not leave with the map's size and current resolution. Then, we create a point geometry from our center coordinates and check for possible intersections. If it does not intersect (that is, it's outside the new extent), we snap it to the nearest border.

You can constrain a number in JavaScript between two values by nesting a `Math.max` method in a `Math.min` method or vice versa. Just make sure that you use the correct extreme in the comparisons.

If you save the code, you will see that you cannot pan outside the edges of the map:

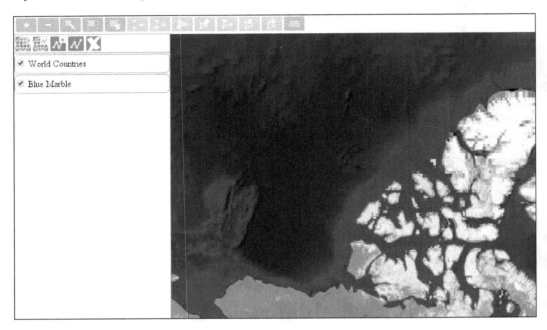

If you use this method, you will have a hard time with rotated maps. To top this, you have to restrict the maximum resolution of the view because if the map size is smaller than the restrictive extent, the application will break.

Creating a navigation history

In the next example, called `ch06_navhist`, we will create a fully functional navigation history. First, as usual, we have to make some considerations. We will store an array in the control containing the view properties for every change. We will also store the current index as we must remember to step our control between view states. A not-so-important property that we will store is a Boolean value, representing whether we should record the new view or not. This is particularly handy when we step between the `history` elements and do not want to double store these states. First, we create the first button for the control:

```
ol.control.NavigationHistory = function (opt_options) {
    var options = opt_options || {};
    var _this = this;
    var controlDiv = document.createElement('div');
    controlDiv.className = options.class || 'ol-unselectable ol-
control';
    var backButton = document.createElement('button');
    backButton.className = 'ol-navhist-back';
    backButton.textContent = options.backButtonText || '◄';
    backButton.title = options.backButtonTipLabel || 'Previous
view';
    backButton.addEventListener('click', function (evt) {
        var historyArray = _this.get('history');
        var currIndex = _this.get('index');
        if (currIndex > 0) {
            currIndex -= 1;
            _this.setProperties({
                shouldSave: false,
                index: currIndex
            });
            _this.getMap().getView().setProperties(historyArray[currI
ndex]);
        }
    });
    backButton.disabled = true;
    controlDiv.appendChild(backButton);
```

This is a usual custom control with a little twist. As we have unicode triangle symbols, we do not have to render a background image to this control. When clicking a button, if we are not in the first state, we will decrease our index and update the view accordingly. We also set our shouldSave Boolean to false as we do not want to save again an already recorded state. Next, we will create the other button:

> If you do not see the triangle symbols properly, check whether your browser uses an UTF-8 encoding. If it does, update it to the latest version.

```
var nextButton = document.createElement('button');
nextButton.className = 'ol-navhist-next';
nextButton.textContent = options.nextButtonText || '►';
nextButton.title = options.nextButtonTipLabel || 'Next view';
nextButton.addEventListener('click', function (evt) {
    var historyArray = _this.get('history');
    var currIndex = _this.get('index');
```

```
            if (currIndex < historyArray.length - 1) {
                currIndex += 1;
                _this.setProperties({
                    shouldSave: false,
                    index: currIndex
                });
                _this.getMap().getView().setProperties(historyArray[currI
ndex]);
            }
        });
        nextButton.disabled = true;
        controlDiv.appendChild(nextButton);
```

This button acts like the previous one; however, it checks whether we are at the end of our history array, and if not, it increases the index. In the next step, we'll finish our control by setting its initial values, adding a listener, and building the inheritance:

```
        ol.control.Control.call(this, {
            element: controlDiv,
            target: options.target
        });
        this.setProperties({
            history: [],
            index: -1,
            maxSize: options.maxSize || 50,
            eventId: null,
            shouldSave: true
        });
        this.on('change:index', function () {
            if (this.get('index') === 0) {
                backButton.disabled = true;
            } else {
                backButton.disabled = false;
            }
            if (this.get('history').length - 1 === this.get('index')) {
                nextButton.disabled = true;
            } else {
                nextButton.disabled = false;
            }
        });
    };
    ol.inherits(ol.control.NavigationHistory, ol.control.Control);
```

We set our initial index to -1, as our control will automatically increment it by one if it saves the first state of the view. Our users can define the maximum size of the history; however, we also set a default value of 50. The listener attached to the changes in the index property makes sure that our control buttons get disabled and enabled appropriately. If we are in the first index, we cannot go back, and if we are in the last one, we cannot step further. Next, we override the control's setMap method, and attach a detachable (stored) event listener to the map:

```
ol.control.NavigationHistory.prototype.setMap = function (map) {
    ol.control.Control.prototype.setMap.call(this, map);
    if (map === null) {
        ol.Observable.unByKey(this.get('eventId'));
    } else {
        this.set('eventId', map.on('moveend', function (evt) {
            if (this.get('shouldSave')) {
                var view = map.getView();
                var viewStatus = {
                    center: view.getCenter(),
                    resolution: view.getResolution(),
                    rotation: view.getRotation()
                };
                var historyArray = this.get('history');
                var currIndex = this.get('index');
                historyArray.splice(currIndex + 1, historyArray.length
- currIndex - 1);
                if (historyArray.length === this.get('maxSize')) {
                    historyArray.splice(0, 1);
                } else {
                    currIndex += 1;
                }
                historyArray.push(viewStatus);
                this.set('index', currIndex);
            } else {
                this.set('shouldSave', true);
            }
        }, this));
    }
};
```

As you are clearly familiar with our event attaching and detaching mechanisms by now, we won't discuss it here any further. The listener attached to the map's moveend event, however, needs to be discussed.

We only act if our `shouldSave` Boolean is set to `true`. We gather the view's center, rotation, and resolution, and store them in an object. This ensures that we can restore them with the view's `setProperties` method, and at the same time, we don't store unnecessary properties.

> Remember: one can assign an arbitrary number of properties to an OpenLayers 3 object.

When we update our history array, we clear out everything from the current index to the end of the array. This operation makes sure that we save the view states correctly from a given index. We also clear the first member of the array if we exceed the maximum size of the history. Finally, we add the new control to our toolbar:

```
var tools = new toolBar({
    map: map,
    target: 'toolbar',
    layertree: tree,
}).addControl(new ol.control.Zoom()).addControl(new
ol.control.NavigationHistory());
```

If you save the code and load it in a browser, you will be able to try out our new navigation history:

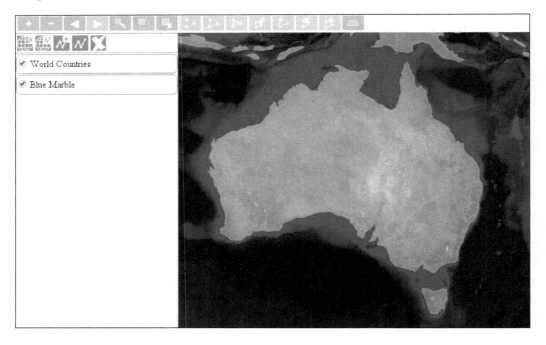

With this method, you can also create geographical bookmarks. You just have to create a control, which creates an object for every named extent and an interface to provide those names.

Working with extents

In a WebGIS application, it is especially feasible to have controls to zoom into various extents. Users are used to the luxury of zooming in to a layer or a feature to the maximum extent with a single click. In this example, called ch06_extent, we will implement such zooming capabilities. We will create a tool to zoom into the validity extent of the current projection, one for zooming into the selected layer, and the other to zoom into the selected feature. First, let's make some CSS rules for our new tools:

```
.toolbar .ol-zoom-extent button {
    background-image: url(../../res/button_zoom_extent.png);
}
.toolbar .ol-zoom-layer button {
    background-image: url(../../res/button_zoom_layer.png);
}
.toolbar .ol-zoom-selected button {
    background-image: url(../../res/button_zoom_selected.png);
}
```

Creating a zoom control

There is a built-in control in OpenLayers 3 to zoom into various extents. However, the main weakness of ol.control.ZoomToExtent lies in its static nature. We can define an arbitrary extent on construction and cannot change it afterwards. There is one strength of this control, however. If we do not provide an extent, it reads the current projection's validity extent. This spark of dynamism makes this control suitable for our first use case. For the rest of the tools, we make our own zoom control, which accepts a function, rather than a static extent, and zooms into the return value of that function:

```
ol.control.ZoomTo = function (opt_options) {
    var options = opt_options || {};
    var _this = this;
    var controlDiv = document.createElement('div');
    controlDiv.className = options.class || 'ol-unselectable ol-
control';
    var controlButton = document.createElement('button');
    controlButton.textContent = options.label || '';
```

```
        controlButton.title = options.tipLabel || 'Zoom to extent';
        controlButton.addEventListener('click', function (evt) {
            var zoomCandidate = _this.get('extentFunction')();
            if (zoomCandidate instanceof ol.geom.SimpleGeometry ||
                (Object.prototype.toString.call(zoomCandidate) ===
'[object Array]' && zoomCandidate.length === 4)) {
                _this.getMap().getView().fit(zoomCandidate,
_this.getMap().getSize());
            }
        });
        controlDiv.appendChild(controlButton);
        ol.control.Control.call(this, {
            element: controlDiv,
            target: options.target
        });
        this.set('extentFunction', options.zoomFunction);
    };
    ol.inherits(ol.control.ZoomTo, ol.control.Control);
```

As the view object's `fit` method can only receive a simple geometry or an extent besides a mandatory size argument, we will check whether the return value of the provided function fits this criteria. Note that we only check this if the returned extent is an array has exactly four members. For a more general control, further checks should be considered.

If you played with JavaScript's `typeof` method, you may know that only primitives are distinguishable from it. Arrays are considered as objects. However, objects have subtypes, which can be extracted by calling `Object.prototype.toString` with an object. Be careful, though. This method is not protected; therefore, any library can overwrite it.

Extending the toolbar

Next, we extend our toolbar with a method, which creates three extent controls:

```
    toolBar.prototype.addExtentControls = function () {
        var _this = this;
        var zoomFull = new ol.control.ZoomToExtent({
            label: ' ',
            tipLabel: 'Zoom to full extent'
        });
        var zoomToLayer = new ol.control.ZoomTo({
            class: 'ol-zoom-layer ol-unselectable ol-control',
```

```
        tipLabel: 'Zoom to layer extent',
        extentFunction: function () {
            var source = _this.layertree.getLayerById(_this.layertree.
selectedLayer.id).getSource();
            if (source.getExtent()) {
                return source.getExtent();
            }
            return false;
        }
    });
```

The first two controls are very simple. For the full extent control, we use OpenLayers 3's mechanism, while for the layer extent control, we provide a function, calling the getExtent method of the layer's source.

 Only vector sources have a factory method to get their extent. However, you can create such a method for any layer with the same functionality. Just make sure that you store the extent of the layer in its source object. For WMS layers, you can parse their extent from their GetCapabilities response.

Next, we create the selection extent control, which is a little more complicated, and close our method appropriately:

```
    var zoomToSelected = new ol.control.ZoomTo({
        class: 'ol-zoom-selected ol-unselectable ol-control',
        tipLabel: 'Zoom to selected feature',
        extentFunction: function () {
            var features = _this.selectInteraction.getFeatures();
            if (features.getLength() === 1) {
                var geom = features.item(0).getGeometry();
                if (geom instanceof ol.geom.SimpleGeometry) {
                    return geom;
                }
                return geom.getExtent();
            }
            return false;
        }
    });
    this.addControl(zoomFull).addControl(zoomToLayer).
addControl(zoomToSelected);
    return this;
};
```

We only accept one feature in this scenario, as allowing more features requires extra calculations. If the feature is a single part, we return it, avoiding unnecessary operations, while if it's multipart, we calculate its extent and return this instead. Finally, we add the new controls to the toolbar:

```
tools.addExtentControls().addSelectControls().addEditingToolBar();
```

If you save the code and run it in your browser, you will see our extent controls up and running:

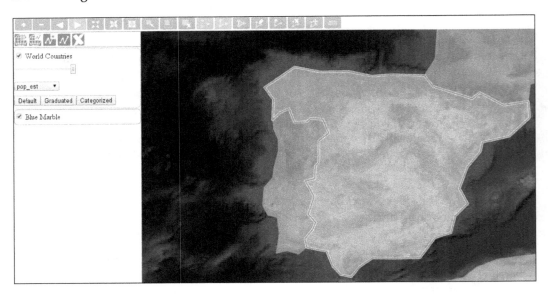

Rotating a view

The penultimate control that we add to our application before we consider it finished, is the rotation control in the next example: ch06_rotate. We will place it in the bottom bar along with the upcoming projection control. In the first step, we extend our HTML file with container elements for them:

```
<div class="notification-bar">
    <div id="messageBar" class="message-bar"></div>
    <div id="projection"></div>
    <div id="rotation"></div>
    <div id="coordinates"></div>
</div>
```

Next, we create some CSS rules for the rotation control:

```css
.notification-bar #rotation {
    width: 10%;
    text-align: center;
}
.notification-bar #rotation input {
    text-align: center;
    outline: none;
    border: 0;
    -moz-appearance: textfield;
}
```

We align the control to the center of the container element and remove any border or outline from it.

 In Firefox, the spinner buttons for numeric inputs exceed the size of the numeric input itself. This is a well-known bug, and it would cause our application to be higher than the height of the screen. To avoid this, we disable these spinner buttons in Firefox.

Next, we create a simple control to change the map's rotation every time our numeric input changes:

```javascript
ol.control.RotationControl = function (opt_options) {
    var options = opt_options || {};
    var _this = this;
    var controlInput = document.createElement('input');
    controlInput.title = options.tipLabel || 'Set rotation';
    controlInput.type = 'number';
    controlInput.min = 0;
    controlInput.max = 360;
    controlInput.step = 1;
    controlInput.value = 0;
    controlInput.addEventListener('change', function (evt) {
        var radianValue = this.value / 180 * Math.PI;
        _this.getMap().getView().setRotation(radianValue);
    });
    ol.control.Control.call(this, {
        element: controlInput,
        target: options.target
    });
    this.set('element', controlInput);
};
ol.inherits(ol.control.RotationControl, ol.control.Control);
```

The only thing we have to make sure here is that we convert the input values from degrees to radians, as OpenLayers 3 uses radian values. We also make sure that our input updates if the map's rotation changes from other sources (for example, from the navigation history):

```
ol.control.RotationControl.prototype.setMap = function (map) {
    ol.control.Control.prototype.setMap.call(this, map);
    if (map === null) {
        ol.Observable.unByKey(this.get('eventId'));
    } else {
        this.set('eventId', map.getView().on('change:rotation',
function (evt) {
            var degreeValue = Math.round(map.getView().getRotation() /
Math.PI * 180);
            this.get('element').value = degreeValue;
        }, this));
    }
};
```

 Note that as we register a listener in the `view` object, we have to register it again every time we use a new `view` object. For example, we will construct a new `view` object in the next example for every change in the projection.

Finally, we add the control to the map with our destination element as the target:

```
var map = new ol.Map({
    [...]
    controls: [
        [...]
        new ol.control.RotationControl({
            target: 'rotation'
        })
        [...]
    ]
});
```

Now, you can try out our new control, and rotate the map between 0 degrees and 360 degrees:

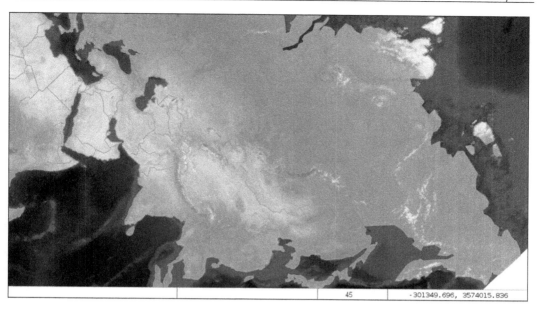

Changing the map's projection

In the next example, called `ch06_projection`, we close our basic WebGIS client with a final control, which is able to change the map's projection dynamically. First, as we will need the `PROJ4JS` library for this example, we include it in the HTML file:

```
<script type="text/javascript" src="../../js/proj4js-2.3.10/proj4.
js"></script>
```

Next, we style the control with CSS:

```
.notification-bar #projection {
    text-align: center;
}
.notification-bar #projection select {
    background: none;
    border: none;
    outline: 0;
}
```

The scheme is the same as the one in the previous example. We will strip the natural look of the select element, which will contain the possible projection options. Next, we start building the control by creating two options for the two default projections:

```
ol.control.Projection = function (opt_options) {
    var options = opt_options || {};
    var _this = this;
    var projSwitcher = document.createElement('select');
    var webMercator = document.createElement('option');
    webMercator.value = 'EPSG:3857';
    webMercator.textContent = 'EPSG:3857';
    projSwitcher.appendChild(webMercator);
    var plateCarree = document.createElement('option');
    plateCarree.value = 'EPSG:4326';
    plateCarree.textContent = 'EPSG:4326';
    projSwitcher.appendChild(plateCarree);
```

The concept here is that we store the projection's string representation as the option's value, and request the appropriate projection from the library. As HTML elements can be overridden in the browser, further checks might be necessary. Next, we add an event listener to the control element and close our control:

```
projSwitcher.addEventListener('change', function (evt) {
    var view = _this.getMap().getView();
    var oldProj = view.getProjection();
    var newProj = ol.proj.get(this.value);
    var newView = new ol.View({
        center: ol.proj.transform(view.getCenter(), oldProj,
newProj),
        zoom: view.getZoom(),
        projection: newProj,
        extent: newProj.getExtent()
    });
    _this.getMap().setView(newView);
    _this.getMap().getLayers().forEach(function (layer) {
        _this.changeLayerProjection(layer, oldProj, newProj);
    });
});
ol.control.Control.call(this, {
    element: projSwitcher,
    target: options.target
});
this.set('element', projSwitcher);
};
ol.inherits(ol.control.Projection, ol.control.Control);
```

When we change the projection, we simply construct a new `view` object with the appropriate projection and a transformed center in order to preserve the previous view. We also loop through the layers and apply a method on them, which we will discuss soon. For now, we set the control element's default value to the current projection:

```
ol.control.Projection.prototype.setMap = function (map) {
    ol.control.Control.prototype.setMap.call(this, map);
    if (map !== null) {
        this.get('element').value = map.getView().getProjection().
getCode();
    }
};
```

As we need to transform vector layers to the new projection and also request new tiles, if available, we will create a `changeLayerProjection` method, which can deal with every case:

```
ol.control.Projection.prototype.changeLayerProjection = function
(layer, oldProj, newProj) {
    if (layer instanceof ol.layer.Group) {
        layer.getLayers().forEach(function (subLayer) {
            this.changeLayerProjection(subLayer, oldProj, newProj);
        });
    } else if (layer instanceof ol.layer.Tile) {
        var tileLoadFunc = layer.getSource().getTileLoadFunction();
        layer.getSource().setTileLoadFunction(tileLoadFunc);
    } else if (layer instanceof ol.layer.Vector) {
        var features = layer.getSource().getFeatures();
        for (var i = 0; i < features.length; i += 1) {
            features[i].getGeometry().transform(oldProj, newProj);
        }
    }
};
```

The method itself is recursive, as it needs to deal with grouped layers, too. If it finds one, it simply calls itself on every member of the group.

The second case is the that of the tile layers. WMS servers often offer tiles in multiple projections. However, there is a truly wonderful but also very sneaky feature in OpenLayers 3, called tile cache. If we do not clear the cache, the application renders tiles from the old projection to the new one's tile grid, which yields bad results. As the tile cache is completely hidden from us, our only chance to tackle this problem is to call a method, which clears the cache as a side effect. There are two such methods: `setTileLoadFunction` and `setTileUrlFunction`. We save the old function, set it back, and thus clear the cache without any other change in the layer.

The last case is the case of vector layers. This is quite straightforward, as our only task is iterating through the features and transforming their geometries from the old projection to the new one.

 OpenLayers 3 is capable of warping raster layers; you just have to provide a projection parameter to the given image source. Note that if you reset the cache of a tile layer and the server cannot give out tiles in the destination projection, you will end up with a blank layer. Sometimes, blurred and ugly labels are better than nothing.

We also need a method to add projections dynamically to the control. Here's how we can do this:

```
ol.control.Projection.prototype.addProjection = function (projection)
{
    ol.proj.addProjection(projection);
    var projSwitcher = this.get('element');
    var newProjOption = document.createElement('option');
    newProjOption.value = projection.getCode();
    newProjOption.textContent = projection.getCode();
    projSwitcher.appendChild(newProjOption);
};
```

 A good implementation should also have a method that can remove a projection. Note that ol.proj does not have a removeProjection method, though.

Next, we will construct our new control in the init function, create a new projection with PROJ4JS, and add the projection to the control:

```
var projControl = new ol.control.Projection({
    target: 'projection'
});
proj4.defs('EPSG:3995', '+proj=stere +lat_0=90 +lat_ts=71 +lon_0=0
+k=1 +x_0=0 +y_0=0 +datum=WGS84 +units=m +no_defs');
var polarProj = new ol.proj.Projection({
    code: 'EPSG:3995',
    extent: [-12382000, -12382000, 12382000, 12382000],
    worldExtent: [-180, 60, 180, 90]
});
projControl.addProjection(polarProj);
```

Do not confuse PROJ.4 with PROJ4JS. PROJ4JS is a JavaScript port of the PROJ.4 desktop application, and it does not contain every transformation from the original software. For example, it cannot recognize the Robinson projection.

OpenLayers 3 and PROJ4JS are so closely integrated that we do not need to implement any wrapper functions; we can construct an OpenLayers 3 projection object directly from a PROJ4JS definition. PROJ4JS definitions can be made with proj4.defs, which are called with two arguments. The first one represents a name, with which the projection will be saved. The second one is the projection's PROJ.4 definition.

 Wondering how to get definition strings and extents? The database behind http://www.epsg.io offers many definitions along with recommended extents. Do not rely blindly on those extents, though. They can fail, especially when the projection is not cylindrical.

Finally, we add the control to our map:

```
var map = new ol.Map({
    [...]
    controls: [
        [...]
        projControl
    [...]
});
```

If you save the code and look it up, you can try out our new projection. Note that the Arctic Polar Stereographic projection's validity extent only covers the northern hemisphere. For features with lower latitudes, the distortion will be ludicrously high.

This is the better case, though, as exceeding some projections' validity extent results in an erroneous transform, destroying the feature's geometry. To make your application more stable, you shouldn't leave geometry handling entirely to the library.

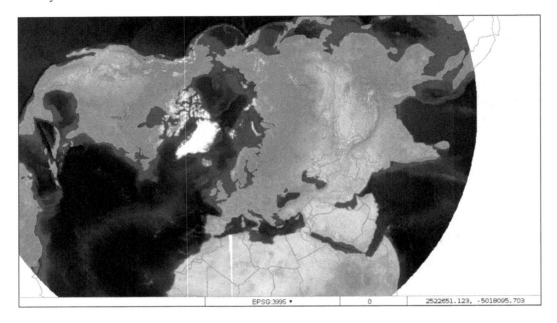

EPSG:3995 ▾	0	2522651.123, -5018095.703

Creating custom animations

In a WebGIS application, animations do not play serious roles; however, in some web mapping applications that are focused on user experience, they can really come in handy. In the last example, called ch06_animation, we will go through the process of making our own special camera effects. The theory behind animations is very important but quite mathematical, so try to keep up with me. First, we declare some CSS rules for our custom animation control:

```
.ol-rocket {
    top: 20px;
    right: 20px;
}
.ol-rocket button {
    background-image: url(../../res/button_rocket.png);
    background-size: contain;
    background-repeat: no-repeat;
    background-position: 50%;
}
```

Building the control

Next, we create a simple control, which will trigger the animation process. Let's make a little revision first. Animations can be triggered by calling the map object's `beforeRender` method with one or more animation functions. We can provide a start time and, occasionally, `source`, `resolution`, or `rotation`. These functions make sure that our view is animated before it switches to the next destination. After the first change in the view, the list of animations gets cleared and changes take place immediately later without animations. In this example, we make two custom animations: one for zooming into the maximum resolution of an OpenSteetMap layer (`rocketTakeOff`) and the other to zoom into my campus (`rocketLanding`):

```
ol.control.RocketFlight = function () {
    var _this = this;
    var controlDiv = document.createElement('div');
    controlDiv.className = 'ol-rocket ol-unselectable ol-control';
    var controlButton = document.createElement('button');
    controlButton.title = 'Launch me';
    controlButton.addEventListener('click', function () {
        var view = _this.getMap().getView();
        _this.getMap().beforeRender(
            ol.animation.rocketTakeoff({
                resolution: view.getResolution(),
                rotation: view.getRotation()
            })
        );
        view.setResolution(39135.75848201024);
```

The first part, as mentioned previously, zooms into the maximum zoom level from the current resolution in an imaginary rocket. Next, we call an animation, which is designated to zoom into the final destination:

```
        setTimeout(function () {
            _this.getMap().beforeRender(
                ol.animation.pan({
                    duration: 2000,
                    source: view.getCenter(),
                    easing: ol.easing.linear
                }),
                ol.animation.rocketLanding({
                    resolution: view.getResolution(),
                    rotation: view.getRotation()
                })
            );
```

```
                view.setProperties({
                    center: [2026883.0676951527, 5792745.55306364],
                    resolution: 0.5971642834779395
                });
            }, 5100);
        });
        controlDiv.appendChild(controlButton);
        ol.control.Control.call(this, {
            element: controlDiv
        });
    };
    ol.inherits(ol.control.RocketFlight, ol.control.Control);
```

As we cannot trigger an animation before the previous one is finished, we delay it by a little more than five seconds. Our first animation will take exactly five seconds to complete, but we do not want the two animations to hook up.

Creating animations

Before we create our first custom animation, let's discuss how animations work in OpenLayers 3. Every animation function returns a function. The returned function receives two arguments. The first is the map object, which is negligible in most of the cases. The second one is the frame state. The returned function gets called in every frame until it returns `false`. From the frame state object, the most important properties that we can decipher is the current time and the view's updated state.

If you are a visual type, this might help you understand animations in OpenLayers 3 better. Imagine a spring. When we start an animation, we fixate one end in the new view. We hold the other end in the previous view where we start animating from. The spring will be in stationary state when both of its ends are in the new view. If we stop animating, we release the spring, which instantly jumps to the new view, as it wants to be in its stationary state. However, until we are animating, we move the end that we hold continuously to the fixated end for a fluent result. But how do we know how much it needs to be moved in a given time? We calculate it from the initial distance and the passed time. Finally, we move closer to the fixed end by the value it needs to be moved. Of course, every spring can be moved in two directions; thus, we can pull the spring in the opposite direction. If we do this, however, we have to calculate with an inverse distance.

There is a very important function, which we will call frequently, called `easing`. An `easing` function in the library expects a number between `0` and `1`, representing the percentage value for which a movement in the animation is completed. It returns a scaling factor that's based on a function curve, with which a linear movement should be multiplied by in order to result in a tween. Now, we create our first custom `animation` function to zoom out of the map in the application:

```
ol.animation.rocketTakeoff = function (options) {
    var now = +new Date();
    return function (map, frameState) {
        if (frameState.time < now + 5000) {
            var delta = 1 - ol.easing.easeIn((frameState.time -
now) / 5000);
            var deltaResolution = options.resolution -
frameState.viewState.resolution;
            frameState.animate = true;
            frameState.viewState.resolution += delta *
deltaResolution;
            if (frameState.time > now + 2000 && frameState.time <
now + 3000) {
                var rotateDelta = ol.easing.linear((frameState.time -
now - 2000) / 1000);
                var deltaRotation = options.rotation - 0.5;
                frameState.viewState.rotation += deltaRotation *
rotateDelta;
            } else if (frameState.time >= now + 3000 && frameState.
time < now + 4000) {
                var rotateDelta = 1 - ol.easing.linear((frameState.
time - now - 3000) / 1000);
                var deltaRotation = options.rotation - 0.5;
                frameState.viewState.rotation += deltaRotation *
rotateDelta;
            }
            frameState.viewHints[0] += 1;
            return true;
        }
        return false;
    };
};
```

As mentioned previously, every frame state comes with a timestamp. There is a twist in the timestamps, though, as it represents the current date in milliseconds.

> In most programming languages, such as JavaScript, the current date represents the elapsed time between 1970, January 1, 00:00:00 and the operating system's current time.

This way, we have to adjust our timing with a new `Date` object, which we can cast to milliseconds by preceding it with + on construction. We save the starting time of our animation with this method and compare every frame state's timestamp to it. As we want our first animation to take 5 seconds, we update our frame states for this time, then return `false`, terminating the animation.

For the resolution change, we use the `ol.easing.easeIn` function, which starts fast and slows down at the end. We must provide the inverse value that's returned by the `easing` function, though, as we move toward our destination.

> In every function call, our `animation` function gets the updated properties of the view object. While the `animation` exists, we can overwrite the view on every frame by modifying the `frameState` object's `viewState` properties. This is how animations work in OpenLayers 3.

We increase our view state's resolution with the delta resolution between the initial and target value multiplied by the value that's returned by our `easing` function. This will make sure that our animation is fluent for the time it takes place.

If the animation is between 2 and 3 seconds, we rotate the view with a linear easing. We do not have to invert the returned value as we are moving from our destination (the updated rotation value). To turn back the rotation between the fourth and the fifth seconds, we take the same procedure with an inverse easing value.

> If you want to use a linear easing, you do not have to use an easing function at all. The `ol.easing.linear` function returns the provided value without any modifications. I'm just using it now for consistency.

As you may have noticed, we changed two values in the frame state's besides its view state's properties. Setting its `animate` property to `true` is mandatory; otherwise, the animation stops. Updating the 0 property of its `viewHints` object is optional, though. That property shows, how many animations are modifying the view at a current frame.

Next, we create our second animation to land in our imaginary rocket's shuttle:

```
ol.animation.rocketLanding = function (options) {
    var now = +new Date();
    var direction = Math.round(Math.random());
    return function (map, frameState) {
        if (frameState.time < now + 15000) {
            var delta = 1 - ol.easing.parachuate((frameState.time
- now) / 15000);
            var deltaResolution = options.resolution -
frameState.viewState.resolution;
            frameState.animate = true;
            frameState.viewState.resolution += delta *
deltaResolution;
            if (frameState.time > now + 5000 && frameState.time <
now + 7000) {
                var rotateDelta = ol.easing.linear((frameState.time -
now - 5000) / 2000);
                var deltaRotation = options.rotation + 2 *
Math.PI;
                frameState.viewState.rotation += deltaRotation *
rotateDelta;
            } else if (frameState.time > now + 7000 &&
frameState.time < now + 10000) {
                var panDelta = ol.easing.linear((frameState.time -
now - 7000) / 3000);
                frameState.viewState.center[direction] += 500 *
panDelta;
            } else if (frameState.time >= now + 10000 &&
frameState.time < now + 12000) {
                var panDelta = 1 -
ol.easing.linear((frameState.time - now - 10000) / 2000);
                frameState.viewState.center[direction] += 500 *
panDelta;
            }
            frameState.viewHints[0] += 1;
            return true;
        }
        return false;
    };
};
```

In this function, at the end of the landing, we swing our capsule on a random axis. The landing takes 15 seconds. For the duration of this period, we decrease the resolution with a custom `easing` function, which we will soon discuss. After 5 seconds, we make a 360 degree turn, which is exactly 2π radians. Between 7 and 10 seconds, we pan our view by 500 meters on the randomly generated axis, while between 10 and 12 seconds, we pan it back to its original place.

Next, we define our custom `easing` function:

```
ol.easing.parachuate = function (t) {
    return 1 - Math.pow(1 - t, 7);
};
```

The basic `ol.easing.easeOut` function is similar to custom easing function; however, it brings the inverted argument to its third power, making the slowdown faster. We slow down the effect drastically by bringing the inverted argument to its seventh power.

 As you may have noticed already, we didn't make an effort to pan our view from our imaginary rocket's launch site to its landing place. This is why we included a built-in pan animation along with a custom landing animation in our control.

Finally, we include the control to the map and change the base layer back to OpenStreetMap:

```
var map = new ol.Map({
    target: 'map',
    layers: [
        new ol.layer.Tile({
            source: new ol.source.OSM({
                wrapX: false
            }),
            name: 'OpenStreetMap'
        }),
        [...]
    controls: [
        [...]
        new ol.control.RocketFlight()
    [...]
});
```

Now, if you save the code and open it, you can fly to my campus from any location.

 For the best experience, start it from a high zoom level!

Summary

Congratulations! You just created your first and very own animation in OpenLayers 3, strictly based on various mathematical functions, proving that you are capable of efficient algorithmic thinking. In this chapter, you learned how to manage your map's view in various ways with some GUI widgets. You learned how to navigate through the map efficiently, zoom to various extents, and most importantly, how to implement new projections and switch between them correctly.

In the next, chapter, we will discuss how rendering, and renderers work in OpenLayers 3. We will see, why we should not use the DOM renderer, and what are the main strengths, and weaknesses of the far more efficient Canvas, and WebGL renderers. After we have learned how to use those renderers properly, and what are the main pitfalls we must overcome, we will learn how to do some basic, and more advanced image manipulations with the Canvas renderer.

7
Mastering Renderers

In the previous chapters, we learned how to create custom controls, and manage the view effectively, but we still don't know how rendering works in OpenLayers 3. In this chapter, we will discuss this subject in greater depth. In order to create a well-optimized, responsive application, we must know how rendering works and how we can make rendering-related considerations for different use cases.

In this chapter, we will cover the following topics:

- Differences between the DOM, the Canvas, and the WebGL renderers
- Limitations of the WebGL renderer
- Operations carried out with the map canvas using the Canvas renderer
- Using raster operations independently from the renderer

Before getting started

In the previous chapter, we finalized our sample WebGIS application. That's it; we won't extend it anymore in this chapter or in future chapters. As we later need to create some controls for different operations, we go back to our layer tree model from *Chapter 3, Working with Layers*. We will use the ch03_layerorder example as our starting point and customize it later according to our needs.

We will not use any third-party library in this chapter; however, we need a large dataset so that we can try out the capabilities of the WebGL renderer. This dataset can be located in the res folder. It's name is switzerland_points_osm.geojson, and it contains 221,291 point features from the OpenStreetMap database.

Using different renderers

As you may already know, there are three different renderers in OpenLayers 3. The DOM renderer is a legacy method that supports pre-HTML5 browsers. The main limitation of this renderer is that it cannot display vector layers. Vector layers are rendered using a canvas if the DOM renderer is used. Only tile and image layers are created as separate DOM elements. If you must support legacy browsers, which cannot use the `canvas` element, OpenLayers 2 is a better choice for you as it supports SVG and VML rendering.

The second one is the Canvas renderer, which is the default. It draws every layer separately on a single `canvas` element, outperforming its predecessor. For now, we don't have to know anything specific about canvas elements; we will see the possibilities of canvas manipulation in further examples.

The third one is a cutting-edge technology called WebGL. WebGL is the browser implementation of OpenGL, making browsers capable of hardware-accelerated rendering. The technology is widely used in client-side 3D applications, but it can drastically increase the rendering performance of OpenLayers 3 too. This renderer has some limitations, which we will see later in this chapter.

 Do not expect too much from the WebGL renderer. OpenLayers 3 is only capable of 2D rendering, and even the WebGL renderer cannot change this behavior.

Creating a WebGL map

In the first example, called `ch07_webgl`, we will create our first WebGL map. We bring our application to its limits, displaying more than 200,000 points on a single map. If you haven't performed this test already, you must be thinking that the magnitude of features will render our application totally unresponsive and useless. Let's make an attempt to perform this test, though. For this example, we only have to modify our map constructor using our new vector layer and the WebGL renderer:

```
var map = new ol.Map({
    target: 'map',
    layers: [
        [...]
        new ol.layer.Vector({
            source: new ol.source.Vector({
                format: new ol.format.GeoJSON({
                    defaultDataProjection: 'EPSG:4326'
                }),
```

```
                    url: '../../res/switzerland_points_osm.geojson',
                    attributions: [
                        new ol.Attribution({
                            html: 'Switzerland Points © OpenStreetMap
Contributors'
                        })
                    ]
                }),
                name: 'Switzerland Points'
            })
        ],
        [...]
        view: new ol.View({
            center: [910000, 5900000],
            zoom: 9
        }),
        renderer: 'webgl'
    });
```

If you save the example and load it in a browser, you will be able to take a look at all the points that are rendered after some processing time. The map is quite hard to handle on lower scales; however, it is still manageable. When we zoom in and out on higher scales, the map becomes responsive again:

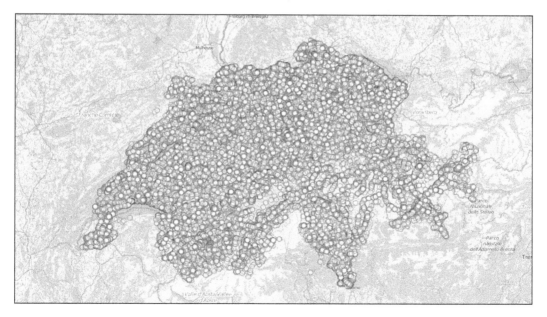

Be patient when you load the example. The library has to parse a lot of points; thus, it will need some time.

The only reason our application didn't freeze was due to the utilization of the GPU via the WebGL renderer. With proper hardware acceleration, we can display bigger datasets with acceptable performance.

There is only one serious limitation of this renderer: it cannot draw lines or polygons. The library will support such rendering methods over time; however, using vector lines and polygons are currently not supported. Furthermore, if we try to use line and polygon datasets with the WebGL renderer, the application will throw an error and stop running.

Drawing lines and polygons with WebGL

In the previous example, we stated that OpenLayers 3 cannot render lines and polygons with the WebGL renderer. However, there is a workaround, which we will use in this example, called ch07_webgl_vector.

Let's add the country boundaries layer with a little twist to our map:

```
var map = new ol.Map({
    [...]
        new ol.layer.Image({
            source: new ol.source.ImageVector({
                source: new ol.source.Vector({
                    format: new ol.format.GeoJSON({
                        defaultDataProjection: 'EPSG:4326'
                    }),
                    url: '../../res/world_countries.geojson',
                    attributions: [
                        new ol.Attribution({
                            html: 'World Countries © Natural
Earth'
                        })
                    ]
                })
            }),
            name: 'World Countries'
        })
    ],
    [...]
```

As you can see, we converted our vector layer to an image layer. The `ol.source.`
`ImageVector` class takes a legal vector source as input and renders it as a set of
images. The class creates internal `canvas` elements for the provided or default
resolutions, draws the underlying vector data on them, and exports their content as
images. From there, the vector layer can be used and rendered as a regular image
layer. This way, the WebGL renderer can easily handle the underlying shapes
without knowing how to render lines and polygons:

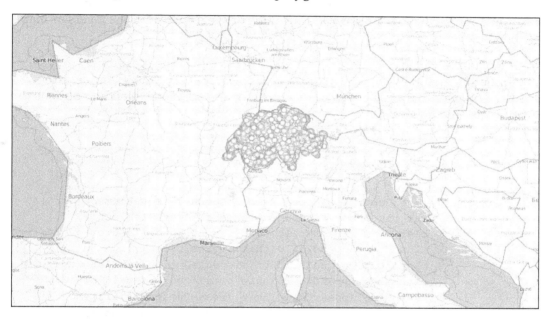

With this little trick, you can use any shape with the WebGL renderer. However, there
are two things you should note. First, converting a vector layer to an image layer does
not increase the application's performance noticeably when used with big datasets.
Furthermore, the line and polygon-based features, like the draw interaction, will still
not work with WebGL. If you need to use them, you have to reinvent the wheel and
implement them in such a way that they are forced to use an image vector source.

> OpenLayers 3 cannot wrap image vectors on the *x* axis. Furthermore,
> they will be a little blurry when they're rendered, which is the result of
> the image conversion. However, when they're rendered with WebGL,
> you won't see the difference as only the Canvas renderer can draw
> sharp shapes.

Blending layers

In the next three examples, we will fall back on the Canvas renderer. It is the most developed and stable one, providing a lot of perks by allowing canvas manipulation methods. The map and every layer is rendered on a different canvas, while in the end, they are aggregated into a single composition. This pattern, the existence of `precompose`, and the `postcompose` events (rendering hooks) enable us to manipulate the context of any layer or the map as a whole. We can basically use any canvas manipulation method as long as we can get the original context of the layers or map with these events.

In this example, called `ch07_blend`, we will discuss one of the most useful canvas manipulation methods, the `globalCompositionContext`. For this example, we modify our layer tree's `createRegistry` method, and add some blending options to every registered layer:

```
var layerTree = function (options) {
    [...]
        this.createRegistry = function (layer, buffer) {
            [...]
            layerControls.appendChild(document.createElement('br'));
            var blendMode = document.createElement('select');
            blendMode.appendChild(this.createOption('source-over'));
            blendMode.appendChild(this.createOption('lighten'));
            blendMode.appendChild(this.createOption('darken'));
            blendMode.appendChild(this.createOption('multiply'));
            blendMode.appendChild(this.createOption('difference'));
            blendMode.addEventListener('change', function () {
                if (layer.get('blendMode')) {
                    ol.Observable.unByKey(layer.get('blendMode'));
                    layer.unset('blendMode');
                }
                layer.set('blendMode', layer.on
('precompose', function (evt) {
                    evt.context.globalCompositeOperation =
blendMode.value;
                }));
                _this.map.render();
            });
            layerControls.appendChild(this.stopPropagationOnEvent
(blendMode, 'click'));
            [...]
```

We create a `select` element for a limited number of blending options. When we change the element's value, we remove the current event listener, if we have one, and then register a new listener on the layer's `precompose` event. In the listener, we simply change the `canvas` element's context `globalCompositeOperation` property.

> The default composite operation is `source-over`. You can find a description for every valid operation on the MDN site at `http://developer.mozilla.org/en-US/docs/Web/API/ CanvasRenderingContext2D/globalCompositeOperation`.

Remember: only one composite operation can be used on a single canvas. Because of the rendering pattern of OpenLayers 3, we can apply a different operation on every layer. However, the library keeps the last operation for every layer from there. Due to this phenomenon, we should explicitly define an operation for every layer. This can be done by registering a listener with the default value (`source-over`) in every layer that's added to the map or leaving the whole process to the users for the purpose of experimenting.

If you load the example, you can experiment with blending methods too. For a better experience, you can change or extend the blending options with the help of more legal operations, load more layers, and try to create complex compositions:

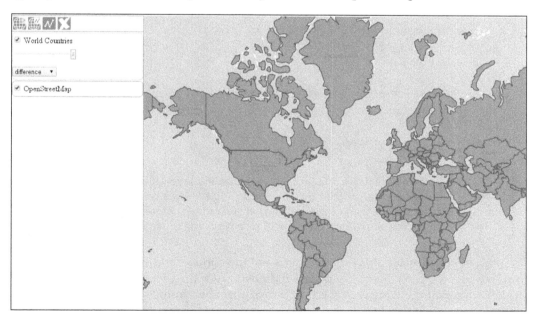

Clipping layers

In the next example, called `ch07_clip`, we will use another useful canvas operation. We will use a clipping mask to restrict a layer to a small square, creating a peeking window, just like the one in the Google Maps application.

 There are way more canvas operations than those described in the examples. However, I tried to pick out the most useful ones for web mapping applications.

For this example, we extend our `init` function with a custom layer. We register the required `precompose` and `postcompose` events on it, and then silently add it to the map:

```
var clippedLayer = new ol.layer.Tile({
    source: new ol.source.MapQuest({
        layer: 'osm'
    }),
    zIndex: 9999
});
clippedLayer.on('precompose', function (evt) {
    var ctx = evt.context;
    ctx.save();
    ctx.beginPath();
    ctx.rect(20, 20, 100, 100);
    ctx.clip();
});
clippedLayer.on('postcompose', function (evt) {
    evt.context.restore();
});
clippedLayer.setMap(map);
```

 You can provide a `zIndex` property for any layer. If it is not 0, it alters the rendering order of the layer, ignoring the layer order. For this example, we provide an arbitrary high number; therefore, the clipped layer (the peeking window) will be always the top layer.

The trick of clipping a context is this: we save the context and then draw a rectangle. First, we begin a path. Next, we define the position of the rectangle relative to the top-left corner of the canvas in the first two arguments. In the second two arguments, we define the width and the height of the rectangle, respectively. Instead of drawing the rectangle on the canvas by calling the `stroke` or `fillRect` methods, we convert the path to a clipping mask using the context's `clip` method.

When the layer is drawn (the `postcompose` event), we restore the saved context, disabling the clipping mask for every other layer. If we skip this step, the entire map is clipped to the defined mask.

If you load the example, you can see our peeking window showing a MapQuest layer over our base map:

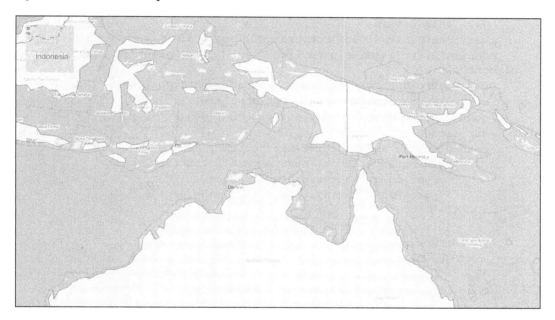

 Most of the canvas operations are can be achieved with the WebGL renderer too (except for blending). However, manipulating the map via WebGL requires adequate expertise in OpenGL programming.

Exporting a map

The third useful canvas operation we will discuss is saving the content of the canvas as an image. As you may already know, traditionally, files can be saved by downloading them from a server. There are serious security considerations behind the restriction of saving anything to the hard drive that's created on the client side. However, there is no restriction in displaying a dynamically created image.

In this example, called `ch07_print`, we will create a control that dynamically creates an image based on the map canvas's context and opens it in a new tab. This way, we can download the image just like any other plain image from a web page. First, we will create a new control to save map states:

```
ol.control.Print = function (opt_options) {
    var options = opt_options || {};
    var _this = this;
    var controlDiv = document.createElement('div');
    controlDiv.className = options.class || 'ol-print ol-unselectable
ol-control';
    var controlButton = document.createElement('button');
    controlButton.textContent = options.label || 'P';
    controlButton.title = options.tipLabel || 'Print map';
    var dataURL;
    controlButton.addEventListener('click', function (evt) {
        _this.getMap().once('postcompose', function (evt) {
            var canvas = evt.context.canvas;
            dataURL = canvas.toDataURL('image/png');
        });
        _this.getMap().renderSync();
        window.open(dataURL, '_blank');
        dataURL = null;
    });
    controlDiv.appendChild(controlButton);
    ol.control.Control.call(this, {
        element: controlDiv,
        target: options.target
    });
};
ol.inherits(ol.control.Print, ol.control.Control);
```

The control is very simple. If we push the button, it registers a one-time listener to the map object and converts the content of its canvas to a `png` image. More precisely, it converts it to a Base64 encoded URL of the `png` image, which can be opened by browsers, just like regular websites. After we have the URL, we call a synchronous rendering frame, making sure that the event occurs before we try to open our image. Finally, we simply open our image in a new tab.

 When you try to open something in a new tab or window from JavaScript, your browser will most likely think that it's a popup and try to block it. As we work from a local server now, this problem does not occur, however, when you have to deploy such a feature, you should consider this behavior.

Next, we modify our map constructor a little bit. We deploy two new layers, adjust their views, and add our new control:

```
map = new ol.Map({
    target: 'map',
    layers: [
        new ol.layer.Tile({
            source: new ol.source.TileWMS({
                url: 'http://demo.opengeo.org/geoserver/wms',
                params: {
                    layers: 'ned',
                    format: 'image/png'
                },
                wrapX: false,
                crossOrigin: 'anonymous'
            }),
            name: 'Elevation'
        }),
        new ol.layer.Tile({
            source: new ol.source.TileWMS({
                url: 'http://demo.opengeo.org/geoserver/wms',
                params: {
                    layers: 'nlcd',
                    format: 'image/png'
                },
                wrapX: false,
                crossOrigin: 'anonymous'
            }),
            name: 'Land Cover'
        })
    ],
    controls: [
        […]
        new ol.control.Print({
            target: 'toolbar'
        })
    ],
    view: new ol.View({
        center: [-8604363.40000572, 4741541.738586053],
        zoom: 9
    })
});
```

As you can see, we used an extra property when we constructed the layer objects. The crossOrigin property is very important if we want to access the pixel values of the canvas. This is also a security consideration that does not let us manipulate or export the content of a canvas if we have used a non-CORS image at any point in time. To mark the images of a layer as cross origin, we only have to set the layer's crossOrigin property to anonymous. If we do not implement this step, we end up with a tainted canvas, which we cannot export.

If you save the example and load it up, you can open the map's content in the form of a picture in a new tab:

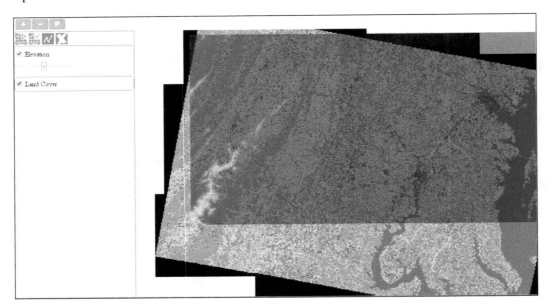

Creating a raster calculator

Now that we are familiar with some of the most useful canvas manipulation methods, let's take a look at a renderer that is independent of any image manipulation. There is a very useful source object in the library that can take multiple sources as input and create a new image based on the provided operations. In this example, called ch07_rastcalc, we will use the ol.source.Raster class to build a basic RasterCalculator function.

Raster 101

To understand the limitations of raster manipulation in OpenLayers 3 or, basically, any web mapping application, we should discuss how rasters work in GIS. If you are familiar with the concept, you can skip this part. If not, this section can give you some basic, but valuable, information, which can help you evaluate better architectural patterns.

First of all, every raster can be translated to a simple matrix. Rasters have a resolution and consist of uniform cells. Therefore, if we know the resolution of a raster, we can handle the underlying data as a matrix, which we can also place in a coordinate reference system if we know the coordinates of one of its corners. Traditionally, this corner is the lower-left one. A raster can only contain one value for every cell it contains. This value can represent anything from elevation to any sort of statistical data. This type of value must be numeric but the subtype is not specified (although it must be uniform for the entire raster).

The main problem when working with rasters in browsers is that browsers can only think in the RGB color space. A browser cannot interpret raster data in its natural form; therefore, map servers convert rasters to a well-recognized RGB format (such as png, jpeg, or gif) and send images in these formats to the client. This way, we can only access the converted RGB values for every pixel of the raster, and without knowing the transformation method exactly, we cannot transform them back to their original values. We can transform them to single band values, making raster calculations possible and showing visually appealing results, but they will not represent the truth.

To sum it up, we can make raster calculations possible in the browser. However, as we do not know the original values by default, just the transformed RGB values, our transformations can only be proportionally correct. This can yield to visually appealing results, but the calculations can only be used to create previews. We can create a preview for an otherwise resource-intensive server-side calculation, thus making users not load the server when the result is clearly dissatisfying.

Operating with pixels

For this example, we will build a static calculator control. This control picks out shades of red from the first map (urban areas in the land classification layer) and keeps the second layer (elevation) only according to the pixels of first layer. In simpler terms, we will mask the elevation layer with the urban areas of the land classification layer. First, we will create the basics of our new control:

```
ol.control.RasterCalculator = function (opt_options) {
    var options = opt_options || {};
    var _this = this;
    var controlDiv = document.createElement('div');
    controlDiv.className = options.class || 'ol-rastercalc ol-
unselectable ol-control';
    var controlButton = document.createElement('button');
    controlButton.textContent = options.label || 'R';
    controlButton.title = options.tipLabel || 'Calculate Raster';
```

Next, we have to write a filter function that checks an input pixel from the mask layer, and if the criteria for this pixel is met, it returns the pixel value of the second layer. If not, it sends back a fully transparent pixel:

```
var filterPixel = function (pixels) {
    var inputPixel = pixels[0];
    var maskPixel = pixels[1];
    if (maskPixel[0] > maskPixel[1] && maskPixel[0] >
maskPixel[2] && Math.abs(maskPixel[1] - maskPixel[2]) < 25) {
        return inputPixel;
    }
    return [0, 0, 0, 0];
};
```

 The value of 25 for the absolute difference in green and blue values is a sensitive default. If you set it to 50 or 100, brownish colors will also get picked.

Next, we add an event listener to the button. If we click on it, our control creates a new layer with a raster source and calculates the layer based on two input layers:

```
controlButton.addEventListener('click', function (evt) {
    var layer = _this.getMap().getLayers().item(0);
    var mask = _this.getMap().getLayers().item(1);
    if (layer && mask) {
        var raster = new ol.source.Raster({
            sources: [layer.getSource(), mask.getSource()],
```

```
            operationType: 'pixel',
            operation: function (pixels, data) {
                return filter(pixels);
            },
            lib: {
                filter: filterPixel
            }
        });
        _this.getMap().addLayer(new ol.layer.Image({
            source: raster,
            name: 'Urban elevation'
        }));
    }
});
```

For the raster source, we have to provide an array of source objects. If we set the operationType attribute to pixels, we will get an array for the operation function with the overlapping pixel values of every provided source. The lib property is optional; however, it is utterly useful. We can separate the most resource-intensive calculations in separate functions and define them in the lib object. OpenLayers 3 can thread these functions via web workers but only if they are defined.

 You can refer to a function provided in the lib object with any function name in the operation function until it is mapped out correctly.

Finally, we finish our control with some routine commands and include it in our map constructor:

```
    controlDiv.appendChild(controlButton);
    ol.control.Control.call(this, {
        element: controlDiv,
        target: options.target
    });
};
ol.inherits(ol.control.RasterCalculator, ol.control.Control);
[…]
var map = new ol.Map({
    […]
    controls: [
        […]
        new ol.control.RasterCalculator({
            target: 'toolbar'
        })
    […]
});
```

If you save the code and try it in a browser, you will see our raster calculator in action. You can also try to perform more complex calculations on input images:

Creating a convolution matrix

In the next example, called ch07_convolution, we will implement a control, which can apply a filter on a single image. We will hardcode a Sobel filter for this example; however, based on the implementation, you will be able to use any kind of filter, even dynamically. Our implementation will have three stages:

- Converting the image to grayscale
- Applying the Sobel filter
- Normalizing the image

How convolution works

Before creating the control, let's discuss how convolution works in a nutshell. When we convolve an image, we calculate some sort of statistics from the image matrix that is based on every pixel's (or raster's) neighborhood. This is why this method is also referred to as focal statistics or a moving window in geoinformatics. There are two things we need to convolve an image: the pixel data arranged in a matrix and a small matrix with weights in it, which is called a kernel. We apply the kernel to every cell in our image and calculate its new value based on the values of its neighbors multiplied by the corresponding kernel value:

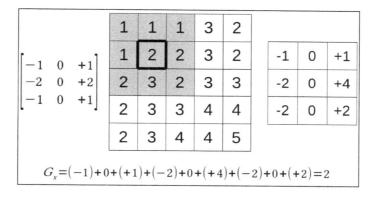

After the operation, we will have a matrix that is equal to the size of the kernel. The matrix contains the values of the original pixel and its neighborhood, which are weighted by the kernel values. If we add these values, we will get the new value for our current cell. The preceding kernel is the horizontal part of a 3 x 3 Sobel filter.

Converting an image to 8-bit

There are tons of cases where applying a convolution matrix to an RGB image just does not work out. In raster calculations or raster algebra, we operated on single band images of various types. This is also the case with the Sobel filter. As it detects edges (that is, the vertical and horizontal changes in pixel values), the easiest and most appropriate way is to clamp our image to a single 8-bit band. Of course, sometimes, storing values in a single byte is just not enough; in such cases, you can create a temporal array with appropriate values. First, we will create the control button:

```
ol.control.Convolve = function (opt_options) {
    var options = opt_options || {};
```

```
    var _this = this;
    var controlDiv = document.createElement('div');
    controlDiv.className = options.class || 'ol-convolve ol-
unselectable ol-control';
    var controlButton = document.createElement('button');
    controlButton.textContent = options.label || 'C';
    controlButton.title = options.tipLabel || 'Convolve bottom
layer';
```

Next, we will define a function in the control, which converts an input RGB matrix to an 8-bit one with the help of an averaging method:

```
    var toGrayScale = function (inputArray) {
        for (var i = 0; i < inputArray.length; i += 4) {
            var grayScaleValue = (inputArray[i] + inputArray[i +
1] + inputArray[i + 2]) / 3;
            inputArray[i] = grayScaleValue;
            inputArray[i + 1] = grayScaleValue;
            inputArray[i + 2] = grayScaleValue;
        }
    };
```

As we only change one pixel at a time, we can overwrite the original values of the provided array. Rounding is not necessary in this case as we operate on typed arrays, which we will see in detail later in the chapter. There is only one consideration that we have to make. As browsers can only think in the RGB color space, we must assign the calculated value to every color band. This way, we end up in a grayscale image. We step our loop with a value of 4 because we get a simple array containing every pixel's RGBA (red, green, blue, and alpha) values in the correct pixel order.

There are two more well-known methods to convert an RGB image to an 8-bit image (desaturating). The first one is called the lightness method, which averages the biggest and smallest value from an RGB pixel. The second one is called the luminosity method, which weighs the values based on the color sensitivity of our eyes. The formula in this case is $0.21 * R + 0.72 * G + 0.07 * B$.

Implementing the Sobel filter

Next, we create a function in our control that applies the Sobel filter to an input pixel and returns its new edge detected value:

```
var applySobel = function (inputArray, index, width) {
    var nh = [inputArray[index - width - 4],
        inputArray[index - width],
        inputArray[index - width + 4],
        inputArray[index - 4],
        inputArray[index],
        inputArray[index + 4],
        inputArray[index + width - 4],
        inputArray[index + width],
        inputArray[index + width + 4]];
    for (var i = 0; i < nh.length; i += 1) {
        if (nh[i] === undefined) {
            nh[i] = inputArray[index];
        }
    }
    var hFilter = nh[0] + 2 * nh[1] + nh[2] - nh[6] - 2 *
nh[7] - nh[8];
    var vFilter = nh[2] + 2 * nh[5] + nh[8] - nh[6] - 2 *
nh[3] - nh[0];
    var pixelValue = Math.sqrt(Math.pow(hFilter, 2) +
Math.pow(vFilter, 2));
    return 255 - pixelValue;
};
```

Our function accepts three parameters. We must grab a reference to the array first as we have to know the values of the input pixel's neighbors. Secondly, we request the current index, which describes the position of our current pixel. Finally, we need a width parameter, also referred to as a stride, which is the numeric representation of the width of the image. This number tells us how many pixels we need to go forward or backward in order to get a pixel above or below our input pixel.

As we have every parameter needed to locate the current pixel's neighborhood, we can set up a temporal array, representing the matrix, which we will weight with a kernel. The Sobel filter has two kernels: one for horizontal edge detection and one for vertical edge detection. In this example, we will hardcode the weighting for the sake of simplicity.

There is one interesting problem we have to deal when we use a convolution matrix. On the edges of the image, we cannot grab a reference to every pixel in the kernel. There are several methods we can use in this particular case. We can shrink the image by n - 2, where n stands for the size of the kernel; however, this method is not simple, especially with OpenLayers 3. Alternatively, we can extrapolate our image, which is easier to implement. In our simple implementation, we do not extrapolate those values properly that are based on the whole neighborhood; we just default it to the current pixel value.

The last step of calculating the final value of the pixel is getting the geometric mean of the two filter values. This will automatically clamp our value to a byte range. Rounding off the value is still not necessary as the typed array will do this for us automatically.

 Inverting the color of the result is optional. We only do this because black edges on a white background is more visually appealing.

Normalizing an image

When the pixel values are finely distributed, the result (display model) is visually appealing. We have a black contour on hard edges and a white representation on homogeneous pixels. However, as we can zoom into the image, this will not be the case on higher zoom levels. On a subset of the image, we can have only soft edges, and if we do not normalize the image, we will barely see them or won't see them at all. The normalization process stretches out the resulting pixel values to a predefined interval; in our case, this is from 0 to 255:

```
var normalizeImage = function (inputArray, min, max) {
    for (var i = 0; i < inputArray.length; i+=4) {
        var newIntensity = (inputArray[i] - min) * 255 / (max
- min);
        inputArray[i] = newIntensity;
        inputArray[i+1] = newIntensity;
        inputArray[i+2] = newIntensity;
    }
};
```

In this example, we use a linear normalization method, which is the easiest to implement. There are some cases, however, when a normalized image with a linear method does not reflect the truth. If there is a nonlinear correlation between the image and the display model, you should use a more complex normalization method.

For a more dynamic application, you should implement some different normalization algorithms, map them to a control, and let the users decide which one is the most adequate for them.

Finalizing a control

In the final step, we add an event listener to the control button, which creates a new raster layer and applies the Sobel filter to it:

```
controlButton.addEventListener('click', function (evt) {
        var layer = _this.getMap().getLayers().item(0);
        if (layer) {
            var raster = new ol.source.Raster({
                sources: [layer.getSource()],
                operationType: 'image',
                operation: function (image, data) {
                    var imageData = image[0];
                    var inputArray = imageData.data;
                    toGrayScale(inputArray);
                    var outputArray = new
Uint8ClampedArray(inputArray);
                    var min = Infinity, max = -Infinity;
                    for (var i = 0; i < inputArray.length; i += 4)
{
                        var edgeValue = calculateValue(inputArray,
i, imageData.width * 4, imageData.height);
                        outputArray[i] = edgeValue;
                        outputArray[i + 1] = edgeValue;
                        outputArray[i + 2] = edgeValue;
                        min = outputArray[i] < min ? outputArray[i] :
min;
                        max = outputArray[i] > max ? outputArray[i] :
max;
                    }
                    normalizeImage(outputArray, min, max);
                    return new ImageData(outputArray, imageData.width,
imageData.height);
                },
                lib: {
                    calculateValue: applySobel,
                    toGrayScale: toGrayScale,
                    normalizeImage: normalizeImage
                }
```

```
        });
        _this.getMap().addLayer(new ol.layer.Image({
            source: raster,
            name: 'Sobel filter'
        }));
    }
});
controlDiv.appendChild(controlButton);
ol.control.Control.call(this, {
    element: controlDiv,
    target: options.target
});
};
ol.inherits(ol.control.Convolve, ol.control.Control);
```

The process resembles the one described in the previous example; however, we now use the `image` operation type. There is a fundamental difference between the two operations. When we use a pixel type, we get one pixel value for every provided layer at a time, but in the case of image type, we get the whole image matrix for every provided layer at once.

As we use an image type operation, we get the whole image data, which is a JavaScript `ImageData` type object. The object contains the matrix of the image in its `data` property. The matrix is a little tricky as it must be a typed array. Typed arrays in JavaScript are low-level interfaces, granting access to *real* arrays stored in the memory. These arrays are the ones you are used to if you have used some lower-level languages, such as C. They are raw binary data whose content depends on the interpretation. To interpret these arrays, JavaScript offers some typed array constructors, such as 8, 16, or, 32-bit integer arrays or 32 and 64-bit floating point arrays. `ImageData` must contain `Uint8ClampedArray` more explicitly, which is an 8-bit unsigned integer array.

 You can learn more about typed arrays in JavaScript on the MDN website at `http://developer.mozilla.org/en-US/docs/Web/JavaScript/Typed_arrays`.

In the raster operation, we convert the input array to grayscale. We can overwrite that array as the original RGB values of the input image can be discarded. For the output array, however, we must create a new array based on the grayscale one. As the convolution must be made on the original values, we must not make the modifications in place of original values. While we calculate the new values for our convolved image, we also store the minimum and maximum values of the current view: our image's range.

 There are several valid use cases of the `Infinity` and `-Infinity` numeric types. One of them is when you want to initialize a counter with arbitrary high or low numeric starting values, which will be certainly overwritten by real numbers.

When we are done with the convolution, we normalize the image in place with the stored minimum and maximum values. Note that if you would like to create a GUI option to change the normalization algorithm, this operation should not overwrite the result. Next, we can return our new, modified image. This must be done with an `ImageData` object, which must contain the image's dimensions.

As seen in the previous example, we provide every external function that's used in the raster operation in the source's `lib` property. Finally, we construct our map with our new control in it. We also change the base layer to OpenStreetMap in order to see nice, sharp edges:

```
var map = new ol.Map({
    target: 'map',
    layers: [
        new ol.layer.Tile({
            source: new ol.source.OSM(),
            name: 'OpenStreetMap'
        })
    ],
    controls: [
        [...]
        new ol.control.Convolve({
            target: 'toolbar'
        })
    [...]
});
```

If you save the code and use our new tool, you will see how edge detection works with the Sobel filter:

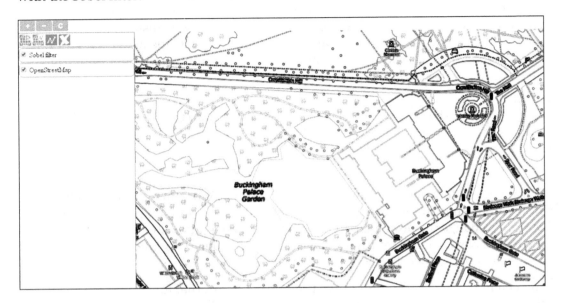

 With a layer that has sharp edges, such as a categorized one, normalization of the result is often unnecessary. However, when you convolve a gradually changing layer, such as a Digital Elevation Model (DEM), the normalization process suddenly becomes indispensable.

Clipping a layer with WebGL

In the last example, called `ch07_clip_webgl`, we will go through some of the key aspects of working with WebGL and OpenLayers 3. WebGL is an exceptionally rich JavaScript port of OpenGL, which is capable of performing advanced 3D GPU calculations. However, as the OpenLayers 3 library already uses it and parameterizes it, when we use the WebGL renderer in the `precompose` and `postcompose` rendering hooks, we have only a limited number of possibilities. For example, OpenGL can automatically blend textures into each other with some blending options. However, as OpenLayers 3 already uses this capability in order to draw the layers on each other with a possible transparency option, we cannot change the global blending property without messing up the entire rendering process.

Clipping, or in this case, masking parts of a layer, is a possible WebGL operation with the library. Our goal is identical to the previous clipping example: we create a 100 x 100 pixels peeking window, which displays a silently added layer above our other layers.

This part can be considered as a bonus example, in which, we will learn about some of the fundamental aspects of WebGL programming. Unfortunately, covering the entire basics of WebGL is out of the scope of this book. There are great sources on the Internet if additional reference is needed. One of the greatest tutorials out there can be found at http:// webglfundamentals.org/.

When we operate with WebGL, we have to deal with two entirely different concepts. First, we need some OpenGL programs, which are transferred and run by the GPU. If we have our programs up and running, we can parameterize them and communicate with them through JavaScript. In JavaScript, we can set global flags and attributes, and send shapes (primitives), colors, textures, and other things to the GPU for rendering.

Learning WebGL can be difficult if you are used to OOP. If a concept is unclear in the example, research on it before moving on in order to understand it better. Remember: knowing the basics of WebGL can really pay off in the field of frontend development.

Writing programs

There are two kinds of programs we can create with WebGL. The first one, the vertex shader, is a vector program, which is responsible for drawing shapes based on vector coordinates. The second one, called fragment shader, is a raster program. It defines the color of the drawn shapes. In this example, we do not need to color the mask; therefore, our fragment shader is an empty function, although, we can define the precision of our calculations. In OpenLayers 3, the default precision is medium because it is sufficient for texture rendering; however, if we need to create a high-precision WebGL extension, we can define it as precision highp float:

```
var fragmentShaderSource = [
    'precision mediump float;',
    'void main() {',
    '}'
].join('');
```

As you can see, when we provide a program, we have to write it as a single string in the language of OpenGL (GLSL), which is similar to the C language. Unlike JavaScript, this language is strongly typed; therefore, make sure that you always work with the right type when you create or assign variables.

Next, we create the vertex shader program, which is a little more tricky. First, we have two variables: one for the position of the current drawing (cursor) and the other for the resolution of the canvas. The resolution is very important as OpenGL uses a clipping space when it draws on the canvas, which ranges from -1 to 1. It is DPI-independent, and as we would like to define our peeking window in pixels, rather than in percentage values, we have to convert the absolute pixel values that we will provide to the clipping space values:

```
var vertexShaderSource = [
    'attribute vec2 a_position;',
    'uniform vec2 u_resolution;',
    'void main() {',
    '    vec2 pixelPos = a_position / u_resolution * 2.0 - 1.0;',
    '    gl_Position = vec4(pixelPos, 0, 1);',
    '}'
].join('');
```

Variables in GLSL are similar to C declarations. There are, however, qualified variables with special meanings. From the four types (`const`, `attribute`, `uniform`, and `varying`), we've used two. A variable with the `attribute` qualifier can only be used by the vertex shader, and it is read only by the shader. It can be modified between drawing vertices; therefore, it is great for the updating of the position of the cursor. Variables with the `uniform` qualifier can be used by both of the shaders but can only be updated between drawing primitives. This peculiarity makes this type suitable for us to store the resolution of our canvas.

Only qualified GLSL variables can be updated from JavaScript.

This conversion is a three-step task. First, we divide the pixel position by the resolution of our canvas, getting a value between 0 and 1. Then, we stretch the interval to 2 by multiplying the value. Finally, we clamp the stretched interval between -1 and 1 (the clipping space) by subtracting 1 from the result. Next, we update the position of the OpenGL cursor with our calculated clipping space position, and we're finally done.

Note that we have to provide the OpenGL programs in a string format. This can be done by concatenating the lines of the program, but the official OpenLayers 3 WebGL clipping example provided a nice, more readable method for this purpose, which we could adapt. This method uses an array of lines and concatenates them right after the array is filled with content.

Creating a clipping mask

Now that we have some programs for OpenGL, we can proceed and use them to clip our layer. The procedure starts similarly to the previous clipping example. We create a layer and register some events to its rendering hooks. The only significant difference is that we use WebGL methods to clip the layer this time. First, we create the layer:

```
var clippedLayer = new ol.layer.Tile({
    source: new ol.source.MapQuest({
        layer: 'osm'
    }),
    zIndex: 9999
});
```

Next, we attach a `precompose` event to it. Before the layer is drawn on the canvas, we initialize our mask using a WebGL stencil. First things first: we construct some proper shader programs from the program strings, create a WebGL program, and attach the shaders to it. We also link our complete program to the context:

```
clippedLayer.on('precompose', function (evt) {
    var context = evt.glContext;
    var gl = context.getGL();
    var program = gl.createProgram();

    var vertexShader = gl.createShader(gl.VERTEX_SHADER);
    gl.shaderSource(vertexShader, vertexShaderSource);
    gl.compileShader(vertexShader);
    gl.attachShader(program, vertexShader);

    var fragmentShader = gl.createShader(gl.FRAGMENT_SHADER);
    gl.shaderSource(fragmentShader, fragmentShaderSource);
    gl.compileShader(fragmentShader);
    gl.attachShader(program, fragmentShader);

    gl.linkProgram(program);
    context.useProgram(program);
```

Next, we save the qualified variables of our vertex shader to JavaScript variables. This operation asks for the memory space where these variables are stored. After this, those memory spaces are mapped to JavaScript variables from where everything is handled by the browser's JavaScript engine:

```
    var resolutionLocation = gl.getUniformLocation(program,
'u_resolution');
    gl.uniform2f(resolutionLocation, context.A.width,
context.A.height);
    var positionLocation = gl.getAttribLocation(program,
'a_position');
```

In the second line, we provide our canvas's width and height to the OpenGL program as the resolution variable. Note that OpenLayers 3 does not expose the `canvas` element when the WebGL renderer is used; it does this only when the canvas renderer is in action. It is stored, however, and can be accessed from the context object's A property.

 OpenLayers 3 is compiled with the Closure Compiler, part of the Closure Library. Therefore, no one can ensure that the canvas element will be obfuscated to the A property of the context object in future versions.

Let's stop here a little bit and think about the second line. We spoke a little about passing the resolution of the canvas to OpenGL, but we passed our canvas's height and width. That's right; we do not use *resolution* in its cartographic or geoinformatic meaning. We send the dimensions of our canvas to the GPU. Take a look at the vertex shader again. The resolution variable is a `vec2` type, which is a simple numeric array with two members. As the clipping space ranges from -1 to 1 in every dimension, we can only calculate the clipping space coordinates from the pixel coordinates in one command in this way. As the position variable and result variable have matching types, we can execute arithmetic operations on the entire arrays. OpenGL will automatically iterate through them and perform the operations on the corresponding members. In the next step, we initialize our stencil test:

```
gl.enable(gl.STENCIL_TEST);
gl.colorMask(false, false, false, false);
gl.stencilOp(gl.KEEP, gl.KEEP, gl.REPLACE);
gl.stencilFunc(gl.ALWAYS, 1, 255);
```

We enable stencil testing, and set the color mask to `false` in every color band (RGBA). We do this as we do not want to draw anything on the canvas; therefore, we do not need the fragment shader to apply colors to our shapes. We only want to create a square to mask some pixels. The stencil is initialized with a stencil operation and a stencil function. The stencil operation needs to know what should be done in the three different test results. If our stencil test fails, we will keep the original value. If our stencil test passes but the depth test fails (there is a layer above the peeking window), we will also keep the original value. Finally, if both of the tests pass, we will replace the original value.

Now, we need a stencil function that determines the conditions under which the stencil test can pass. In our case, the stencil test should be always passed when a pixel is in the peeking window. The second argument is called the reference value. It contains a value that is compared to every pixel if we use a comparison function in the first argument. It also represents the replace value if we call `gl.REPLACE` in our stencil operation. The third value is the mask. Both the reference and the original values are bitwise AND-ed with it before comparison. As a direct comparison is enough for us, we use a 255 mask value. After these operations, our stencil buffer is initialized with a bunch of 0 values, and every pixel will get a 1 value from the shapes using which we will draw from now on.

 If you bitwise AND an 8-bit value with 255, you will get back the provided 8-bit value.

Next, we draw our rectangle, which will act as a stencil for the peeking window layer:

```
var buffer = gl.createBuffer();
gl.bindBuffer(gl.ARRAY_BUFFER, buffer);
gl.bufferData(gl.ARRAY_BUFFER, new Float32Array([
    20, 20, 120, 20, 20, 120, 120, 120
]), gl.STATIC_DRAW);
```

In OpenGL, when we want to provide an array of vertices or colors, we need to do this with a vertex buffer. This is a simple typed array from the aspect of JavaScript, containing the values of the provided data. First, we create an empty buffer. Then, we link it to our program and fill it with values. This is another tricky part. We have to create a square but as a primitive. However, only points, lines, and triangles can be drawn as primitives in OpenGL. This way, we have to create an array with the vertex coordinates of two triangles building a square.

Now, things get a little interesting. If you look at the array, it does not contain six pairs of coordinates, which would be required for three triangles; it only contains four pairs. OpenGL can draw three kinds of triangles. If we have triangles with shared line segments, we can draw triangle strips. This method allows code not being redundant, and only pass the final point of the second triangle without repeating the shared segment. Now, we draw our triangles:

```
gl.enableVertexAttribArray(positionLocation);
gl.vertexAttribPointer(positionLocation, 2, gl.FLOAT, false,
0, 0);
gl.drawArrays(gl.TRIANGLE_STRIP, 0, 4);
```

First, we turn on our cursor with the position attribute of our vertex shader. Next, we set the metadata of our vertex buffer. The index will be stored in the position attribute. The size of the coordinates is two (two dimensional coordinates); the type of the coordinates is a floating point since they aren't normalized, and finally, their stride and offset are 0. Now that OpenGL knows everything about our triangles, we can instruct it to draw them.

As we have our stencil initialized at this point, the only thing we have to do is prepare it to mask the pending content:

```
gl.bindBuffer(gl.ARRAY_BUFFER, null);
gl.deleteBuffer(buffer);

gl.colorMask(true, true, true, true);
gl.stencilFunc(gl.NOTEQUAL, 0, 255);
});
```

We remove the vertex buffer containing the vertices of our triangles as we do not need it anymore. Next, we override the stencil function. From now on, we only keep values that do not result in a 0 after the stencil test. Remember: in the square, every value is 1; outside of it, every value is 0. Finally, we register an event listener to the layer's postcompose event and add it to the map silently:

```
clippedLayer.on('postcompose', function (evt) {
    var context = evt.glContext;
    var gl = context.getGL();
    gl.disable(gl.STENCIL_TEST);
});
clippedLayer.setMap(map);
```

After the layer has been rendered, we simply disable the stencil testing, allowing the library to properly render any other pending content. If you save the code and look it up in a browser, you will see our peeking window rendered entirely with WebGL:

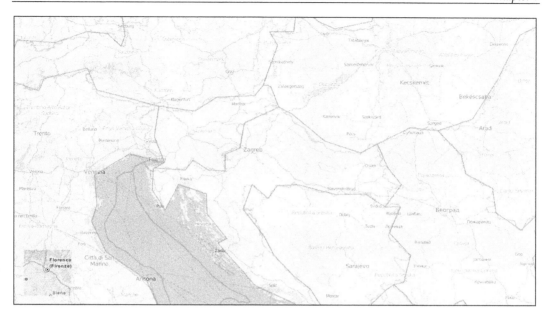

As you can see, the peeking window is in the lower-left corner this time. Unlike the 2D Canvas, OpenGL has a starting point in the lower-left corner. If you need to place it in the upper-left corner, you have to invert the y axis in the vertex shader.

Summary

Congratulations! You not only learned when it's appropriate to use the Canvas or WebGL renderer but also how to create local modifications with the rendering hooks of the library. You learned the basics of the 2D and 3D Canvas and also learned how to use a renderer independent of pixel manipulation methods. We can definitely say that if you can solve the problems lined up in this chapter, you have mastered the renderers of OpenLayers 3.

In the next chapter, we will travel to a completely different part of the library and learn how to create mobile-friendly web mapping applications. We will get the most out of the geolocation capabilities of your smartphone and design a basic geocaching application based on randomly generated data.

8
OpenLayers 3 for Mobile

Now that we are through with the hardest parts of this book, and you have mastered a lot of very important aspects of the library, we will discuss an entirely different concept of OpenLayers 3 in this chapter. We will create a geocaching application that can be used on handheld devices and desktop computers too. We will write this application from scratch and utilize some of the knowledge we just harnessed from the previous chapters.

For those who don't know what exactly geocaching is, let's start with a brief explanation. Geocaching is a great outdoor activity. A player needs two essential things: a device with GPS and a database of geocaches. There are plenty of little boxes hidden in Nature, marked with a point, and uploaded in a geocaching database. The game is usually played as follows: the player picks a cache on the device; if the location is found, the cache still needs to be located as it is usually well-hidden. When the player finds the box, there is usually a notebook in it, along with some trinkets. The player then can read the content of the notebook, write something into it, take some of the items, or put something in the box. Finally, the player puts the cache back to its original place and moves on.

In this chapter, we will discuss the following topics:

- Responsive web design with OpenLayers 3
- Using the HTML5 Geolocation API through the library
- Creating multipurpose web mapping applications

Before getting started

As stated previously, we will write a brand new application in this chapter. However, there are some general considerations we made in an early stage of our learning. We will use these considerations and also the very simple code built with them. In this chapter, we will use the final code, produced in *Chapter 2, Applying Custom Styles*, called `ch02_webgis`, as a basis.

Basic considerations

One of the most challenging problems in responsive web design is detecting the type of the client's device. There are several effective approaches such as adjusting the style of the web page to the screen's dimensions with CSS media queries, or detecting the type of the hardware from the `navigator.userAgent` property in JavaScript (device detection). These methods are quite practical for a blog, news page, or shopping page, but not effective in our case.

The goal of our application is to adapt to the different capabilities of handheld and desktop computers. If we are working on a desktop computer, we will be dispatchers, able to modify the locations and the attributes of the geocaches. However, if we use a handheld device, we are geocachers and would like to have an application that can help us find those caches.

As technology rapidly develops, it is hard to separate desktop devices from handheld devices based on common attributes. For example, the dimensions of a modern handheld device's screen in pixels surpass the dimensions of an old monitor. Scanning for touch and orientation capabilities also yields false results, as nowadays some of the modern laptops also have touch screens and built-in GPS receivers. However, we do have to separate the two roles in a simple manner; thus, we make this false assumption and nominate every touch device as a receiver and every non-touch device as a dispatcher. This way, we can use feature detection to issue roles.

Responsive styling with CSS

In the first example, called `ch08_css`, we will create the layout of our application. We differentiate three styling methods. If the device is a desktop computer, we use regular styling, as in *Chapter 2, Applying Custom Styles*. If we come through a touch screen device, though, we use different rules for controls. Furthermore, we apply a slightly different style to the application in portrait mode than in landscape mode.

Firstly, we create the required elements in the HTML file in our example:

```
<body>
    <div id="map" class="map">
        <div id="toolbar" class="toolbar"></div>
    </div>
</body>
```

This part is more simple than ever before. However, in this case, we create our toolbar inside the map element. We will discuss the importance of this step later in this chapter.

Writing the style sheet

Now that we have our HTML elements in place, let's head to the CSS file in this example. As you can see, we completely removed the map container from our design, putting everything in the map element. This way, we have to size our map element to have a full screen application:

```
.map {
    width: 100%;
    height: 100%; /*Fallback*/
    height: 100vh;
}
```

The rule for our tool bar is almost identical to the one used in *Chapter 2, Applying Custom Styles*. However, as we place it on top of our map, we position it accordingly and use an arbitrary high z-index. This way, our control buttons won't get covered up by the map canvas:

```
.toolbar {
    height: 2em;
    padding: .2em;
    position: absolute;
    z-index: 999;
}
```

For the control buttons, we stop displaying them as table elements as we do not have to align them vertically anymore. Furthermore, we remove the distracting background color from them:

```
.toolbar .ol-control {
    position: static;
    display: inline-block;
    padding: 0;
}
```

```
.toolbar .ol-control {
    background-color: rgba(0,0,0,0);
}
.toolbar .ol-control button {
    border-radius: 2px;
    width: 2em;
    background-color: rgba(219,63,63,.5);
    display: inline-block;
}
```

Next, we define some touch screen-only rules. We handle touch screen devices by adding an ol-touch class to the map element when we encounter one. As hovering does not make sense on touch devices, we disable that feature:

```
.ol-touch .toolbar .ol-control button {
    background-color: rgba(219,63,63,0.5);
}
.ol-touch .toolbar .ol-control button:hover {
    background-color: rgba(219,63,63,0.5);
}
```

 Remember the rule of specificity! As always, the most specific rule applies; we can easily override the styling on touch devices by declaring more specific rules for them.

Finally, we separate portrait styling from landscape styling with some media queries. When we have a portrait orientation, we make the control buttons look similar to the desktop styling, just bigger:

```
@media only screen and (orientation: portrait) {
    .ol-touch .toolbar {
        height: 2rem;
    }
    .ol-touch .toolbar .ol-control {
        height: 2rem;
    }
    .ol-touch .toolbar .ol-control button {
        width: 3rem;
        height: 2rem;
    }
}
```

In OpenLayers 3, the em values change in full screen mode. However, if we adjust the style to the root element by using `rem` values, we get better results.

If we change our device's orientation to landscape, however, we make our controls appear on the left-hand side as we have rotated the tool bar by 90 degrees clockwise. This way, we create a feeling in the users that our controls cover up the least space possible from the application:

```
@media only screen and (orientation: landscape) {
    .ol-touch .toolbar {
        width: 2rem;
    }
    .ol-touch .toolbar .ol-control {
        display: block;
        width: 2rem;
    }
    .ol-touch .toolbar .ol-control button {
        height: 3rem;
        width: 2rem;
    }
}
```

 There are better ways and a lot of optimization methods in responsive web design. Covering this topic is out of the scope of this book, though there are other great and detailed literatures to learn from. Also, optimizing the design for every browser is harder on smartphones than desktop computers. Our code is only optimized for Webkit-based browsers, such as Google Chrome, Opera, or Safari.

Constructing the map

As a final step, we construct our `map` object. It is simple, just like in *Chapter 2, Applying Custom Styles*. The only modification lies in touch detection. OpenLayers 3 grants some convenient browser feature detection methods in the namespace `ol.has`. One of them can easily detect touch screen devices, which we will use in this chapter:

```
var map = new ol.Map({
    target: 'map',
    layers: [
        new ol.layer.Tile({
            source: new ol.source.OSM()
        })
```

```
    ],
    controls: [
        new ol.control.Zoom({
            target: 'toolbar'
        })
    ],
    view: new ol.View({
        center: [0, 0],
        zoom: 2
    })
});
if (ol.has.TOUCH) {
    document.getElementById('map').classList.add('ol-touch');
}
```

If we detect a touch screen, we add the `ol-touch` class to our `map` element, just like we mentioned previously. Now, if you save the code and load it in a browser, you will see our new design in action, as shown in the following screenshot. Don't forget to check it with a smartphone (or a smartphone simulator) and a desktop computer too:

The only requirement for checking the code on your smartphone is connecting to the same network as your server. You can query your computer's IP from the command line of your OS. In Windows, you have to type the ipconfig command on Linux type ip addr show; while on OSX, you have to use the ifconfig command.

Don't worry about the small buttons in portrait mode and the address bar covering up valuable map space in landscape mode. Our application will look great in full screen mode, just after we implement it.

Simulating mobile devices is quite easy, you just need to know your tools. In Google Chrome, you can select a touch device after enabling emulation with the Toggle device mode button (smartphone icon) in the developer tools. In Firefox, you can start emulating by clicking on the Responsive Design Mode button in the dev tools and simulate touch events after that. In Internet Explorer 11 or Microsoft Edge, though, you can only change the user agent string, making those browsers inappropriate to test web pages with feature detection, such as our application.

Generating geocaches

In the next example, called ch08_points, we create some random geocaches based on the user's location. As server-side scripting and client-server connections are also out of the scope of this book, we make our application viable by adding random points within 500 meters of our position. Firstly, we create an empty layer for the points and initialize Geolocation:

```
var geoloc = new ol.Geolocation({
    projection: map.getView().getProjection(),
    tracking: true
});
var geoCaching = new ol.layer.Vector({
    source: new ol.source.Vector()
});
map.addLayer(geoCaching);
```

The `ol.Geolocation` constructor creates a simple wrapper object around the HTML5 Geolocation API. It is capable of everything the Geolocation API can do, and provides convenience methods to register listeners on changes and access Geolocation-related information. As we need our position to generate local points, we must register a listener to the `Geolocation` object's `change:position` event. As we do not want our application to generate new points on every change, we do this only once:

```
geoloc.once('change:position', function (evt) {
    var altitude = this.getAltitude() || 100;
    var myPos = this.getPosition();
    map.getView().setCenter(myPos);
    map.getView().setZoom(17);
    for (var i = 0; i < 50; i += 1) {
        geoCaching.getSource().addFeature(new ol.Feature({
            geometry: new ol.geom.Point([myPos[0] - 500 + Math.
random() * 1000, myPos[1] - 500 + Math.random() * 1000, altitude - 150
+ Math.random() * 300]),
            loot: 'Treasures of the Seven Seas'
        }));
    }
});
```

Firstly, we read out all useful information from the `Geolocation` object. Altitude information will only be present if we have a GPS in our device and proper satellite coverage. Therefore, we default our altitude to a predefined value if we cannot extract it from the object.

Next, we center the map to the measured position, zoom in, and generate 50 random points. As we want to generate points within a 500 meter radius of our location, we calculate a position from a 1000 meter range with a random number. We also calculate a random altitude for every point within the 150 meters from the measured or the predefined altitude value. Finally, we provide a loot attribute just for fun.

 You can provide two, three, or four values with every coordinate. Just remember: you must be consistent in a single geometry object and in the entire layer.

If you save and load the example, you will see a map to the one in the following screenshot. You will get the generated geocaches in your area. Just make sure that the application can access your location:

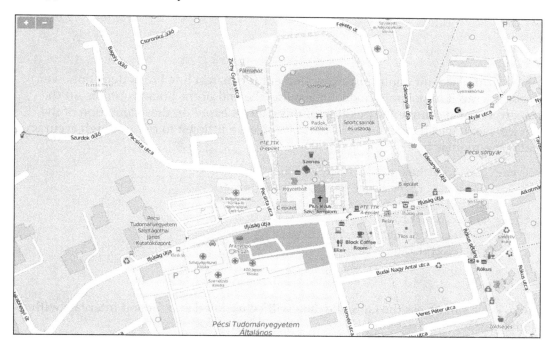

Adding device-dependent controls

In the next example, called `ch08_controls`, we create some roles for the different devices identified by OpenLayers 3. Firstly, we add some CSS rules for our new text-based control:

```
@media only screen and (orientation: portrait) {
    […]
    .ol-geoloc {
        bottom: 0;
        right: .5em;
        white-space: pre-wrap;
    }
}
```

```css
@media only screen and (orientation: landscape) {
    [...]
    .ol-geoloc {
        top: 0;
        right: .5em;
    }
}
```

As we will place our control in a `pre` element for correct line break detection, we need to wrap it in portrait mode. Otherwise, the end of the lines would be off the screen. We also change the position of this control based on the orientation of the device. Next, we change our `Geolocation` object a little bit to request high accuracy data on a regular basis:

```javascript
var geoloc = new ol.Geolocation({
    projection: map.getView().getProjection(),
    tracking: true,
    trackingOptions: {
        enableHighAccuracy: true,
        maximumAge: 2000
    }
});
```

Now, if we can access the GPS, the data will be updated at 2-second intervals with high accuracy.

There are three tracking options in OpenLayers 3's `Geolocation` object, just like in the HTML5 Geolocation API. The `enableHighAccuracy` parameter requests data from GPS results in higher-precision and higher-power consumption. The `timeout` parameter defines how old the received data can be before it is considered outdated. The `maximumAge` parameter denotes how old a cached position can be before it is considered outdated. The last two parameters are accepted in milliseconds.

Adding controls for touch devices

As a next step, we define some controls that will only be added when we open our application from a touch device. We add a full screen control for maximum usability and a custom control to display Geolocation-related data:

 The full screen control of OpenLayers 3 uses the HTML5 full screen API. This API can request full screen mode for an element in a web page, displaying its content in full screen. As OpenLayers 3 requests full screen for the map element, we must put our tool bar in it for a proper display.

```
if (ol.has.TOUCH) {
    document.getElementById('map').classList.add('ol-touch');
    map.addControl(new ol.control.FullScreen({
        target: 'toolbar'
    }));
    var geolocData = document.createElement('pre');
    geolocData.className = 'ol-geoloc ol-unselectabble ol-control';
    geoloc.on('change', function (evt) {
        var dataString = 'Position: ' + this.getPosition() +
'\nError: ' + this.getAccuracy() + 'm\nAltitude: ' + this.
getAltitude() + 'm\nAltitude error: ' + this.getAltitudeAccuracy() +
'm';
        geolocData.textContent = dataString.replace
(/undefined/g, 'N/A');
    });
    map.addControl(new ol.control.Control({
        element: geolocData
    }));
}
```

As we concatenate Geolocation-related data to a single string with line breaks, we provide them in a `pre` element; thus, the browsers will follow those breaks. If we cannot access a value and the library returns `undefined`, we simply replace that value to N/A with a regular expression. If you save the code in this state and load it up from your smartphone, you will see uniform control buttons and a nice text output in full screen. This is the way our application should be used on touch devices:

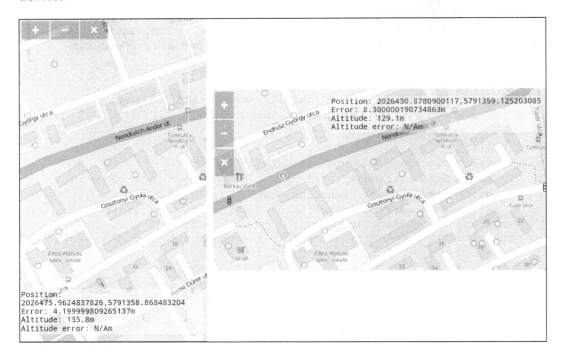

Adding controls for desktop computers

If the library detects a regular device, it gives that a dispatcher role. A dispatcher should be able to move points and edit the loot of the geocaches in our scenario. Therefore, we add two such interactions to our map. We also disable Geolocation as we do not need it from a desktop computer:

```
} else {
    geoloc.once('change', function (evt) {
        this.setTracking(false);
        map.addInteraction(new ol.interaction.Modify({
            features: new ol.Collection(geoCaching.getSource().
getFeatures())
        }));
    });
```

Finally, we create our next interaction by registering a listener to the map's
`click` event. We query every feature under the click location, which has a `loot`
attribute, and create an output with its value. We wrap this output in an overlay
and display it on the map anchored on the clicked feature. We use the usual
`forEachFeatureAtPixel` method that accepts a layer filter function and, thus, only
queries our geocaches:

 The `ol.Overlay` constructor has quite a lot of customizing possibilities.
Make sure that you check it out in the API documentation.

```
map.on('click', function (evt) {
    map.getOverlays().clear();
    this.forEachFeatureAtPixel(evt.pixel, function (feature) {
        if (feature && feature.get('loot')) {
            var overlayElem = document.createElement('div');
            var lootElem = document.createElement('textarea');
            lootElem.textContent = feature.get('loot');
            overlayElem.appendChild(lootElem);
            overlayElem.appendChild(document.createElement('br'));
            var saveButton = document.createElement('button');
            saveButton.textContent = 'Save';
            overlayElem.appendChild(saveButton);
            var overlay = new ol.Overlay({
                position: feature.getGeometry().getCoordinates(),
                element: overlayElem
            });
            saveButton.addEventListener('click', function (evt) {
                feature.set('loot', lootElem.value);
                map.removeOverlay(overlay);
            });
            map.addOverlay(overlay);
        }
    }, this, function (layer) {
        if (layer === geoCaching) {
            return true;
        }
        return false;
    });
});
}
```

As we added an interaction that creates an overlay with an alternative styling, every click returns two almost identical features. However, as in `overlay` object, only the selected feature's geometry is added, we can discard the dummy feature by querying its `loot` attribute.

If you save the code and load it up on your desktop computer, you can move the geocaches and edit their `loot` attribute:

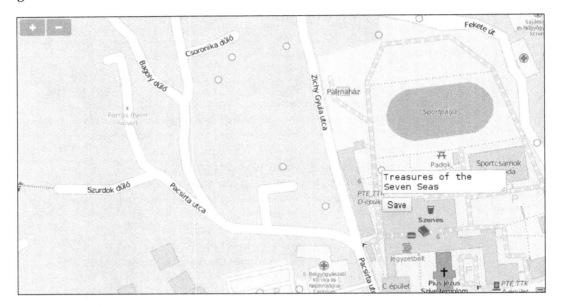

 Note that, without a server-side component, the points won't be updated in the mobile appliation when we update them in the desktop version. Writing a server-side component is, however, beyond the scope of this book.

Vectorizing the mobile version

In the next example, called `ch08_styling`, we improve our touch device version with another vector layer and some styling. We display the current position of the user and the accuracy of the position in meters, and style the geocaches based on the height difference of our position and the caches. Firstly, we create a layer containing our position and give it a static style:

```
if (ol.has.TOUCH) {
    [...]
    var positionLyr = new ol.layer.Vector({
        source: new ol.source.Vector(),
        style: new ol.style.Style({
            image: new ol.style.Circle({
                fill: new ol.style.Fill({
                    color: [255, 255, 255, 1]
                }),
                stroke: new ol.style.Stroke({
                    color: [0, 0, 0, 1],
                    width: 2
                }),
                radius: 6
            }),
            stroke: new ol.style.Stroke({
                color: [255, 0, 0, 1],
                width: 2
            })
        })
    });
    map.addLayer(positionLyr);
```

We will have two kinds of features in this layer. If we have to deal with a point feature, it will be our position that we style with the image property. Every other layer, regardless of its type, will be displayed with a red line or an outline. Next, we update our layer every time we receive a new position:

```
geoloc.on('change', function (evt) {
    [...]
    var positionSrc = positionLyr.getSource();
    positionSrc.clear(true);
    positionSrc.addFeatures([
        new ol.Feature({
            geometry: new ol.geom.Point(evt.target.getPosition())
        }),
        new ol.Feature({
            geometry: new ol.geom.Circle(evt.target.getPosition(),
evt.target.getAccuracy())
        })
    ]);
    geoCaching.setStyle(geoCaching.getStyleFunction());
});
```

The first part is simple: we fast-clear our new layer's source by providing a `true` value to its `clear` method. This way, no `removefeature` events get dispatched, increasing the performance of our application. After this, we add two new features, one for our position and one to display the accuracy of it. Next, we update the style of our geocaches, as styles returned by style functions become static after evaluation.

> Try to replace the accuracy feature's geometry with the geometry returned by the `Geolocation` object's `getAccuracyGeometry` method and observe the difference.

Finally, we provide the style function that will be updated regularly. In this function, we evaluate some common values based on the feature's and the position's altitude. If a cache is almost on the same elevation as us, we symbolize it as a yellow square. If it lies higher, it will be a red triangle pointing upwards. If it is lower than us, it's shape will be a green triangle pointing downwards:

```
geoCaching.setStyle(function (feature, res) {
    if (geoloc.getAltitude()) {
        var altitude = geoloc.getAltitude();
        var zCoord = feature.getGeometry().getCoordinates()[2];
        var shapePts, shapeColor, shapeAngle;
        if (Math.abs(altitude - zCoord) < 1) {
            shapePts = 4;
            shapeColor = [255, 255, 0, 1];
            shapeAngle = Math.PI / 4;
        } else if (zCoord < altitude) {
            shapePts = 3;
            shapeColor = [0, 255, 0, 1];
            shapeAngle = Math.PI;
        } else {
            shapePts = 3;
            shapeColor = [255, 0, 0, 1];
            shapeAngle = 0;
        }
```

Now we can return the appropriate style object for our cache. If we can get an altitude from our `Geolocation` object, we return a style evaluated previously; otherwise, if the GPS signal is not adequate to give an altitude value, we display our caches with red X symbols. We can create such a shape by creating a star with four tips and a great difference between its inner and outer radii:

```
        return [new ol.style.Style({
            image: new ol.style.RegularShape({
                fill: new ol.style.Fill({
                    color: shapeColor
                }),
                stroke: new ol.style.Stroke({
                    color: [0, 0, 0, 1],
                    width: 1
                }),

                points: shapePts,
                radius: 10,
                angle: shapeAngle
            })
        })];
    } else {
        return [new ol.style.Style({
            image: new ol.style.RegularShape({
                fill: new ol.style.Fill({
                    color: [255, 0, 0, 1]
                }),
                stroke: new ol.style.Stroke({
                    color: [0, 0, 0, 1],
                    width: 1
                }),
                points: 4,
                radius1: 5,
                radius2: 10,
                angle: Math.PI / 2
            })
        })];
    }
});
}
```

If you save the code and look it up from your smartphone, you will see the dynamic rendering of our position and symbols:

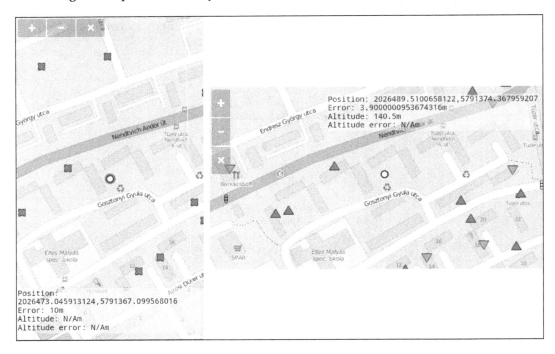

Making the mobile application interactive

In the final example, called ch08_interact, we extend the touch device part of our application and make it more interactive. We want to know our heading when we search for geocaches. Furthermore, it would be a nice feature if our application could give some extra information about a given cache that we could select manually.

Firstly, we extend our listener on the Geolocation object's change event with some necessary modifications. As we would like to track our position and heading, we modify our map's view on every change:

```
geoloc.on('change', function (evt) {
    [...]
    map.getView().setCenter(this.getPosition());
    if (this.getHeading()) {
        map.getView().setRotation(this.getHeading());
    }
```

Just like an altitude value, heading is also a GPS-only feature. As receiving a heading is not guaranteed, you should always put the code responsible for rotating the map in an `if` clause. You can provide the heading to the map's view directly, as it is already in radians that are measured clockwise from north.

Next, we check whether we have a selected feature. Don't worry about the `selectInteraction` object; we will add it to the map just after this part. If we have a selected cache, we grab its coordinates. As our caches have a z coordinate, we can calculate an elevation delta from it and also our position's altitude data. However, we cannot create a geometry with coordinates having different strides. To solve this problem, we simply remove the z coordinate from our cache's position after we calculate the height difference:

```
if (selectInteraction.getFeatures().getLength() === 1) {
    var selectedFeat =
selectInteraction.getFeatures().item(0);
    var selectedCoords =
selectedFeat.getGeometry().getCoordinates();
    var height = selectedCoords[2] - this.getAltitude();
    selectedCoords.pop();
```

Now, we are ready to create a new line between our position and the selected cache, representing the as-the-crow-flies distance between the two locations. We don't have to worry about the styling of our new feature, as we symbolize everything other than a point with a red line:

```
positionSrc.addFeature(new ol.Feature({
        geometry: new ol.geom.LineString([evt.target.
getPosition(), selectedCoords])
        }));
```

Next, we give some more feedback about the cache by extending our output with some new lines. We display the distance between the two locations, the height difference, and the possible loot of the given cache. If we can't get an altitude value, we change the resulting NaN to N/A for added consistency:

```
    var extDataString = '\nDistance: ' +
positionSrc.getFeatures()[2].getGeometry().getLength() +
'm\nHeight: ' + height + 'm\nPossible loot: ' +
selectedFeat.get('loot');
    geolocData.textContent +=
extDataString.replace(/NaN/g, 'N/A');
    }
});
```

Finally, we add a select interaction to our map, so we can select arbitrary caches from the cache layer:

```
var selectInteraction = new ol.interaction.Select({
    layers: [geoCaching]
});
map.addInteraction(selectInteraction);
```

If you save and load up the code, you will be able to select caches and get some information about them:

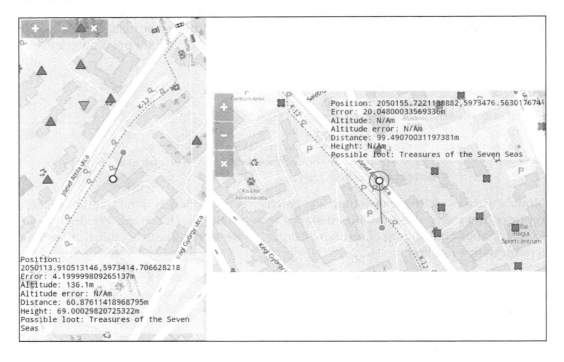

Summary

In this chapter, we learned some architectural patterns to create mobile web mapping applications with OpenLayers 3. We created a simple geocaching application that can adapt to the type of our device. If you want to create an adaptive web mapping application, be creative. Use these examples as a starting point and extend them with animations and a working backend, and you have a great application on your hands. If you think about this concept further and switch the roles of handheld and desktop devices, you can create a field survey application. The data collected by touch devices can be analyzed instantly from a desktop computer, if you have a working server behind your application.

In the next chapter, we will discuss the various third-party applications and libraries that can make your life easier. We will learn to export projects from QGIS to the web using OpenLayers 3, and use some libraries to create richer applications with extended capabilities.

9
Tools of the Trade – Integrating Third-Party Applications

With the knowledge that you've gained from the previous chapters, you can create various rich, web mapping applications for multiple devices. Now that you are aware of the most important aspects of OpenLayers 3, we will dig into some irregular topics that are not strongly related to the library. We will take a look at how we can implement QGIS and some third-party libraries in our workflow in order to make our lives easier or just extend the capabilities of our application.

In this chapter, we will cover the following topics:

- Exporting layers from QGIS as a web map using OpenLayers 3
- Importing shapefile layers on the client side
- Extending topological functionality with Turf and JSTS
- Creating 3D visualizations with Cesium

Before getting started

As we are going to use QGIS in this chapter, you will need to have a working copy installed on your computer. Installing QGIS is straightforward; therefore, we will not discuss the process. For the best possible experience, update the software to its latest version before proceeding further. The example was created with QGIS 2.10 Pisa.

 If you are using Windows or you need the source code, you can download both at http://qgis.org/en/site/forusers/download.html.

We will also use some third-party libraries, which are provided with the examples. You can find them in the `js` folder under the appropriate subdirectory. We will need Shapefile JS, Turf, JSTS, Cesium, and OL3-Cesium. The Cesium library is handled as part of the OL3-Cesium integration library; therefore, it is located in the latter's folder. For this chapter, we will use `ch03_layerorder` for the base of our code, just like we did in the previous one.

Exporting a QGIS project

When we create custom web maps, we cannot always rely on already developed OWS services. Sometimes, we need to publish our own data regardless of whether it is plotted directly from some measurements or processed from existent data. If we have to process our data before publishing it, we usually do it in a desktop GIS environment. However, one of these environments, called QGIS, is not only capable of advanced geoprocessing, but with a little help, we can export our results directly in the form of a web map using OpenLayers 3.

If you are a GIS person, you might be familiar with QGIS. If this is the case, just install the `qgis2web` plugin, load the project provided with the code (`ch09_qgis.qgs`), and skip to the part where we use the plugin to export the layers. If you are not familiar with QGIS, don't worry. Keep reading, and you will be up and running in no time.

Quantum GIS is an open source desktop GIS application. It started slowly, but with enough time and effort from its community, it became the most competent open source GIS application of its time. From version 2.0, it gained very powerful geoprocessing capabilities as developers integrated some other open source GIS applications with it. Now, it harnesses the power of the most capable open source applications and libraries such as GDAL, GRASS, or SAGA, and offers a user-friendly GUI and Python API for enhanced user experience. With these considerations in mind, QGIS is now accepted as valid competition even for the best commercial desktop GIS, ArcGIS.

QGIS's success story is a good example of the importance of integrating other powerful applications instead of trying to reinvent the wheel.

Installing the qgis2web plugin

QGIS is a modular software. It is written in C++ but also has a Python API; thus, people can extend it and write modules in it in any of these languages. Using the Python API, people can create dynamic modules, called plugins, which can be used by anyone via an inner plugin management system. These specialized Python modules, which are created by company employees and enthusiastic individuals, make QGIS an even richer GIS environment.

First, start QGIS. You will see the layer tree on the left-hand side, the map canvas on the right-hand side, and some control buttons at the top and far-left. There is also a notification bar at the bottom with some extra controls. Does this resemble something similar to what you've seen before? We designed our WebGIS application in the last few chapters based on the layout of QGIS, which basically matches the layout of the most popular desktop GIS applications. At the top of the window, you can see a menu bar. From there, access the plugin manager. It's in the **Plugins** menu, called **Manage and Install Plugins...**. After opening the manager, wait for QGIS to fetch the available plugins from the default repository.

Next, scroll down to the plugin named **qgis2web**. This plugin wraps itself around other plugins that are capable of exporting QGIS projects to web maps using OpenLayers 3 (**qgis-ol3**) and Leaflet (**qgis2leaf**). However, the OpenLayers 3 exporter is not available in its original form, and nevertheless, this plugin ships with a great preview window to check the results before exporting the map. Click on **Install plugin** to download it, and you will see a new button in your toolbar as a result:

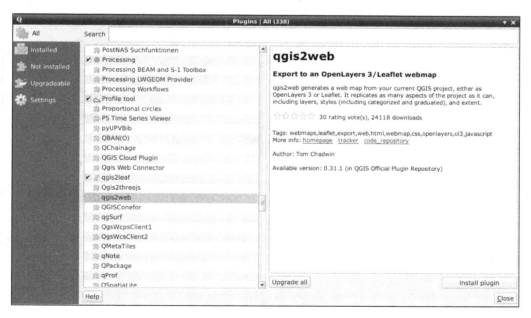

Inspecting the project

Now that you have the plugin installed, open the QGIS project provided with the code, called ch09_qgis.qgs, and inspect its contents. You can open a project by clicking on the yellow folder icon in the toolbar, the **Open...** button in the **Project** menu, or just by pressing *Ctrl + O*. You can also drag and drop the project file into the application window. As you can see, there are two vector layers and one raster layer included in various projections. With an elevation map, a choropleth country map, graduated capitals map, and some labels from the countries map, we can test the plugin against the most basic display types.

 Cannot see the elevation map? Right-click on it in the layer tree and select the **Zoom to Layer** option.

With the toolbar on the left-hand side of the window, you can add additional layers, while in the layers' **Properties** window, you can adjust the styling. You can access this window by right-clicking on a layer element in the layer tree and selecting the corresponding menu entry:

 QGIS projects store the reference of the resources with relative paths. As long as you do not modify the structure of the directory, you don't have to worry about inaccessible resources in other systems.

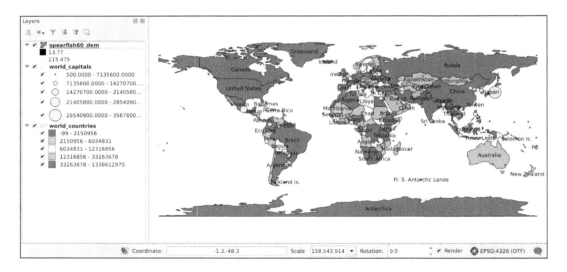

Exporting a map

Next, we open the `qgis2web` plugin to customize our map before exporting it. You can access the plugin from the toolbar or the `Web` menu's `qgis2web` entry. In the plugin's main window, you will see our layers nicely aligned in the preview window. However, there is something weird about them. The plugin can export maps in Web Mercator or the project's projection. When it exports the project, it transforms and warps every layer to the chosen projection before showing them.

> Did you notice that Antarctica in the countries' layer only extends to 85 degrees south instead of 90 degrees? Web Mercator's validity extent only extends to 85.06 degrees north and south. Beyond these limits, transformations produce great errors, ending in 90 degrees, which is equal to infinity in Web Mercator. This phenomenon also has an effect on the plugin. If we provide a layer with an extent outside Web Mercator's validity extent, we won't see anything in the preview window.

Let's make a thorough test and check checkboxes everything aside from the **Show popups on hover** and **Match project CRS** options. This way, we have to click on the map to identify its features. However, to have popups, we need some attributes to expose. In the top window, we add some attributes to the popups (**Info popup content**). Finally, we define a base layer in the bottom window, and then we export the composition:

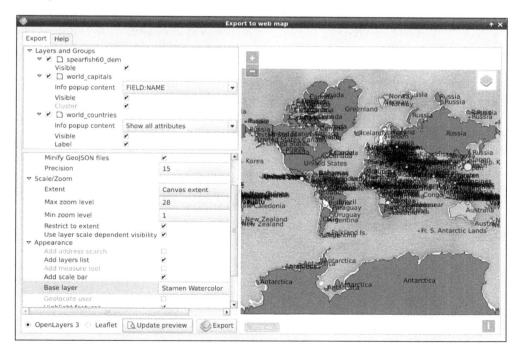

In the latest version of qgis2web (0.39.0), the plugin lacks the capability of exporting or displaying raster layers in the preview window. If you see an error message in the preview window, simply disable the raster layer in the top window, and click on **Update preview**. Naturally, by doing this, the raster layer won't be exported.

Salvaging the results

Once you click on **Export**, the plugin will open the exported map in your default browser. The first thing we can see in the preview already is that this composition is ugly and cannot be used as a map. Nevertheless, the plugin works great and can render every display type we provided in our project. The result is good as a quick preview but nothing more. However, there is valuable information coded in the created files. Let's navigate to the export folder and examine those files.

First, there is the index.html file, which contains two libraries, some styling, and the JavaScript part of the aggregated map. One of the libraries is OpenLayers 3. As we requested a layer switcher in the plugin, it also linked an extension to the library called OpenLayers 3 LayerSwitcher. This is a lightweight layer switcher, capable of handling base layers and overlays. It allows us to select from multiple base layers and toggle the visibility of overlays.

 You can download OpenLayers 3 LayerSwitcher from the GitHub repository at https://github.com/walkermatt/ol3-layerswitcher/releases.

If we further examine the index file, we can see that there are other local JavaScript files included from the layers and styles folder. Let's check these scripts for additional valuable information. In the layers folder, we can see that our elevation map is in a JPEG format, our vector layers in GeoJSON (saved to variables), and there is a layers.js file. Let's open the third file in a text editor:

 If you do not see the raster layer, ensure that you have zoomed to the full extent in QGIS.

As we can see, the layer objects are created in this script. The most valuable information, which can be salvaged from this script, is our exported elevation layer's extent. It is in Web Mercator; however, we can transform it to any projection with OpenLayers 3:

```
var lyr_spearfish6dem = new ol.layer.Image({
                        opacity: 1,
                        title: "spearfish60_dem",
                        source: new ol.source.ImageStatic({
                           url: "./layers/spearfish6dem.jpg",
                           projection: 'EPSG:3857',
                           alwaysInRange: true,
                           imageSize: [634, 477],
                           imageExtent: [-11562879.041972,
    5523336.351119, -11535975.014406, 5543008.947284]
                        })
                      });
```

As we now have the extent of the layer, we can export it in any browser-capable format from QGIS and have a better, but already georeferenced, image. For example, we could export it in PNG for a lossless result.

If you are familiar with our elevation map from the Spearfish60 example of GRASS, you must be wondering why it has floating point values and why those values range from 13.77 to 215.475. Well, QGIS, and, therefore, qgis2web, use GDAL to export images. The GDAL JPEG exporter only accepts rasters with values between 0 and 255. If you try to export an image with a wider value range, lower and higher values are set to 0 and 255, respectively.

Finally, let's navigate to the `styles` folder. In this folder, we can see a separate script for every vector layer that we have. If we open one of the scripts, we can also see the symbology for the graduated layers that are stored in these files. They are quite verbose and complicated; however, everything is in one place. We can get the intervals but also the associated colors or circle radii:

```
var ranges_worldcountries = [[-99.000000, 2150955.800000, [ new
ol.style.Style({
                                stroke: new ol.style.Stroke({color:
"rgba(0,0,0,1.0)", lineDash: null, width: 0}),
                        fill: new ol.style.Fill({color:
"rgba(5,113,176,1.0)"})
                        })
                        ]],
[...]
```

Importing shapefiles

In the next example, called `ch09_shp`, we implement a method to import binary layers to our maps. Shapefile is an old specification to store vector data; however, it is still a very common and popular exchange format. It stores the geometry in a binary file, which has an `shp` MIME type. There are usually at least three more files along with the geometry. The `shx` file stores the shape indexes of the geometries in a binary format, providing an internal spatial indexing for faster lookups. The `prj` file is an ASCII file containing the projection string of the layer, while the `dbf` file is a dBASE database file containing attribute data. For this example to work, we will need at least the `shp` and `dbf` files of a shapefile.

Editing the HTML file

First, let's edit the HTML file of the example. In this example, we will implement an easy way and replace the function associated with the **Add Vector Layer** button in our layer tree. This way, we don't have to touch the GUI elements, just modify the form and the function. As we will use the Shapefile JS library to load our shapefiles, we have to link it in our HTML file's `head` section:

```
<head>
    [...]
    <script type="text/javascript" src="../../js/shp-3.3.1/shp.min.
js"></script>
</head>
```

You can grab the latest version of the Shapefile JS from the GitHub repository at `https://github.com/calvinmetcalf/shapefile-js/releases`.

The next consideration we have to make before we continue with reshaping the form is how we would like to handle the user-provided files. Shapefile JS offers three mechanisms for inputs. It can handle a path with the name of the shapefile, individual shp, dbf, and optional prj files, or a zip file, which contains one or more shapefiles. Providing a path is the most convenient; however, it is only possible if the shapefile is located in our server. As requiring the three files individually is quite annoying, we will require a simple zip file from our users:

```html
<div id="addvector" class="toggleable" style="display: none;">
    <form id="addvector_form" class="addlayer">
        <p>Add Shapefile</p>
        <table>
            <tr>
                <td>Vector file:</td>
                <td><input name="file" type="file"
required="required" accept=".zip"></td>
            </tr>
            <tr>
                <td>Display name:</td>
                <td><input name="displayname" type="text"></td>
            </tr>
            <tr>
                <td>Projection:</td>
                <td><input name="projection" type="text"></td>
            </tr>
            <tr>
                <td><input type="submit" value="Add layer"></td>
                <td><input type="button" value="Cancel" onclick="this.
form.parentNode.style.display = 'none'"></td>
            </tr>
        </table>
    </form>
</div>
```

 With the `accept` parameter of the file `input` element, you can restrict the accepted file types in various ways. Note that users can easily override this filter, thus using it for extra convenience and not replacing further checks.

Replacing a function

Now that our form is in its place, the only thing left to do is replace the old `addVectorLayer` method with a new one. Let's open the JavaScript file of the example and navigate to line 305. The structure of the function remains the same. We read the form, create a file reader and, once it has finished reading the file, we parse its content and display it as a layer in our map. However, in this case, we only read shapefiles; therefore, we do not need to switch between multiple formats. As Shapefile JS returns the parsed binary data in GeoJSON, we only need this particular format:

```
layerTree.prototype.addVectorLayer = function (form) {
    var file = form.file.files[0];
    var currentProj = this.map.getView().getProjection();
    var fr = new FileReader();
    var sourceFormat = new ol.format.GeoJSON();
    var source = new ol.source.Vector();
```

Once we have the right variables and constructors, we can create the file reader's `onload` listener and read the file right away:

```
    fr.onload = function (evt) {
        var vectorData = evt.target.result;
        var dataProjection = form.projection.value ||
sourceFormat.readProjection(vectorData) || currentProj;
        shp(vectorData).then(function (geojson) {
            source.addFeatures(sourceFormat.readFeatures(geojson,
{
                dataProjection: dataProjection,
                featureProjection: currentProj
            }));
        });
    };
    fr.readAsArrayBuffer(file);
    [...]
};
```

Now, there are two things we should discuss from the listener in more detail. First, we've called the Shapefile JS's `shp` method with the input file and placed the loading mechanism inside its `then` method. If you know some of the perks and new features of ES6 (EcmaScript, which is the official name of JavaScript), you may have identified the returned object of the `shp` method as a promise. Promises, in a nutshell, are the new way to handle asynchronous functions. They offer a simple and clean interface to make nestable asynchronous calls and handle occasional errors. To learn more about promises, you can consult the MDN page at `http://developer.mozilla.org/en-US/docs/Web/JavaScript/Reference/Global_Objects/Promise`.

Don't worry about using Shapefile JS in browsers that do not have the ES6 features implemented yet. The library uses another library, called `lie`, to create and handle promises. However, it does not use the polyfill version of `lie`; therefore, Shapefile JS cannot use the ES6 `Promise` constructor even if a browser has one.

The second thing is that we read our data using the file reader's `readAsArrayBuffer` method. As we have to deal with a set of binary files packed into a single binary file, we need a binary representation of our content. This way, the library can read our shapefiles correctly. Shapefile JS uses another third-party JavaScript library, JSZip, to read `zip` files from the client side. With the file reader's `readAsArrayBuffer` method, we simply request a read-only buffer object with the binary content of the opened `zip` file.

Now that we have our replaced method in place, we can test our new capability. Open up the result in a browser, and try to load a zipped shapefile in our application. You can find one in the `res` folder, called `glaciated.zip`.

Don't worry about the layer's projection if your shapefile has a `prj` file included. Shapefile JS is capable of automatic coordinate transformations with PROJ4JS, and if it can recognize the layer's projection, it will always return the GeoJSON object in EPSG:4326 (WGS84).

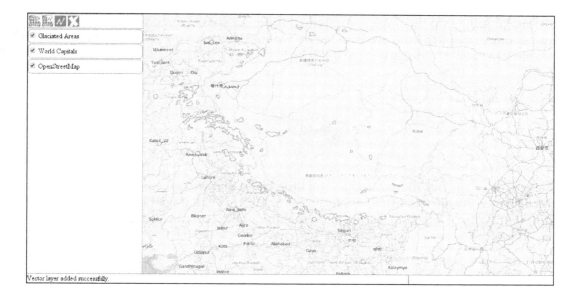

Spatial analysis with Turf

In the next example, called `ch09_turf`, we will extend our application's topological capabilities with Turf. Turf is a well-documented, simple, but capable, library for geospatial analysis. All the basic topological functions are in the library along with some more advanced and scarce functions. Turf uses GeoJSON not only as its exchange format but also as its internal format. This enables it to skip the overhead caused by data conversion.

 You can grab the most recent version of Turf from the GitHub repository at `https://github.com/Turfjs/turf/releases`.

First, we open the HTML file and resolve the dependencies. We have an easy job with Turf as we only have to provide one extra JavaScript file:

```
<head>
    [...]
    <script type="text/javascript" src="../../js/turf-
2.0.0/turf.min.js"></script>
</head>
```

Preparing an example

Before jumping into the implementation of different spatial operations, we need to tweak our example a little bit. First, as we wouldn't want to involve our layer tree, we simply hack it in order to save the selected layer in the map object:

```
layerTree.prototype.addSelectEvent = function (node, isChild) {
    [...]
        _this.map.set('selectedLayer',
_this.getLayerById(targetNode.id));
        [...]
};
```

Next, we rewrite our map constructor a little bit so that we can add one additional vector layer. As we will implement different kinds of spatial operations, we will need different types of layers to test them on. Additionally, you can add a further line layer, too:

```
var map = new ol.Map({
    [...]
```

```
        new ol.layer.Vector({
            source: new ol.source.Vector({
                format: new ol.format.GeoJSON({
                    defaultDataProjection: 'EPSG:4326'
                }),
                url: '../../res/world_capitals.geojson'
            }),
            name: 'World Capitals'
        }),
        new ol.layer.Vector({
            source: new ol.source.Vector({
                format: new ol.format.GeoJSON({
                    defaultDataProjection: 'EPSG:4326'
                }),
                url: '../../res/world_countries.geojson'
            }),
            name: 'World Countries'
        })
    ],
    [...]
});
```

We also add every layer created in this way to the layer tree manually, and then register an interaction with the countries' layer as we would like to be able to modify it:

```
var tree = new layerTree({map: map, target: 'layertree', messages:
'messageBar'})
    .createRegistry(map.getLayers().item(0))
    .createRegistry(map.getLayers().item(1))
    .createRegistry(map.getLayers().item(2));

map.getLayers().item(2).getSource().once('change', function (evt)
{
    if (this.getState() === 'ready') {
        map.addInteraction(new ol.interaction.Modify({
            features: new ol.Collection(evt.target.getFeatures())
        }));
    }
});
```

Implementing a buffer operation

In this example, we will create a single control for three spatial operations. The first one creates a buffer around the input elements, the second one merges an entire layer, while the third one checks for self-intersections in the input polygons.

 The operations presented in this example are just a little subset of the true capabilities of Turf. If you want to get introduced to the library, you can browse its API page at http://turfjs.org/static/docs/.

First, we only create a control for buffering, then we proceed and extend this control. This way, you can check every functionality before we go on to the next. First, we create the required DOM elements for our control:

```
ol.control.Turf = function (opt_options) {
    var options = opt_options || {};
    var _this = this;
    var controlDiv = document.createElement('div');
    controlDiv.className = options.class || 'ol-turf ol-
unselectable ol-control';
    var bufferButton = document.createElement('button');
    bufferButton.textContent = 'B';
    bufferButton.title = 'Buffer selected layer';
```

Next, we define what will happen if we click on the buffer button. As we can access the selected layer without getting the layer tree object, this makes our job easier. The Turf API documentation says that we can provide a feature or feature collection to the `buffer` method; thus, we won't make any checks, just pass the content of an entire layer to the method in GeoJSON. As we need a GeoJSON object, rather than the string representation of the GeoJSON, we can use the format object's `writeFeaturesObject` method instead of the more commonly used `writeFeatures` method:

```
bufferButton.addEventListener('click', function (evt) {
    var layer = _this.getMap().get('selectedLayer');
    var units =
_this.getMap().getView().getProjection().getUnits();
    if (layer instanceof ol.layer.Vector) {
        var parser = new ol.format.GeoJSON();
        var geojson =
parser.writeFeaturesObject(layer.getSource().getFeatures());
```

```
var buffered = turf.buffer(geojson, 10000, units);
var bufferedLayer = new ol.layer.Vector({
    source: new ol.source.Vector({
        features: parser.readFeatures(buffered)
    }),
    name: 'Buffer result'
});
_this.getMap().addLayer(bufferedLayer);
}
});
controlDiv.appendChild(bufferButton);
```

After the buffering is done, we load the result in a new layer. In this example, we will work with a fixed radius of 10,000 meters.

 The `buffer` method requires three parameters: the feature(s) in GeoJSON, a buffer radius, and the units that the radius is in. We can easily get the current map units from the map's projection object.

Finally, we close our control with the ordinary method, and add it to our map:

```
controlDiv.appendChild(selfIntersectButton);
ol.control.Control.call(this, {
    element: controlDiv,
    target: options.target
});
};
ol.inherits(ol.control.Turf, ol.control.Control);
[…]
    var map = new ol.Map({
        […]
        controls: [
            […]
            new ol.control.Turf({
                target: 'toolbar'
            })
        ],
        […]
```

If you test our example in this state (in the **World Capitals** layer first), you can try out our new buffering capability. Note that this is an expensive operation; therefore, if you provide a big dataset as input, you have to wait for it to finish for quite a bit of time:

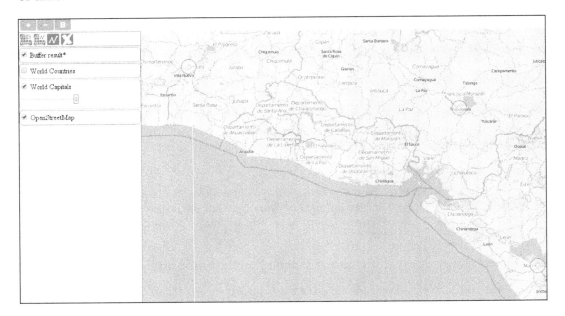

 As you can see, there are some points that were not processed by the algorithm. To test it further, use the world countries' layer as an input. What do you observe? Turf returned an error and did not create the buffers. The algorithm cannot process multipart geometries correctly. Fear not! We will learn how to split up these geometries in the third operation.

Implementing a merge operation

Next, we implement an additional operation to merge entire polygon layers. Let's take a look at the Turf API documentation's merge operation. It requires a set of polygons in a geometry collection and returns a simple polygon or a multipart polygon. First, we create the DOM elements of the new control button:

```
ol.control.Turf = function (opt_options) {
    […]
    var mergeButton = document.createElement('button');
    mergeButton.textContent = 'M';
    mergeButton.title = 'Merge selected layer';
```

Next, we register a listener on the button's `click` event as usual. As we can pass a geometry collection to this method and the OpenLayers 3 GeoJSON's format returns a geometry collection when its `writeFeaturesObject` method is called, we don't check anything; we just pass the GeoJSON object to Turf:

```
mergeButton.addEventListener('click', function (evt) {
    var layer = _this.getMap().get('selectedLayer');
    if (layer instanceof ol.layer.Vector) {
        var parser = new ol.format.GeoJSON();
        var geojson = parser.writeFeaturesObject(layer.
getSource().getFeatures());
        var merged = turf.merge(geojson);
        var mergedLayer = new ol.layer.Vector({
            source: new ol.source.Vector({
                features: parser.readFeatures(merged)
            }),
            name: 'Merge result'
        });
        _this.getMap().addLayer(mergedLayer);
    }
});
controlDiv.appendChild(mergeButton);
```

If you save the example and try out our new functionality, you will see that we can execute the merge operation on both of the vector layers. You can also observe that we do not get a simple continuous polygon for every continent but multipart polygons with some inner borders, instead. This can easily mean that we have some topology errors inside our dataset:

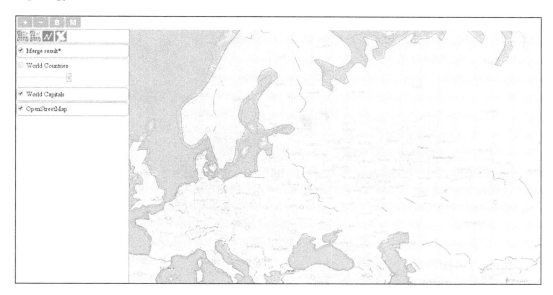

Once the API documentation is stated, the merge method expects a set of simple polygons as input. However, we could manage to use it in point features and multipart polygons, too. As the API documentation does not cover every use case correctly, you should always experiment with it before deploying an application.

Implementing the self-intersect operation

Now that we've discovered an algorithm to detect topological integrity in Turf, we will further implement an operation that's dedicated to such a purpose. The kinks method checks one simple polygon at a time, according to the API documentation, and returns a collection of points at self-intersections. First, let's create the DOM elements for the last control button:

```
var selfIntersectButton = document.createElement('button');
selfIntersectButton.textContent = 'S';
selfIntersectButton.title = 'Check self intersections';
```

Next, as we would like this method to work correctly, we limit the operation to two types of features: simple polygons and multipart polygons. We get the selected layer's features if it is a vector:

```
selfIntersectButton.addEventListener('click', function (evt) {
    var layer = _this.getMap().get('selectedLayer');
    if (layer instanceof ol.layer.Vector) {
        var parser = new ol.format.GeoJSON();
        var selfIntersectLayer = new ol.layer.Vector({
            source: new ol.source.Vector(),
            name: 'Self intersects'
        });
        _this.getMap().addLayer(selfIntersectLayer);
        var features = layer.getSource().getFeatures();
```

Next, we iterate through the features, convert them to GeoJSON one by one, and perform additional checks on them. If we meet a simple polygon, we just call the kinks method on it, and add occasional results to a new layer. If we have to deal with a multipart polygon, we make a second loop and get the coordinates of every part. From the coordinates, we create a simple GeoJSON polygon with Turf's polygon method and call kinks on it:

```
        for (var i = 0; i < features.length; i += 1) {
            var geojson =
parser.writeFeatureObject(features[i]);
            if (geojson.geometry.type === 'MultiPolygon') {
                for (var j = 0; j <
geojson.geometry.coordinates.length; j += 1) {
                    var selfIntersect =
turf.kinks(turf.polygon(geojson.geometry.coordinates[j]));
                    if
(selfIntersect.intersections.features.length > 0) {
                        selfIntersectLayer.getSource().
addFeatures(parser.readFeatures(selfIntersect.intersections));
                    }
                }
            } else if (geojson.geometry.type === 'Polygon') {
                var selfIntersect = turf.kinks(geojson);
                if (selfIntersect.intersections.features.length >
0) {
                    selfIntersectLayer.getSource().
addFeatures(parser.readFeatures(selfIntersect.intersections));
                }
            }
        }
    });
    controlDiv.appendChild(selfIntersectButton);
```

According to the API documentation, `kinks` returns a collection of GeoJSON points. However, it returns an object that occasionally has a set of GeoJSON points in its `intersections` attribute. Always use the API documentation and the rich examples hand in hand for quick and satisfying results.

If you load the final code in your browser, you can test all of our geospatial operations implemented with Turf. For the last operation, use the modify interaction, which we added to our map at the beginning of the example, and mess up one or more polygons horribly (create a lot of self-intersections):

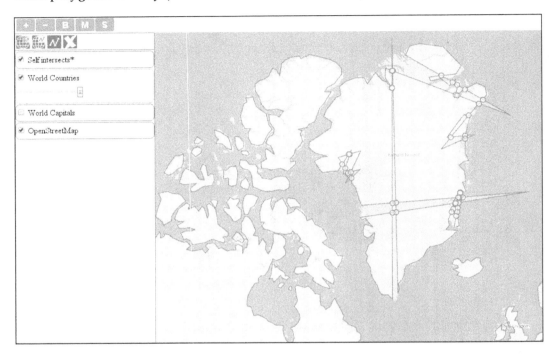

You will notice that the asterisk remains next to the new layer. This does not mean that it is still processing; we just did not bother to create a hack that removes it. If you can see the points on the places of self-intersections, the analysis has succeeded.

Spatial analysis with JSTS

Now that we are kind of familiar with Turf, let's take a look at another topological library: JSTS. In this example, called ch09_jsts, we will reproduce the first two spatial operations from the previous example with JSTS. As we would like to make the least replicated code, we will use ch09_turf as the basis for this example.

JSTS Topology Suite (JSTS) is another reasonably mature topology library out there. It is the JavaScript port of the famous desktop topology application, Java Topology Suite (JTS). The most important difference between Turf and JSTS is that JSTS is more robust but less capable of implementation. It uses an internal format to handle geometries and offers some I/O capabilities. It can traditionally read from Well-Known Text (WKT), but now it can also read from GeoJSON, OpenLayers 2, and OpenLayers 3's internal geometry formats. It can also write to these formats. As JSTS can directly read and write OpenLayers 3's geometries, the overhead of converting geometries to an exchange format is minimal. The biggest downside of JSTS is its terribly poor documentation. It is old and highly outdated; therefore, the newest features can only be explored by reading the source code or experimenting from the console.

> You can download the latest release of JSTS from the GitHub repository at `https://github.com/bjornharrtell/jsts/releases`.

First, like in the previous examples, we will resolve the dependencies of JSTS in the HTML file. For JSTS, we have to include two JavaScript files, and as JSTS initializes itself with the other utility library, the order really matters:

```
<head>
    [...]
    <script type="text/javascript" src="../../js/jsts-0.17.0/
javascript.util.min.js"></script>
    <script type="text/javascript" src="../../js/jsts-0.17.0/jsts.min.
js"></script>
</head>
```

Implementing operations

As we have gone through the implementing process already, we will now only discuss the changes between the previous implementation and this one. First, we initialize our control and define some variables for the buffer operation:

```
ol.control.JSTS = function (opt_options) {
    [...]
    controlDiv.className = options.class || 'ol-jsts ol-unselectable
ol-control';
    [...]
    bufferButton.addEventListener('click', function (evt) {
        var layer = _this.getMap().get('selectedLayer');
        if (layer instanceof ol.layer.Vector) {
            var parser = new jsts.io.olParser();
            var features = layer.getSource().getFeatures();
            var buffered = [];
```

JSTS can read and write OpenLayers 3's geometries but not its features. This way, if we would like to keep the attributes of the original features, we need to clone them first and set their geometries for the result of the operation. To store these features, we initialize an empty array. Next, we iterate through the features and buffer them one by one:

```
for (var i = 0; i < features.length; i += 1) {
    buffered.push(features[i].clone());
    var geom = parser.read(features[i].getGeometry());
    buffered[i].setGeometry(parser.write(geom.
buffer(10000)));
}
```

We create a clone of every feature, add it to our array, and override its geometries dynamically. In JSTS, we can call topological methods from the converted geometry objects. The `buffer` method of JSTS needs only one parameter: the radius in map units. It has two optional parameters: the number of segments that the approximation of a circular line end should be made up of and the line end (cap) style. Finally, we finish our control by creating a new layer, adding the content of our array to it, and adding it to the map:

```
var bufferedLayer = new ol.layer.Vector({
    source: new ol.source.Vector({
        features: buffered
    }),
    name: 'Buffer result'
});
_this.getMap().addLayer(bufferedLayer);
    }
});
```

Next, we implement the merge operation. It is available in JSTS under the `union` method and accepts one argument: another JSTS geometry. Theoretically, it can calculate a union of a geometry collection if it is called on one without any arguments; however, in practice, it throws an error. This way, we can merge our layer by calling the union method with every feature. First, we will set up the required variables:

```
[...]
mergeButton.addEventListener('click', function (evt) {
    var layer = _this.getMap().get('selectedLayer');
    if (layer instanceof ol.layer.Vector) {
        var parser = new jsts.io.olParser();
        var features = layer.getSource().getFeatures();
        var unionGeom = parser.read(features[0].getGeometry());
```

We initialize our operation with the first feature of the layer that's converted to a JSTS geometry. This variable will store the union of the processed features and will be extended for every iteration. Next, we create the iteration, and add a new, merged layer to the map. Note that we will only have one geometry in the end; therefore, we will lose every attribute that's associated with the original dataset:

```
            for (var i = 1; i < features.length; i += 1) {
                unionGeom = unionGeom.union(parser.read(features[i].
    getGeometry())));
            }
            var mergedLayer = new ol.layer.Vector({
                source: new ol.source.Vector({
                    features: [
                        new ol.Feature({
                            geometry: parser.write(unionGeom)
                        })
                    ]
                }),
                name: 'Merge result'
            });
            _this.getMap().addLayer(mergedLayer);
        }
    });
    [...]
};
ol.inherits(ol.control.JSTS, ol.control.Control);
```

If you save the code and load it in your browser, you can try out the topological functions that we implemented with JSTS. Don't forget to try out buffering with the help of the polygon layer:

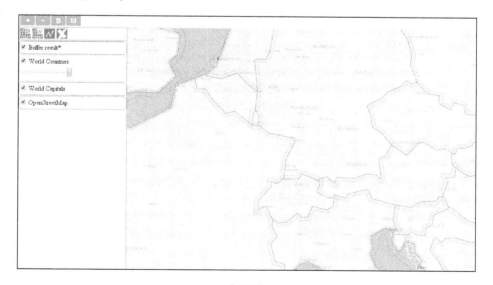

3D rendering with Cesium

In our final example, called ch09_cesium, we will integrate Cesium into our application. Cesium is a 3D web mapping application, capable of rendering ordinary OWS layers and features on a globe and creating DEM visualizations with elevation tiles. It can display various spatial data in 2D and 3D, knows some projections, and on top of visualizing elevation data, it can also render 3D objects using various 3D-capable formats.

The only problem with Cesium is that it would be very hard to synchronize with OpenLayers 3. Luckily, the OpenLayers 3 developer team created an integration library, which can utilize the 3D capabilities of Cesium. The downside of this approach is the limitation of the capabilities of Cesium. We can use the 3D renderer, Web Mercator, and the WGS84 projections (EPSG:3857 and EPSG:4326), and we can access the currently used Cesium scene. The library automatically synchronizes the scene with our OpenLayers 3 map, and if we know how to use Cesium, we can also use some Cesium-only features with the object of the exposed scene.

Preparing a map

First, we include the Cesium and OL3-Cesium libraries in our HTML file. We must include both of the libraries, but in this case, theoretically, the order does not matter. However, loading Cesium before OL3-Cesium is the least error-prone; therefore, we will do this.

> OL3-Cesium ships with the exact versions of OpenLayers 3 and Cesium that it was compiled against. On the top of this, from OL3-Cesium 1.10.0, OpenLayers 3 is bundled in ol3cesium.js. This way, we do not have to include ol.js in a script tag. The integration library will be error-free when we use it with the proper OpenLayers 3 and Cesium versions. However, if we want to use a custom version that is compatible with the given OL3-Cesium version, we can do this by including our custom library after OL3-Cesium.

```
<head>
    [...]
    <script type="text/javascript" src="../../js/ol3-cesium-
1.10.0/Cesium/Cesium.js"></script>
    <script type="text/javascript" src="../../js/ol3-cesium-
1.10.0/ol3cesium.js"></script>
    <script type="text/javascript" src="ch09_cesium.js"></script>
</head>
```

Next, we load some additional layers in our JavaScript file to test the rendering capabilities of the library. We will use MapQuest's OpenStreetMap layer because it has some nice hillshade effects. As an overlay, we will use a GeoJSON point layer containing capitals. We will use a marker to represent these capitals instead of the default blue circles:

```javascript
var map = new ol.Map({
    target: 'map',
    layers: [
        new ol.layer.Tile({
            source: new ol.source.MapQuest({
                layer: 'osm'
            }),
            name: 'MapQuest'
        }),
        new ol.layer.Vector({
            source: new ol.source.Vector({
                format: new ol.format.GeoJSON({
                    defaultDataProjection: 'EPSG:4326'
                }),
                url: '../../res/world_capitals.geojson'
            }),
            name: 'World Capitals',
            style: new ol.style.Style({
                image: new ol.style.Icon({
                    anchor: [0.5, 46],
                    anchorXUnits: 'fraction',
                    anchorYUnits: 'pixels',
                    src: '../../res/marker.png'
                })
            })
        })
    ],
    [...]
});
var tree = new layerTree({map: map, target: 'layertree', messages: 'messageBar'})
    .createRegistry(map.getLayers().item(0))
    .createRegistry(map.getLayers().item(1));
```

For the images representing the capital cities, we used some extra parameters for styling. The anchor property represents the offset of the image. As OpenLayers 3 snaps the upper-left corner of the image to the feature, we define an offset, and thus the cusp of the marker is snapped to the capital it represents. We can use different units for different dimensions, therefore we also define them as extra parameters. The preceding style definition indicates that the library should offset the image by 50% (0.5 fraction) to the left and 46 pixels upward (the height of the image is 48 pixels).

> In OpenLayers 3, we can use cross-origin images, but Cesium will throw an error when it tries to access them. This way, the marker is provided as part of the example and is downloaded from the OpenLayers 3 official page.

Creating a control

Next, we continue creating the control. First, as usual, we create the element of the control and parameterize it correctly:

```
ol.control.Cesium = function (opt_options) {
    var options = opt_options || {};
    var _this = this;
    var controlDiv = document.createElement('div');
    controlDiv.className = options.class || 'ol-cesium ol-
unselectable ol-control';
```

The next step is to initialize the 3D visualization of our map. The only problem with this is that the OL3-Cesium library requires the map object to read out the layers and view properties. However, if we provide the control in the map's constructor, we will not have the map object yet when this code block is run. To avoid such errors, we call this part of the code asynchronously; thus, we put the construction of the Cesium scene after the construction of the map object.

> Alternatively, you can use a promise to achieve the same result but with nicer code.

The initialization of the Cesium scene via OL3-Cesium is quite automatic. We only have to define one thing: the source of the elevation tiles. By default, Cesium can use two kinds of elevation formats: quantized mesh and height map. Both of these formats are supported by the `CesiumTerranProvider` constructor:

```
setTimeout(function () {
    var ol3d = new olcs.OLCesium({map: _this.getMap()});
    var scene = ol3d.getCesiumScene();
    scene.terrainProvider = new Cesium.CesiumTerrainProvider({
        url: 'http://assets.agi.com/stk-terrain/world'
    });
    _this.set('cesium', ol3d);
}, 0);
```

Next, we create the control button and define its `click` event. We can easily read the status of the visualization; therefore, we can enable or disable it according to its status. The only extra command we include is the `setBlockCesiumRendering` method. When we disable the visualization, we also block the dynamic rendering of the current viewport in Cesium. This consideration improves the performance of the 2D application but makes the rendering longer when we activate the 3D visualization:

```
var controlButton = document.createElement('button');
controlButton.textContent = '3D';
controlButton.title = 'Toggle 3D rendering';
controlButton.addEventListener('click', function (evt) {
    var cesium = _this.get('cesium');
    if (cesium.getEnabled()) {
        cesium.setBlockCesiumRendering(true);
        cesium.setEnabled(false);
    } else {
        cesium.setBlockCesiumRendering(false);
        cesium.setEnabled(true);
    }
});
```

Finally, we close our control in the usual way and add it to the map:

```
controlDiv.appendChild(controlButton);
ol.control.Control.call(this, {
    element: controlDiv,
    target: options.target
});
};
```

```
ol.inherits(ol.control.Cesium, ol.control.Control);
[...]
    var map = new ol.Map({
        [...]
        controls: [
            [...]
            new ol.control.Cesium({
                target: 'toolbar'
            })
        ],
        [...]
    });
```

If you load the example and enable 3D rendering, you can browse the capitals on the globe and have a nice visualization of the terrain due to the elevation tiles and shaded base layer. You can also check how the atmosphere is rendered in Cesium:

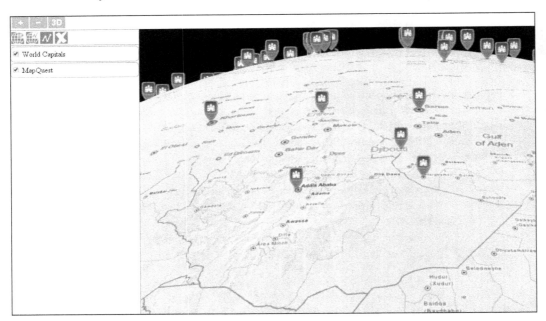

Observing a terrain

Now that we have taken a look at the 3D visualization of our map on a global scale, let's also examine the minor details of it. There is another example, called `ch09_ cesium_terrain`, in which we will load some more layers. First, we extend our map with two more layers. The first one is the topological map of the Grand Canyon, while the second is a vector layer in TopoJSON, representing the major rivers on the Earth:

```
var map = new ol.Map({
    target: 'map',
    layers: [
        [...]
        new ol.layer.Tile({
            source: new ol.source.XYZ({
                url: 'http://tileserver.maptiler.com/grandcanyon/{z}/
{x}/{y}.png'
            }),
            name: 'Grand Canyon'
        }),
        new ol.layer.Vector({
            source: new ol.source.Vector({
                format: new ol.format.TopoJSON({
                    defaultDataProjection: 'EPSG:4326'
                }),
                url: '../../res/rivers.topojson'
            }),
            name: 'Rivers',
            altitudeMode: 'clampToGround'
        }),
        [...]
```

Next, as we do not expect anyone to know the coordinates of the Grand Canyon, we center our view in this way:

```
    [...]
    view: new ol.View({
        center: [-12488000, 4308000],
        zoom: 12
    })
});
```

We also add our new layers to the layer tree for a nice visual feedback:

```
var tree = new layerTree({map: map, target: 'layertree', messages:
'messageBar'})
    .createRegistry(map.getLayers().item(0))
    .createRegistry(map.getLayers().item(1))
    .createRegistry(map.getLayers().item(2))
    .createRegistry(map.getLayers().item(3));
```

Now, if you load the extended example and enable 3D rendering, you will see the Grand Canyon's terrain with the topological map and shaded MapQuest layer draped around it:

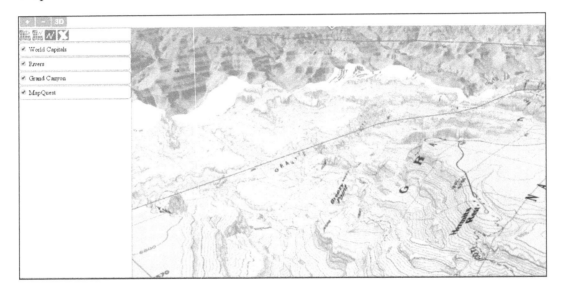

As you can see, there is one odd thing in the composition. The Colorado River is not masked by the terrain. There is an option in Cesium to create geometries, which are draped around the terrain, and a depth test is executed against them. You can invoke this option even from OL3-Cesium by adding a property to a vector layer, named `altitudeMode`, and setting its value to `clampToGround`. However, Cesium does not support draping line geometries yet, just polygons. Alternatively, you can set the `globe.depthTestAgainstTerrain` property of the Cesium scene to `true`, but you will need a vector layer with altitude data for this to work correctly.

Extending the Cesium scene

In the final task, let's look into what we can do easily with the Cesium scene. In this example, which has a dedicated JavaScript file like the previous one, we will focus on Cesium and create some stars, a Sun, Moon, some water effects, and lighting effects. This example is called `ch09_cesium_extend`.

First, let's extend our control and modify the exposed Cesium scene. We will request some additional data from the terrain provider:

```
ol.control.Cesium = function (opt_options) {
    [...]
        scene.terrainProvider = new Cesium.CesiumTerrainProvider({
            url: 'http://assets.agi.com/stk-terrain/world',
            requestWaterMask: true,
            requestVertexNormals: true
        });
```

The water mask is quite an expressive name; we use it to request the shorelines of the terrain. With this option set to `true`, Cesium will render a more water-like texture to water bodies and even animate waves on higher zoom levels. Vertex Normal is a bit of a different term. With this option, we can request information in order to shade the terrain. Next, we will create the sky along with the stars:

```
        scene.skyBox = new Cesium.SkyBox({
            sources: {
                positiveX:
Cesium.buildModuleUrl('Assets/Textures/SkyBox/tycho2t3_80_px.jpg'),
                negativeX:
Cesium.buildModuleUrl('Assets/Textures/SkyBox/tycho2t3_80_mx.jpg'),
                positiveY:
Cesium.buildModuleUrl('Assets/Textures/SkyBox/tycho2t3_80_py.jpg'),
                negativeY:
Cesium.buildModuleUrl('Assets/Textures/SkyBox/tycho2t3_80_my.jpg'),
                positiveZ:
Cesium.buildModuleUrl('Assets/Textures/SkyBox/tycho2t3_80_pz.jpg'),
                negativeZ:
Cesium.buildModuleUrl('Assets/Textures/SkyBox/tycho2t3_80_mz.jpg')
            }
        });
```

Cesium ships with some default textures, such as one for water bodies, another for the Moon, and multiple JPEG images for a darkly colored sky. We have to supply these images manually since there are no default values for the `SkyBox` sources. There is a convenient method, however, that lets us use the path from the Cesium directory, called `buildModuleUrl`. Finally, we add the Moon and Sun as well as enable lighting effects on the Earth. To achieve this, we have to use the scene's `globe` property, which represents the Earth. For the Moon, we disable the lighting effect; otherwise, we would only see a black disk in its place:

```
scene.moon = new Cesium.Moon({
    onlySunLighting: false
});
scene.sun = new Cesium.Sun();
scene.globe.enableLighting = true;
[...]
```

If you load this example, you can admire the multiple textures and effects provided by Cesium directly in your browser:

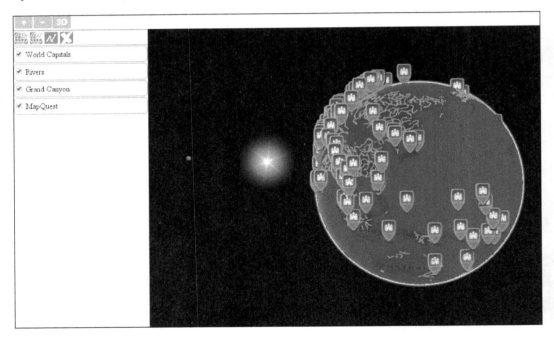

Summary

Congratulations! You are almost there! In this chapter, you learned a bit about extendibility and modularity. You learned about the perks of modular applications and how to bring third-party libraries into your workflow. You also learned a few things about QGIS, including not only creating a quick preview of your project but also salvaging valuable information from it. You explored the usage of some of the most useful third-party libraries for a WebGIS application built in OpenLayers 3. To top this, we managed to create beautiful 3D visualizations with Cesium and OpenLayers 3, which was the most exciting part of this chapter.

In the final chapter, you will learn how to use the Closure Compiler and create custom builds of OpenLayers 3. This is useful to create lightweight versions when we do not need the full capability of this robust library. Additionally, you will learn how to extend the source code or expose originally hidden functions, which we would like to access for our project. Finally, you will also learn how to automatically create rich documentation for our project based on OpenLayers 3 using JSDoc.

10
Compiling Custom Builds with Closure

Welcome to the last chapter of *Mastering OpenLayers 3*. In your journey to master this library, you became familiar with quite a lot of concepts of OpenLayers 3. Until now, we used a full build of the library for our various purposes. This is good for learning, but it's not very effective in cases where we'd like to deploy an application. In most of cases, you will only need a small subset of the library's capabilities. To have a firm grip on the required subset, you will learn how to compile a custom build with Closure Compiler. You will also learn a few tricks to minimize your application even better and create documentation.

In this chapter, we will cover the following topics:

- Building OpenLayers 3 with only a subset of features
- Bundling an application with OpenLayers 3
- Extending OpenLayers 3
- Creating a rich API documentation automatically with JSDoc

Before getting started

As we are going to compile the library from source code, we will need the source code of OpenLayers 3 for this chapter. You can find the source code of OpenLayers 3.11.1 in the src folder of the code appendix. Alternatively, you can download the source of the most recent version from the OpenLayers 3 GitHub repository at https://github. com/openlayers/ol3/releases. For the compiling, we will use Google's Closure Compiler, which is bundled with OpenLayers 3. On the top of this, the library offers convenience tools that are tailored for this specific library. As these tools are JavaScript files, we have to use a desktop JavaScript interpreter to use them. For this task, we will install Node JS, which is based on Google Chrome's JavaScript engine (V8).

Configuring Node JS

As a first task, we will need a copy of Node JS running on our system. We can get this piece of software in different ways on different systems. This book covers the installation process on Windows and Linux systems. After the installation, everything will work similarly from the command line or terminal.

> If you use the Mac OS X, there are great tutorials to install Node JS on the Web. The `http://coolestguidesontheplanet.com/installing-node-js-on-osx-10-10-yosemite/` website shows you how to install it with a precompiled binary (do not be misled by the title; it's the one for El Capitan), while `http://sourabhbajaj.com/mac-setup/Node.js/README.html` shows you how to install it using `brew`.

Installing Node JS on Windows

To get Node JS on Windows, we have to download the installer from its home page. First, we navigate to `https://nodejs.org/en/`, where the site tries to detect our system configuration and automatically offers a version to download. In most cases, this version is the appropriate one.

> If the site misinterprets your system, navigate to the download's site where you can choose the right installer.

Next, we download the installer and run it. Then, the installation wizard leads us through the installation process. We can leave every option in their default values. After the installation is finished, we get some shortcuts for different purposes:

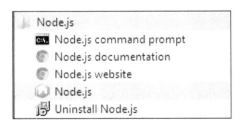

From the available shortcuts, we will need the command prompt (**Node.js command prompt**) as we will need to start various JavaScript programs. When we start a program, we get a default command line with the message: the command line is configured to work with Node JS. The only thing left to do is navigate to the folder containing the source code of OpenLayers 3. We can easily do this with the `cd` command and a relative path from the current directory.

If you have your source code on a different partition, you have to change the current partition first. You can do this by simply typing in the letter of the partition. For example, if you have your source code on partition D and you are in partition C, just type D: in the command prompt before changing the current directory.

Installing Node JS on Linux

In Linux, we can easily install Node JS if we have a distribution with a package management system. The only restriction is that we must have superuser privileges to install new packages. Therefore, we have to change to a superuser with su or prepend sudo to the following commands. For Debian-based distributions (such as Ubuntu), we have to run the following command in the terminal:

```
apt-get install node
```

In systems based on Fedora and Red Hat, we can use the yum package manager to achieve the same results:

```
yum install node
```

 Most of the common distributions have their own package management systems. For example, Arch Linux has pacman. If your distribution does not have one, you have to build Node JS from its source code. You can download the source code from the Node JS download page.

If we used su to switch to the superuser, we switch back with the exit or logout commands, and navigate to the source code's directory using cd.

Resolving dependencies

The installation process of Node JS gave us two programs for our use: node and npm. **npm** stands for Node Package Manager, and we will use it to install every dependency of OpenLayers 3. npm can be used to install packages globally or only for a single project. We will use the latter option as it is a cleaner solution for our case. From now on, every step will be almost identical on different operating systems.

 When we say almost identical, we mean that on Windows, you have to replace every forward slash (/) representing a folder delimiter with a backward slash (\). You only have to do this for command-line commands. In configuration files, you have to use a forward slash as usual.

To resolve the dependencies of OpenLayers 3, we only have to type the following command in the terminal from the directory of the source code (`src/ol3-3.11.1`):

```
npm install
```

If we wait for the command to finish, we will notice that there are two new folders in the directory, called `node_modules` and `build`. The `node_modules` folder contains every node package used by OpenLayers 3 on compilation. The other folder contains some external JavaScript libraries, which are bundled with OpenLayers 3.

Compiling OpenLayers 3

Now that we have resolved every dependency, let's build some versions of the library. First, we will build the minified and debug versions of the library just to see whether everything works fine. In the `tasks` folder, we can see a bunch of JavaScript files used in various stages of development. There are some test programs, serve commands, and the command that we will use to compile the library: `build.js`. This program requires two parameters to run. The first is a `configuration` file, while the second is the name of the result.

As the Closure Compiler is a quite complex library built in Java and Python, OpenLayers 3's developers created some utilities to make our lives easier. With `build.js`, we do not have to directly parameterize the Closure Compiler, we just have to write a configuration file in the JSON format. The program reads our configuration file and writes every exportable symbol (constructor, method, and so on) from the `src` folder to a file named `info.json`. This file can be located in the `build` folder. Then it goes on to parameterize the Closure Compiler based on the parameters of our configuration file's `compile` section and builds the library.

There is another utility called closure-utils. This program contains all the programs from the tasks folder in one place. It uses a slightly different syntax from `build.js`. You can watch a great tutorial to use this program on the OpenLayers 3 official site at `http://openlayers.org/en/master/doc/tutorials/closure.html`. It covers everything from creating a new Node project with OpenLayers 3 as a dependency to creating debug builds.

Building default versions

Next, as we now know how to use the `build.js` program, we can build the default versions of OpenLayers 3. For this, we only need the default configuration files, which are located in the `config` folder. From the source directory, we can build the two versions with the following commands:

```
node tasks/build.js config/ol.json ol.js
```

```
node tasks/build.js config/ol-debug.json ol-debug.js
```

```
Terminal - debian@mapserver: ~/ol3-3.11.1

File  Edit  View  Terminal  Go  Help

debian@mapserver:~/ol3-3.11.1$ node tasks/build.js config/ol.json ol.js
info ol Parsing dependencies
info ol Compiling 365 sources
debian@mapserver:~/ol3-3.11.1$ node tasks/build.js config/ol-debug.json ol-debug
.js
info ol Parsing dependencies
info ol No compile options found.  Concatenating 365 sources
debian@mapserver:~/ol3-3.11.1$
```

In the examples for this chapter, you will find an example named `ch10_test`. It is a simple copy of the simple map example from the first chapter. If you copy your freshly compiled library to this example and link it to the HTML file, you will see the map show up. You can test your debug version in a similar manner.

 If you use Windows, you will most likely run into an error if you have one or more whitespaces in your full path. You have to remove them prior to compiling the code.

Understanding a configuration file

Before we create a smaller build, let's take a look at the configuration file first. Open the `ol.json` file from the `config` folder of the source code in a text editor. We can see that there are three parameters in the file. The first one is called `exports`. It defines an array of symbols which we would like to export. Every other symbol will be obfuscated in the compiled library. The second one is `umd`. UMD stands for Universal Module Definition, and it should be used when we would like to use our library in a modular way, for example, with Browserify or ReactJS. The third symbol is `compile`, which contains the Closure Compiler-related parameters.

There is one extra parameter that we should discuss. It is called `src`, and it contains an array of paths. The JavaScript files under these paths are used in the compilation process. For now, its default value is sufficient; however, if we have some files outside the `src` folder, it has to be defined.

 Note that symbols are only exported from JavaScript files located in the `src` folder.

Building OpenLayers 3 with a subset of features

In the configuration file, we saw that the `exports` parameter had a single member: `*`. This means that every exportable symbol should be exported and there is no filter applied. To compile only the necessary features for a project, we can define an array of features in this parameter. In this example, we will compile a small library with only the features needed for our geocaching application from *Chapter 8, OpenLayers 3 for Mobile*. First, there is a configuration file called `ch10_geocaching_conf.json`. If we open this configuration file, we can see that every feature of it is used in a mobile application in the order of occurrence. The other thing that we recognize instantly is that we have to export methods besides constructors. Methods are annotated after a corresponding constructor that is delimited by #:

```
{
  "exports": [
    "ol.Map",
    "ol.layer.Tile",
    "ol.source.OSM",
    "ol.control.Zoom",
    "ol.View",
    "ol.Geolocation",
    "ol.Map#getView",
    "ol.View#getProjection",
    "ol.layer.Vector",
    "ol.source.Vector",
    "ol.Map#addLayer",
    "ol.Geolocation#once",
    "ol.Geolocation#getAltitude",
    "ol.Geolocation#getPosition",
    [...]
```

Now that we have a nice list of features to export, we can compile a smaller library. We copy this configuration file to the `config` folder of the source code and build a new version of it with the following command:

```
node tasks/build.js config/ch10_geocaching_conf.json ol-geocaching.js
```

> Note that copying the configuration file into the `config` folder is not mandatory; we just do this for added consistency.

If we examine the resulting library, we will see that it's only 205.6 kilobytes. This is a great result compared to the original library, which is 497.3 kilobytes. Finally, we test our custom version. There is an example, called `ch10_geocaching`, which we use for testing purposes. Let's link this version in the example's HTML file and check whether it works:

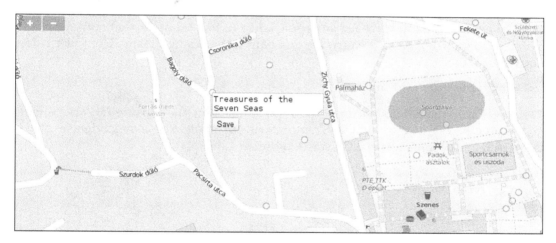

> We could get such a small library with a defined set of exports because Closure Compiler checks for the exported symbols in the advanced mode. It exports the unchanged symbols and packs every other related code next to them in an obfuscated form. If a piece of code is entirely unrelated to the exported symbols, Closure removes it from the resulting library.

Bundling an application with OpenLayers 3

Now, as we know how to build custom libraries, let's take a step forward and learn how to compile our application with OpenLayers 3. This process has two steps. First, we have to edit our application as it has to be compatible with the Closure Compiler. Next, we have to create a custom configuration file, which can create a library with just the features that our application needs.

Editing the application

To make our application Closure-compatible, we have to make two modifications to it. You can either make these modifications in the JavaScript file of the previous example, called ch10_geocaching.js, or open the provided modified file to check the result. The modified version is called ch10_geocaching_reworked.js. First, we have to provide a namespace for our application. In this example, that namespace will be geocaching. Next, we provide that namespace to the Closure Compiler using the Closure Library:

```
goog.provide('geocaching');
```

Next, we build the dependencies of the application using the Closure Library. Similar to the previous syntax, we will also require some symbols. These dependencies will be parsed and resolved by the Closure Compiler:

```
goog.require('ol.Map');
goog.require('ol.layer.Tile');
goog.require('ol.source.OSM');
goog.require('ol.control.Zoom');
goog.require('ol.View');
goog.require('ol.Geolocation');
goog.require('ol.layer.Vector');
goog.require('ol.source.Vector');
goog.require('ol.Feature');
goog.require('ol.geom.Point');
goog.require('ol.has');
goog.require('ol.control.FullScreen');
goog.require('ol.style.Style');
goog.require('ol.style.Circle');
goog.require('ol.style.Fill');
goog.require('ol.style.Stroke');
goog.require('ol.geom.Circle');
goog.require('ol.geom.LineString');
goog.require('ol.interaction.Select');
```

```
goog.require('ol.control.Control');
goog.require('ol.style.RegularShape');
goog.require('ol.interaction.Modify');
goog.require('ol.Collection');
goog.require('ol.Overlay');
```

As we can see, the number of dependencies are lower than the number of exports from the previous example. As we wouldn't like to export anything now, we only have to provide the constructors that our application uses. The methods of these constructors get included automatically if they are used. Finally, let's add the main parts of our application to the provided geocaching namespace:

```
function init() {
    document.removeEventListener('DOMContentLoaded', init);
    geocaching.map = new ol.Map({
        [...]
    });
    var map = geocaching.map;
    geocaching.geoloc = new ol.Geolocation({
        [...]
    });
    var geoloc = geocaching.geoloc;
    geocaching.geoCaching = new ol.layer.Vector({
        source: new ol.source.Vector()
    });
    var geoCaching = geocaching.geoCaching;
```

 Namespacing your application is important. No matter how complex it will be in the end, if you create a nice structure for it, you will still be able to read it easily. Namespaces can help you develop a good structure for your application.

Creating a configuration file

The only thing left is building a new configuration file for our application. First, create a folder, called app, in the source code's directory. Next, move the modified JavaScript file (ch10_geocaching_reworked.js) to this folder. If you look at the examples, you will see a file named ch10_geocaching_reworked_conf.json. This will be our new configuration file, which we will discuss in the following lines. You can either create your own or use this file. The first thing we can see in the modified configuration file is the new src parameter. If we override the default parameter with our own array, we have to provide the two default values. Additionally, we provide the path to our application:

If you use closure-utils, the `src` parameter becomes `lib` and mandatory. The rest of the syntax is the same. Here, `**` indicates every folder, while `*` indicates every file.

```
{
  "src": [
    "src/**/*.js",
    "build/ol.ext/**/*.js",
    "app/**/*.js"
  ],
```

The next change we can notice is that the `exports` parameter is an empty array. That's right: we do not export any symbol, just make a big compiled JavaScript application:

```
"exports": [],
```

We did not discuss the `compile` parameter before, but as we have to change the parameters of the Closure Compiler, we should do it now. First of all, there is a new parameter called `closure_entry_point`. It defines the namespace and whether the Closure Compiler should resolve the dependencies recursively. The `goog.provide` function must be called on it:

```
"compile": {
  "closure_entry_point": "geocaching",
```

There are some slight changes in the `defines` property. This property contains every variable that can be changed at the time of compilation. These are some of the configuration options built in the library. As we compile a mobile application with a Canvas renderer, we do not need WebGL or DOM support:

```
"define": [
  "goog.array.ASSUME_NATIVE_FUNCTIONS=true",
  "goog.dom.ASSUME_STANDARDS_MODE=true",
  "goog.json.USE_NATIVE_JSON=true",
  "goog.DEBUG=false",
  "ol.ENABLE_DOM=false",
  "ol.ENABLE_WEBGL=false"
],
```

 You can find every OpenLayers 3-related compile time parameter with its default values in the source code (`src/ol/ol.js`). They are marked with `@define` in their headers.

Next, you will notice quite an extensive list of values under the jscomp_warning, jscomp_error and jscomp_off parameters. These important parameters instruct the compiler on whether it should throw an error for various check types. As we did not make any effort to structure our application in the Closure syntax, we define most of the checks as warnings. Closure will only throw an error if we do not require or provide appropriate classes. Furthermore, we will disable the error checks that are disabled in the default configuration file:

```
"jscomp_warning": [
  "accessControls",
  "ambiguousFunctionDecl",
  "checkEventfulObjectDisposal",
  "checkRegExp",
  "checkTypes",
  "checkVars",
  "const",
  [...]
],
"jscomp_error": [
  "missingRequire",
  "missingProvide"
],
"jscomp_off": [
  "useOfGoogBase",
  "unnecessaryCasts",
  "lintChecks"
],
[...]
  }
}
```

> You can find every valid Closure Compiler parameter on the closure-utils GitHub page at https://github.com/openlayers/closure-util/blob/master/compiler-options.txt.

This way, the Closure Compiler will not run if we've missed out a dependency but specifies it in the error statement. It will also tell us about every other error in our code from the aspect of Closure but compiles the code anyway. As our application worked before the compilation, it will work after it as well. Or won't it? Let's copy the configuration file into the source code's config directory, and make a custom build with the following command:

```
node tasks/build.js config/ch10_geocaching_reworked_conf.json
ol_geocaching_rw.js
```

If everything is in place, the compiler creates a build with some warnings. Those warnings are the result of the poor structure of our application. However, our new library is only 178 kilobytes, which is great:

```
Terminal - debian@mapserver: ~/ol3-3.11.1

File Edit View Terminal Go Help
tFeatures()[2].getGeometry().getLength() + 'm\nHeight: ' + height + 'm\nPossible
 loot: ' + selectedFeat.get('loot');
ERR! compile
                        ^

ERR! compile
ERR! compile /home/debian/ol3-3.11.1/app/ch10_geocaching_reworked.js:141: WARNIN
G - Property getCoordinates never defined on (null|ol.geom.Geometry|ol.render.Fe
ature|undefined)
ERR! compile            var zCoord = feature.getGeometry().getCoordinates()
[2];
ERR! compile
ERR! compile
ERR! compile /home/debian/ol3-3.11.1/app/ch10_geocaching_reworked.js:192: WARNIN
G - actual parameter 1 of ol.Collection does not match formal parameter
ERR! compile found    : (Array<(null|ol.Feature)>|null)
ERR! compile required: (Array<(null|ol.Feature)>|undefined)
ERR! compile            features: new ol.Collection(geoCaching.getSource().
getFeatures())
ERR! compile                                                ^
ERR! compile
ERR! compile
ERR! compile 0 error(s), 7 warning(s), 97.4% typed
ERR! compile
debian@mapserver:~/ol3-3.11.1$
```

Finally, let's test the application in the example, named `ch10_geocaching`, by linking the new library in the HTML file. Don't forget to replace the OpenLayers 3 library with our new one, and remove the link to `ch10_geocaching.js`. As you can see, everything works well, except for the functionalities related to the `loot` attribute.

Fixing the application

So, what could go wrong in our application? Let's put ourselves in a compiler's shoes. It shrinks the library aggressively by replacing every variable in it with a few letter representations. When it comes to the part where we've declared the `loot` property, it sees the following:

```
geoCaching.getSource().addFeature(new ol.Feature({
    [...]
    loot: 'Treasures of the Seven Seas'
}));
```

It replaces `loot` with a shorter representation and goes on. When it comes to the part of calling this attribute, it sees the following:

```
saveButton.addEventListener('click', function
(evt) {
        feature.set('loot', lootElem.value);
        map.removeOverlay(overlay);
    });
```

It's also `loot`, but as a string. The compiler cannot find a shorthand for `'loot'`; therefore, it shortens it as another variable. Thus, when we run our application, it declares `loot` as variable A and calls `'loot'` variable B. To fix our application, we simply have to declare `loot` as a string:

```
geoCaching.getSource().addFeature(new ol.Feature({
    [...]
    'loot': 'Treasures of the Seven Seas'
}));
```

If you recompile the library with the fixed application, you will see that everything works fine. The global scope is filled with some obfuscated functions, but it is also the result of the poor structure of our application.

> This was quite an easy problem to fix. However, it could be worse. If you write a complex application and already know in the beginning that you will have to compile it with Closure, you might want to become familiar with the Closure Library and write your application with it.

As the last check, let's take a look at how error handling works in Closure. Modify the application and remove one or more of the dependencies. If you run the compiler, you will see that it does not fill the terminal with warnings, it just throws the errors. This way, you can resolve the missing dependencies quite easily:

```
1    goog.provide('geocaching');
2
3    goog.require('ol.Map');
4    goog.require('ol.layer.Tile');
5    goog.require('ol.source.OSM');
6    goog.require('ol.control.Zoom');
7    goog.require('ol.View');
8    goog.require('ol.Geolocation');
9    goog.require('ol.layer.Vector');
10   goog.require('ol.source.Vector');
11   goog.require('ol.Feature');
12   //goog.require('ol.geom.Point');
13   goog.require('ol.has');
14   goog.require('ol.control.FullScreen');
15   goog.require('ol.style.Style');
16   goog.require('ol.style.Circle');
17   goog.require('ol.style.Fill');
18   goog.require('ol.style.Stroke');
19   goog.require('ol.geom.Circle');
20   goog.require('ol.geom.LineString');
21   goog.require('ol.interaction.Select');
22   goog.require('ol.control.Control');
23   goog.require('ol.style.RegularShape');
24   goog.require('ol.interaction.Modify');
25   goog.require('ol.Collection');
26   goog.require('ol.Overlay');
27
28   function init() {
```

```
Terminal - debian@mapserver: ~/ol3-3.11.1           ↑ _ □ ✕
File  Edit  View  Terminal  Go  Help
debian@mapserver:~/ol3-3.11.1$ node tasks/build.js ch10_geocaching_reworked_conf
.json ol_geocaching_rw.js
info ol Parsing dependencies
info ol Compiling 366 sources
ERR! compile /home/debian/ol3-3.11.1/app/ch10_geocaching_reworked.js:108: ERROR
- 'ol.geom.Point' used but not goog.require'd
ERR! compile                     geometry: new ol.geom.Point(evt.target.getPosit
ion())
ERR! compile                              ^
ERR! compile
ERR! compile 1
ERR! compile  error(s), 0 warning(s)
ERR! compile
ERR! Process exited with non-zero status, see log for more detail: 1
debian@mapserver:~/ol3-3.11.1$
```

Extending OpenLayers 3

In the previous examples, we worked hard to reduce the size of the library by cutting out some irrelevant parts. Now, let's do the contrary and extend the library with additional functionality. Remember the example where we measured distance on an ellipsoid? We used the debug library of an older OpenLayers 3 version to achieve this. Now, we will build the `ol.Ellipsoid` class in our next custom build. You can find a JavaScript file, named `ellipsoid.js`, in the `examples` folder and an example named `ch10_test_ellipsoid`. The latter is the exact copy of `ch05_measure` with `ch05_measure_vincenty.js`. First, open up `ellipsoid.js`. This is how a well-structured code looks from the aspect of the Closure Compiler. There are headers everywhere with type definitions and additional information. These headers are written in the syntax of JSDoc, but JSDoc and Closure Compiler go hand in hand.

The first part of the code resolves the dependencies of this constructor and provides a name for it:

```
goog.provide('ol.Ellipsoid');

goog.require('goog.math');
goog.require('ol.Coordinate');
```

Then, the constructor is defined with every parameter and method. The important part is the header. It is clearly defined. Closure has to deal with a constructor that has two input parameters:

```
/**
 * @constructor
 * @param {number} a Major radius.
 * @param {number} flattening Flattening.
 */
```

However, as there is nothing else specified, this constructor won't get exported unless we modify this header. The standard Closure way to do this is by declaring the symbol as exportable and setting the `generate_exports` compiler parameter to `true`. However, this won't work with the library. As the exportable symbols are preprocessed with the custom build tools, we have to use an OpenLayers 3-only tag: `api`. Let's extend the header with the new tag:

```
/**
 * @constructor
 * @param {number} a Major radius.
 * @param {number} flattening Flattening.
 * @api
 */
```

We are not yet done with the code. As we would like to expose the ellipsoid object's `vincentyDistance` method, we have to make it exportable, too:

```
/**
 * Returns the distance from c1 to c2 using Vincenty.
 *
 * @param {ol.Coordinate} c1 Coordinate 1.
 * @param {ol.Coordinate} c2 Coordinate 1.
 * @param {number=} opt_minDeltaLambda Minimum delta lambda for
convergence.
 * @param {number=} opt_maxIterations Maximum iterations.
 * @return {number} Vincenty distance.
 * @api
 */
```

Next, we create a `plugins` folder inside the source code directory's `src` folder. We copy the modified `ellipsoid.js` to this folder. We're almost there. The only thing left to do is remove the `info.json` file from the `build` folder. This file is generated by the build tool if it does not exist. If it is there, the tool simply parses the exportable symbols from it and builds the library accordingly. However, as we try to extend the library, the symbols in that file will not correspond with the truly exportable symbols. As a result, if we extend a library and compile it without removing the file, the new symbols won't be exported. If we remove something from the source code and compile it without removing the file, the Closure Compiler will throw an error:

 If you accidentally remove a dependency from the `build` folder or anywhere else, don't panic. Just rerun `npm install`, and npm will take care of fixing those files for you.

```
Terminal - debian@mapserver: ~/ol3-3.11.1                    ↑ _ □ ✕
File  Edit  View  Terminal  Go  Help
debian@mapserver:~/ol3-3.11.1$ node tasks/build.js config/ol.json ol_ellipsoid.js
info ol Parsing dependencies
info ol Compiling 366 sources
debian@mapserver:~/ol3-3.11.1$ node tasks/build.js config/ol.json ol.js
info ol Parsing dependencies
info ol Compiling 365 sources
ERR! compile /tmp/exports1151017-6248-l0lzhs.js:17: ERROR - required "ol.Ellipsoid"
namespace never provided
ERR! compile goog.require('ol.Ellipsoid');
ERR! compile ^
ERR! compile
ERR! compile
ERR! compile 1 error(s),
ERR! compile 0 warning(s)
ERR! compile
ERR! Process exited with non-zero status, see log for more detail: 1
debian@mapserver:~/ol3-3.11.1$
```

Now that everything is in place, we can run the compiler with the default configuration file. We run the compiler with the following command:

```
node tasks/build.js config/ol.json ol_ellipsoid.js
```

If you copy the resulting library in the examples' folder and link it in `ch10_test_ellipsoid.html` in the place of the original OpenLayers 3 library, you will see that `ol.Ellipsoid` is now exposed:

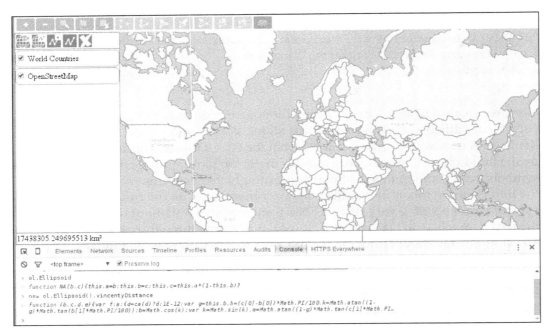

Creating rich documentation with JSDoc

In our last example, we will automatically create documentation for OpenLayers 3. As we saw in `ellipsoid.js`, the headers resemble to the structure of the API documentation. The explanation is simple: Closure Compiler and JSDoc use the same headers to compile the library and create documentation for them. When we extended the constructor and the `vincentyDsitance` method with the `@api` tag, we not only make them exportable but also define that they should appear in the API documentation.

JSDoc is defined as an OpenLayers 3 dependency; therefore, it can be found in the `node_modules` folder. We will use it to generate documentation for our customized version. It also needs a configuration file, which is different from the one used for compiling. The default JSDoc configuration file can also be found in the `config` folder (`config/jsdoc/api/conf.json`). First, let's create a documentation with the default configuration file. For this, type the following command into the terminal:

```
node node_modules/jsdoc-fork/jsdoc.js -c config/jsdoc/api/conf.json
```

If you wait for the program to be completed, you will notice that there is a new folder in the directory, called `out`. This is the default output directory for JSDoc. If you open `index.html` inside this folder, you will see the generated API documentation with the `ol.Ellispoid` constructor and its `vincentyDistance` method:

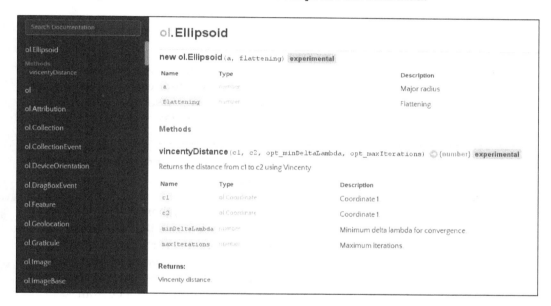

Customizing the documentation

We can tell from the first API documentation export that JSDoc uses the same headers, just like Closure. However, it uses a different syntax in the configuration file and command line. Now, we customize the documentation template a little bit, starting with a few simple steps. First, let's add a little description to the `ol.Ellipsoid` constructor in `ellipsoid.js`:

```
/**
 * @classdesc
```

```
 * Class to create an ellipsoid to measure accurate geodesic
distances,
 * where accuracy is more important, than performance.
 *
 * To create the WGS84 ellipsoid:
 *
 * ```js
 * var ellipsoid = new ol.Ellipsoid(6378137, 1 / 298.257223563);
 * ```
 *
 * @constructor
 * @param {number} a Major radius.
 * @param {number} flattening Flattening.
 * @api
 */
```

With the `@classdesc` tag, we can write an extensive class description for a symbol. The content marked by this tag gets a different class name in the generated documentation, and, thus, it can be distinguished from other descriptions with the help of CSS. With a special syntax, we can also embed a code snippet, which is not only displayed as a code in the documentation but also syntax that's highlighted based on the language we define.

Next, we modify the default template of OpenLayers 3. The library uses a modified version of the Jaguar template (`https://github.com/davidshimjs/jaguarjs/tree/master/docs/templates/jaguar`). First, we navigate to the template in the source code (`config/jsdoc/api/template`). In this folder, there are two folders of interest. First, let's navigate to the `tmpl` folder, which contains the skeleton of various parts of the API documentation. The main template is called `layout.tmpl`, which is our main target. When you open that template, you will see that there are two main parts in the body of the skeleton. The first one describes the navigation bar, while the second one is for the content. The horizontal navigation bar is a custom OpenLayers 3 feature; therefore, we remove it. To also add something to the documentation, we add an attribute footer with a timestamp:

```
<body>
    <div id="wrap" class="clearfix">
        <?js= this.partial('navigation.tmpl', this) ?>
        <div class="main">
            <h1 class="page-title" data-filename="<?js= filename
?>"><?js= title ?></h1>
            <?js= content ?>
            <footer>
```

```
            Documentation generated by <a href="https://github.
com/jsdoc3/jsdoc">JSDoc <?js=
env.version.number ?></a> on <?js= (new Date()) ?>
            </footer>
        </div>
    </div>
    <script>prettyPrint();</script>
    <script src="scripts/linenumber.js"></script>
    <script src="scripts/main.js"></script>
</body>
```

 As these documents are just templates, you can call JavaScript variables and methods in them. Just use the right syntax (<?js= for an opening tag and ?> for a closing tag).

Now, we've gotten rid of the horizontal navigation bar, but we also lost the name of the application. Without a horizontal navigation bar, the best fixed place to put such an annotation is in the vertical navigation bar. To do this, we have to modify navigation.tmpl a little bit:

```
<div class="navigation">
    <p class="applicationName"><a href="index.html"><?js=
env.conf.templates.applicationName ?></a></p>
    <div class="search">
        <input id="search" type="text" class="form-control input-sm"
placeholder="Search Documentation">
    </div>
    [...]
```

With this extension, our application's name, which is read out from the configuration file and stored in the env.conf.templates.applicationName variable at the time of being generated, will always appear on the top of the vertical navigation bar.

If we'd like to generate our modified API documentation now, we would notice that everything is working nice, aside from the white space in the place of the horizontal navigation bar. As both of the navigation bars are in a fixed position, the body of the document has a padding of 50px. This way, the horizontal navigation bar fits nicely at the top of the documentation. To fix this, we have to modify one of the template's CSS files. This can be found in the other folder of interest under the static/styles/jaguar.css path. In this CSS file, we only have to remove the padding from the body element:

```
body {
  padding-top: 50px;
}
```

Finally, before generating the new API documentation, let's change the configuration file a little bit. Most of the options are good to go; we only need to change the name of the application and the `outputSourceFiles` parameter. If this parameter is set to `true`, the source files get bundled along with the documentation and will be accessible from the corresponding symbol. The configuration file that we modify is located in the parent of the `template` folder (`config/jsdoc/api/conf.json` from the source code's root directory):

```
{
    [...]
    "templates": {
        [...]
        "default": {
            "outputSourceFiles": true
        },
        "applicationName": "OL3 with Ellipsoid"
    },
```

Now, at last, we run JSDoc again. This time, we specify another parameter: the output directory. We can do this with the -d argument. Don't forget to run this command from the source code's root directory:

```
node node_modules/jsdoc-fork/jsdoc.js -c config/jsdoc/api/conf.json -d
apidoc
```

If we wait for the program to finish and look at the newly created `apidoc` folder, we can take a look at our new documentation:

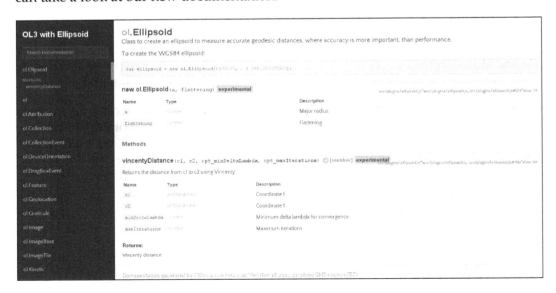

The new API documentation is customized with a class description added to the `ol.Ellipsoid` constructor, and there is a source code page associated with every class. This is very nice; however, if we check the size of this new, extended documentation, it's the double of the one without the source code included. It seems like linking everything to the appropriate GitHub source file is a good practice.

 Curious about the long, ugly, and partially broken links? The OpenLayers 3 API documentation tries to link every source to the appropriate GitHub source file. Take a look at `config/jsdoc/api/template/static/scripts/main.js` to discover and, optionally, modify/turn off this feature.

Summary

Congratulations! You are at the end of a long journey of mastering OpenLayers 3. In this last chapter, we extended our knowledge even further and learned how to customize, shrink, and extend the source code of the library as well as compile our own version. We also learned how to compile our own application with the library and create a standalone documentation for our customized product.

There is only one thing left for you to do. As every book has a physical limit, we could not cover every little part of the library. As now you have a solid basis in application development with OpenLayers 3, go on, and create your own great applications. Practice, find the best solution for your case, and always keep up with the changes, and the new, cutting edge features. Good luck!

Index

Symbols

3D rendering, with Cesium
about 248
Cesium scene, extending 255, 256
control, creating 250-252
map, preparing 248-250
terrain, observing 253, 254

A

animations
control, building 163, 164
creating 164-169
custom animations, creating 162
API documentation
URL 9
using 9
application
building, with OpenLayers 3 266
configuration file, creating 267-270
editing 266, 267
fixing 270, 271
arbitrary formats 96
attributes, accessing
about 76
code, writing 77, 78
attributes, setting
about 80
code, writing 81-84
form, styling 80, 81
attributes, validating
about 84
code, writing 86-88
headers, building 85
styles, adjusting 85

C

canvas-based web mapping library 13, 14
categorized maps
creating 94-96
Cesium 248
choropleth maps
creating 91-94
clipping mask
creating 197-201
Closure Compiler parameter
URL 269
code
debugging 11, 12
controls
adding 107
creating 105, 106
interactions, mapping 104
removing 107
selection control, adding 108
convolution matrix
control, finalizing 191-194
creating 186
image, converting to 8-bit 187, 188
image, normalizing 190
Sobel filter, implementing 189
working 187
Cross Origin Resource Sharing (CORS) 2

D

default appearance
attribution, modifying 26-28
attribution control, customizing 18
classes, identifying 15
controls, styling 15-17

Thank you for buying
Mastering OpenLayers 3

About Packt Publishing

Packt, pronounced 'packed', published its first book, *Mastering phpMyAdmin for Effective MySQL Management*, in April 2004, and subsequently continued to specialize in publishing highly focused books on specific technologies and solutions.

Our books and publications share the experiences of your fellow IT professionals in adapting and customizing today's systems, applications, and frameworks. Our solution-based books give you the knowledge and power to customize the software and technologies you're using to get the job done. Packt books are more specific and less general than the IT books you have seen in the past. Our unique business model allows us to bring you more focused information, giving you more of what you need to know, and less of what you don't.

Packt is a modern yet unique publishing company that focuses on producing quality, cutting-edge books for communities of developers, administrators, and newbies alike. For more information, please visit our website at www.packtpub.com.

About Packt Open Source

In 2010, Packt launched two new brands, Packt Open Source and Packt Enterprise, in order to continue its focus on specialization. This book is part of the Packt Open Source brand, home to books published on software built around open source licenses, and offering information to anybody from advanced developers to budding web designers. The Open Source brand also runs Packt's Open Source Royalty Scheme, by which Packt gives a royalty to each open source project about whose software a book is sold.

Writing for Packt

We welcome all inquiries from people who are interested in authoring. Book proposals should be sent to author@packtpub.com. If your book idea is still at an early stage and you would like to discuss it first before writing a formal book proposal, then please contact us; one of our commissioning editors will get in touch with you.

We're not just looking for published authors; if you have strong technical skills but no writing experience, our experienced editors can help you develop a writing career, or simply get some additional reward for your expertise.

open source
community experience distilled

PACKT
PUBLISHING

OpenLayers 3 Beginner's Guide

ISBN: 978-1-78216-236-0   Paperback: 512 pages

Get started with OpenLayers 3 and enhance your web pages by creating and displaying dynamic maps

1. Create and display maps online with the latest HTML5 features available, using the OpenLayers 3 library.

2. Learn how to interact with the map and learn best practices to improve the loading time for a map.

3. A practical beginner's guide, which also serves as a quick reference with useful screenshots and detailed code explanations.

Instant OpenLayers Starter

ISBN: 978-1-78216-510-1   Paperback: 58 pages

Web Mapping made simple and fast!

1. Learn something new in an Instant! A short, fast, focused guide delivering immediate results.

2. Visualize your geographical data.

3. Integrate with third party map services to create mash-ups.

4. Stylize and interact with your maps.

Please check **www.PacktPub.com** for information on our titles

OpenLayers Cookbook

ISBN: 978-1-84951-784-3   Paperback: 300 pages

60 recipes to create GIS web applications with the open source JavaScript library

1. Understand the main concepts about maps, layers, controls, protocols, events etc.

2. Learn about the important tile providers and WMS servers.

3. Packed with code examples and screenshots for practical, easy learning.

OpenLayers 2.10
Beginner's Guide

ISBN: 978-1-84951-412-5   Paperback: 372 pages

Create, optimize, and deploy stunning cross-browser web maps with the OpenLayers JavaScript web mapping library

1. Learn how to use OpenLayers through explanation and example.

2. Create dynamic web map mashups using Google Maps and other third-party APIs.

3. Customize your map's functionality and appearance.

4. Deploy your maps and improve page loading times.

Please check **www.PacktPub.com** for information on our titles